What is it to deceive someone? And how is it possible to deceive oneself? Does self-deception require that people be taken in by a deceitful strategy that they know is deceitful? The literature is divided between those who argue that self-deception is intentional and those who argue that it is non-intentional. In this study, Annette Barnes offers a challenge to both the standard characterization of other-deception and current characterizations of self-deception, examining the available explanations and exploring such questions as the self-deceiver's false consciousness, bias, and the irrationality and objectionability of self-deception. She arrives at a non-intentional account of self-deception that is deeper and more complete than alternative non-intentional accounts and avoids the reduction of self-deceptive belief to wishful belief.

CAMBRIDGE STUDIES IN PHILOSOPHY

Seeing through self-deception

CAMBRIDGE STUDIES IN PHILOSOPHY

RECENT TITLES

WILLIAM G. LYCAN *Judgement and justification*
GERALD DWORKIN *The theory and practice of autonomy*
MICHAEL TYE *The metaphysics of mind*
DAVID O. BRINK *Moral realism and the foundations of ethics*
W. D. HART *Engines of the soul*
PAUL K. MOSER *Knowledge and evidence*
D. M. ARMSTRONG *A combinatorial theory of possibility*
JOHN BISHOP *Natural agency*
CHRISTOPHER J. MALONEY *The mundane matter of the mental language*
MARK RICHARD *Propositional attitudes*
GERALD E. GAUS *Value and justification*
MARK HELLER *The ontology of physical objects*
JOHN BIGELOW & ROBERT PARGETTER *Science and necessity*
FRANCIS SNARE *Morals, motivation and convention*
CHRISTOPHER S. HILL *Sensations*
JOHN HEIL *The nature of true minds*
CARL GINET *On action*
CONRAD JOHNSON *Moral legislation*
DAVID OWENS *Causes and coincidences*
ANDREW NEWMAN *The physical basis of predication*
MICHAEL JUBIEN *Ontology, modality and the fallacy of reference*
WARREN QUINN *Morality and action*
JOHN W. CARROLL *Laws of nature*
M. J. CRESSWELL *Language in the world*
JOSHUA HOFFMAN & GARY S. ROSENKRANTZ *Substance among other categories*
PAUL HELM *Belief policies*
NOAH LEMOS *Intrinsic value*
LYNNE RUDDER BAKER *Explaining attitudes*
HENRY S. RICHARDSON *Practical reasoning about final ends*
ROBERT A. WILSON *Cartesian psychology and physical minds*
BARRY MAUND *Colours*
MICHAEL DEVITT *Coming to our senses*
SYDNEY SHOEMAKER *The first-person perspective and other essays*
MICHAEL STOCKER *Valuing emotions*
ARDA DENKEL *Object and property*
E. J. LOWE *Subjects of experience*
NORTON NELKIN *Consciousness and the origins of thought*
PIERRE JACOB *What minds can do*
ANDRE GALLOIS *The world without, the mind within*
D. M. ARMSTRONG *A world of states of affairs*
DAVID COCKBURN *Other times*
MARK LANCE & JOHN O'LEARY-HAWTHORNE *The grammar of meaning*

Seeing through self-deception

Annette Barnes
University of Maryland, Baltimore County

PUBLISHED BY THE PRESS SYNDICATE OF THE UNIVERSITY OF CAMBRIDGE
The Pitt Building, Trumpington Street, Cambridge CB2 1RP, United Kingdom

CAMBRIDGE UNIVERSITY PRESS
The Edinburgh Building, Cambridge CB2 2RU, United Kingdom
40 West 20th Street, New York, NY 10011–4211, USA
10 Stamford Road, Oakleigh, Melbourne 3166, Australia

First published 1997

Printed in the United Kingdom at the University Press, Cambridge

Typeset in 10.5/12pt Monotype Bembo [SE]

A catalogue record for this book is available from the British Library

Library of Congress cataloguing in publication data

Barnes, Annette.
Seeing through self-deception / Annette Barnes.
p. cm. – (Cambridge studies in philosophy)
Includes bibliographical references and index.
ISBN 0 521 62014 7 hardback
1. Self-deception. I. Title. II. Series.
BD439.B37 1998
128′.3 – dc21 97–20457 CIP

ISBN 0 521 62014 7 hardback

For GWB

Contents

Acknowledgments *page* x

Introduction 1

1 Other-deception 4

2 Two models of self-deception 18

3 The need for an alternative model of self-deception 34

4 Functioning to reduce an anxiety; satisfying a desire 59

5 Self-deceptive belief formation: non-intentional biasing 77

6 False consciousness 98

7 Intentional and non-intentional deception of oneself 110

8 Irrationality 135

9 What, if anything, is objectionable about self- and other-deception? 158

References 176

Index 181

Acknowledgments

My greatest debt in writing this book has been to Gerald Barnes. His criticisms and suggestions were invaluable. I am also indebted to two readers, Alfred Mele and William Talbott. Their generously detailed and pointed commentaries prompted much-needed clarifications and revisions. I am grateful to All Souls College, Oxford, for a visiting fellowship to work on the manuscript.

Introduction

I argue that while a given interaction between people is deceptive, i.e., is an example of interpersonal or other-deception, only if one of the parties in the interaction engages in some essentially intentional activity, such as lying or pretending, intentionality is not necessary for a given activity to be self-deceptive, i.e., to be an example of self-deception.

The literature on self-deception is divided between those who argue, as I do, that self-deception is non-intentional and those who insist that self-deception must be intentional. Difficulties, however, await proponents on either side of this particular divide.

The common consensus has been that if self-deception must be intentional, then self-deception cannot be explained without introducing some sort of division.[1] One who insists, as I do, that self-deception need not be intentional can find it tempting to suppose that self-deception can be explained only by assimilating it to wishful thinking.[2] But if, as I believe, no satisfactory account of the requisite division can be given, and reducing self-deception to wishful think-

[1] David Pears (*Motivated Irrationality* [Oxford: Clarendon Press paperback, 1986]) and Donald Davidson ("Deception and Division," in *The Multiple Self*, edited by Jon Elster [Cambridge: Cambridge University Press paperback, reprinted 1988], pp. 79–92) both give intentional accounts of self-deception which require some sort of division. William Talbott, "Intentional Self-Deception in a Single Coherent Self," *Philosophy and Phenomenological Research*, vol. 55, no. 1 (March 1995), pp. 27–74, has recently challenged the common consensus. Talbott believes that self-deception is intentional but can be explained without introducing some sort of division (viz., some sort of division over and above the types of divisions invoked in the explanation of non-self-deceptive phenomena). I discuss Talbott's alternative in Chapter 5.

[2] It is tempting to suppose this if one looks, for example, at Mark Johnston's account. See "Self-Deception and the Nature of the Mind," in *Perspectives on Self-Deception*, edited by Brian McLaughlin and Amelie Oksenberg Rorty (Berkeley: University of California Press, 1988), pp. 63–91.

ing does injustice to self-deception, is any satisfactory explanation of self-deception possible?

A satisfactory explanation might be possible if self-deception were not intentional but could, nonetheless, be explained without assimilating it to wishful thinking, that is, without making all self-deceivers wishful believers, believing what they wish were true. While some would not be initially optimistic regarding the prospects for such a strategy,[3] I argue that this strategy can be pursued successfully and should, therefore, be adopted.[4]

I enter the current debate on self-deception by first taking a close look at the claim that self-deception can, without paradox, be modeled on interpersonal deception. In Chapter 1 I consider the suggestion that the seeming paradoxes associated with self-deception may be the result of misconstruing interpersonal deception.[5] The suggestion is that if, despite a general assumption to the contrary, it is not the case that in interpersonal deception the deceiver must believe the denial of something he causes the deceived to believe,

[3] For a discussion of why the prospects for this strategy have been thought dim, see Dion Scott-Kakures, "Self-Deception and Internal Irrationality," *Philosophy and Phenomenological Research*, vol. 56, no. 1 (March 1996), pp. 31–56. Scott-Kakures believes, for example, that "once we admit that the content of desire and belief need not be the same and insist that self-deception need not be intentional, spelling out what counts as [an] intimate enough [connection between belief content and desire content] looks hopeless" (p. 39).

[4] One can regard Alfred Mele as having followed this strategy. While he gives a non-intentional account of self-deception, Mele acknowledges that not all self-deceptive belief is wishful belief. Cf. *Irrationality: An Essay on Akrasia, Self-Deception and Self-Control* (New York: Oxford University Press, 1987). While Mele's account avoids assimilating self-deceptive belief to wishful belief, his account is, I argue, neither deep enough nor complete.

[5] A suggestion made in passing by Bas van Fraassen, "The Peculiar Effects of Love and Desire," in *Perspectives on Self-Deception*, p. 124. Alfred Mele, in "Recent Work on Self-Deception," *American Philosophical Quarterly*, vol. 24, no. 1 (January 1987), p. 2, and in his book *Irrationality*, also makes this suggestion. Mele, however, believes that the misconstrual occurs because people assume that all interpersonal deception must be intentional. If the deception is not intentional, then the interpersonal deceiver need not believe the denial of what he gets the deceived to believe. I argue that in the ***intentional*** deception of others – and indeed I focus on interpersonal deception which is intentional – the deceiver need not believe the denial of what he intentionally gets the deceived to believe. For a discussion of Mele's point, and how it differs from mine, cf. Chapter 1, note 1.

then the seeming paradoxes associated with self-deception would not arise. I argue that the general assumption about interpersonal deception is in fact wrong; the deceiver need not believe the denial of something he causes the deceived to believe. Yet while some of the paradoxes traditionally associated with self-deception would not arise, I show why modeling self-deception on other-deception remains paradoxical.

In Chapter 2 I consider whether the paradox that I suggest remains when self-deception is modeled on other-deception can be resolved by a suitable division. I focus on the division proposed by Donald Davidson.[6] I then examine Mark Johnston's claim that self-deception should not be modeled on interpersonal deception but should be understood as a form of wishful belief.[7] I argue in Chapter 3 that neither a division nor an assimilation to wishful thinking is satisfactory – neither the strategy adopted by Davidson nor that adopted by Johnston allows one to deal adequately with a familiar enough type of self-deception – and I begin to set out an alternative, which focuses on the relation between anxious desire and self-deceptive belief. While Johnston's account also focuses on the relation between anxious desire and self-deceptive belief, I propose a new way of construing this relation. Chapter 4 continues the discussion of anxious desire and self-deceptive belief begun in 3. I show that self-deceptive beliefs must do more than reduce anxiety, and discuss how self-deceptive beliefs can, but need not, facilitate the satisfaction of desires. Chapters 5, 6, and 7 focus on various aspects of both the self-deceiving process and the self-deceived state. Chapter 5 is concerned with the biasing that occurs in self-deceptive belief formation, a biasing that I claim is unintentional; Chapter 6, with a kind of consciousness that is found in self-deception. Necessary and sufficient conditions for self-deceiving are set out in Chapter 7, and self-deceiving is contrasted with other kinds of unintentional self-misleading. Whether self-deceivers are irrational is discussed in Chapter 8; Chapter 9 considers what, if anything, is wrong with self- and other-deception.

6 See "Deception and Division."

7 See "Self-Deception and the Nature of the Mind."

1

Other-deception

At an amateur cricket match, a mature and rather plump philosopher comes in to bat. The bowler who delivers the ball to the batsman mistakenly expects an easy out. We might quite naturally say of the bowler that he was deceived by appearances – he believed the batsman would be a bad cricket player when in fact he was a good one. Although the philosopher was pleased (it is reported that he was very pleased) when his opponent was thus fooled, he did not deceive him into believing that he was a bad player. The philosopher behaved as he normally would. He did not, for example, pretend to be in worse shape than he was. The homeless man in New York City with matted hair and dirty slept-in clothes, whose appearance, the *New York Times* reported, led the pediatrician who passed him to believe that he was not an affectionate father of an infant daughter, did not seek to create this mistaken impression.

While no one would deny that we can be, and often are, deceived by appearances, and that in such cases the deception can be achieved without there being anyone who attempts to bring about the deception, or even anyone who wants the deception to occur, many would deny that self-deception is in this regard like deception by appearances. Among the deniers would be those who believe that self-deception should be strictly modeled on interpersonal deception, a deception which can only occur if there is someone who attempts to bring about the deception.

Using interpersonal or other-deception as the model for self-deception, however, has proved difficult. If we use this model, and if, as is generally assumed, in interpersonal deception deceivers must intentionally get the deceived to believe something which the deceivers know or truly believe is false, then we are led to say that in self-deception self-deceivers must intentionally get themselves to believe something they know or truly believe is false. But it is difficult, at least initially, to comprehend how self-deceivers could believe simultaneously both a proposition and its denial.

Modeling self-deception on interpersonal deception would face fewer obstacles if the initial assumption about other-deception was mistaken. That is, if

> **Claim 1:** ***It need not be the case, when A intentionally deceives B into believing that p, that (a) A knows or truly believes that something is false, and (b) A intentionally gets B to believe that it is true.***

were true, the so called paradox of belief or doxastic paradox, viz., self-deceivers believe simultaneously a proposition and its denial, would not arise in self-deception when self-deception was modeled on other-deception.

While the standard account of interpersonal deception assumes that claim 1 is false,[1] some philosophers have recently pointed out that the following claim, claim 2, is true.

[1] See Alfred Mele's initial formulation of the paradox of belief in *Irrationality*, p. 121. "For any *A* and *B*, when *A* deceives *B* into believing that *p*, *A* knows or truly believes that not-*p* while causing *B* to believe that *p*. So when *A* deceives *A* (i.e., himself) into believing that *p*, he knows or truly believes that not-*p* while causing himself to believe that *p*. Thus, *A* must simultaneously believe that not-*p* and believe that *p*. But how is this possible?"

While Mele does not believe that "when *A* deceives *B* into believing that *p*, *A* knows or truly believes that not-*p* while causing *B* to believe that *p*" is true of *all* cases of interpersonal deception, he seems willing, as I am not, to accept that it may be true of all cases of intentional interpersonal deception ("Although knowledge or true belief may be a prerequisite of intentional deception," p. 122). He does not believe it is true of all cases of interpersonal deception, because he believes it is not true of some cases of unintentional interpersonal deception. Mele suggests that when we speak of *A* deceiving *B* into believing that *p* we sometimes mean roughly that *A* induces a false belief that *p* in *B*. If we use "deceive" in this way, a deceiver need not intentionally deceive the other, nor need the deceiver know or truly believe that *p* is false when he gets the other to believe that *p*. But Mele acknowledges that philosophers tend not to model self-deception on unintentional interpersonal deceiving but on intentional deceiving, for the former deceiving may be accidental while self-deceiving is not. His strategy is to argue that the non-accidentality of self-deception does not imply that the agent must intentionally deceive himself. If the self-deceiver does not intentionally deceive himself, then the self-deceiver need not be in the paradoxical condition of simultaneously believing that *p* and believing that not-*p*. This strategy will be discussed in succeeding chapters. Mele, it should be noted, also believes that "there is no good reason to believe that it [intentional self-deception] involves the subject's being in the peculiar doxastic condition of believing that *p* while believing that not-*p*" (p. 133). He does not, however, claim, as I do, that in intentional

Claim 2: ***It need not be the case, when A intentionally deceives B into believing that p, that (a) A knows or truly believes that p is false and (b) A gets B to believe that it is true.***

Some have thought that the truth of claim 2 was sufficient for the truth of claim 1. I believe that claim 2 is true, and I shall show why it might be tempting to suppose that if claim 2 were true, claim 1 is true; but I shall show also that the truth of claim 2 is not sufficient for the truth of claim 1.

Yet, although it is tempting to concur with the standard account of interpersonal deception in the belief that claim 1 is false,[2] I shall argue that claim 1 is true.[3] There are better grounds than the truth of claim 2 for believing it true. Claim 1 is true; but it does not follow that self-deception can without paradox be modeled on interpersonal deception. The truth of claim 1 does ensure that those who model self-deception on other-deception do not have to confront the paradox of belief, a paradox that "is often regarded as *the* paradox of self-deception."[4] The truth of claim 1 does not, however, ensure that those who model self-deception on other-deception do not have to confront another paradox.

It is generally assumed that if I intentionally deceive you into believing that *p*, then you must be taken in by a strategy which I know, but which you do not know, is deceitful. As Alfred Mele observes, "In general, *A* cannot successfully employ a deceptive strategy against *B* if *B* knows *A*'s intention and plan."[5] If we model self-deception on other-deception, then as deceived, I must be taken in by a deceitful

interpersonal deception the deceiver need not know or truly believe the denial of what he gets the deceived to believe.

In the discussion of interpersonal deception that follows I focus exclusively on *intentional* interpersonal deception. *A*'s inducing a false belief that *p* in *B* is neither a necessary nor a sufficient condition for *A*'s intentionally deceiving *B* into believing that *p*. That is, if *A* intentionally deceives *B* into believing that *p*, it need not be the case that *A* induces a false belief that *p* in *B*. Nor is it the case that if *A* gets *B* to believe that *p* when *p* is false, then *A* has deceived *B* in the relevant sense into believing that *p*.

2 It is a temptation to which I previously succumbed. Cf. Annette Barnes, "When Do We Deceive Others?" *Analysis*, vol. 50, no. 3 (June 1990), pp. 197–202, and "On Deceiving Others," *American Philosophical Quarterly*, vol. 29, no. 2 (April 1992), pp. 153–61.

3 Comments made by Richard Moran, Jonathan Barnes, and an anonymous reader helped to persuade me that claim 1 is true.

4 Mele, *Irrationality*, p. 121.

5 Ibid., p. 138.

strategy that, as deceiver, I know to be deceitful. If claim 1 is true, however, I need not in self-deception be engaged in the deceitful strategy of getting myself to believe something that I know or truly believe is false. We shall see what paradoxical-seeming strategy is, nonetheless, required of the self-deceiver if self-deception is modeled on interpersonal deception.

Why is it a mistake to believe that claim 1 is false? I first show why someone might believe that claim 1 is obviously false, yet be mistaken about that. I then show that while it is relatively easy to show that claim 1 is not obviously false, it is not as easy as some have thought to show that claim 1 is true.

I. WHY IT IS A MISTAKE TO BELIEVE THAT CLAIM I IS OBVIOUSLY FALSE

One who focuses on certain kinds of case might easily suppose that one person, *A*, deceives another person, *B*, into believing that *p* only if (1) *A* knows or truly believes that something is false, and (2) *A* intentionally gets *B* to believe that it is true. Suppose I ***inadvertently*** get you to believe something false. A telephone conversation I am having with you is cut short. Although I believe the proposal we were discussing is a good one, I had time only to apprise you of some of its shortcomings. You believe that the proposal is bad, but had the conversation continued I would have convinced you that it was good. If we are reluctant to say that I have deceived you in this case, it is because we believe that in interpersonal deception the deceiver's getting someone to believe something false must be ***intentional***.

Suppose further that I get you to believe something I ***mistakenly believe*** is true. For example, I believe, mistakenly, that an American businessman recently spent a total of $23 million in his attempt to win his party's presidential nomination and I intentionally get you to believe this. It seems wrong to say that I have deceived you here. Although I intentionally got you to believe something, and the something I got you to believe was false, I did not know that I was getting you to believe something false. This suggests that one must intentionally get another to believe something false when one knows that this is what one is doing. One knows that this is what one is doing when one knows or truly believes that the proposition one intentionally gets the other to believe true is false.

If one reasons along these lines it seems plausible to suppose that in interpersonal deception deceivers must not only intentionally deceive others, they must know or truly believe that the propositions which they get the deceived to believe are false. It seems natural to conclude that claim 1 is clearly false.

However, as I indicated earlier, some have thought that the truth of claim 2 was sufficient for the truth of claim 1. And examples are readily available which show that claim 2 is true (i.e., which show that *it is not the case that if A intentionally deceives B into believing that p, then (a) A knows or truly believes that p is false, and (b) A intentionally gets B to believe that it is true*).

Suppose I do not know whether what I get you to believe is false. It seems possible, nevertheless, for me to deceive you into believing it. I do not know whether your friend is being honest with you, but knowing that you would be distressed to learn that he wasn't, I get you to believe he is honest.[6]

Suppose I believe, mistakenly, that what I get you to believe is false. It seems possible, nevertheless, to deceive you into believing it. I believe, mistakenly, that your friend is honest, but for some reason I want you to believe that he is dishonest. I invent examples of his dishonesty and intentionally get you to believe that he is dishonest. While I have deceived you into believing he is dishonest, I did not know or truly believe that it was false that your friend was dishonest. For it was true that your friend was dishonest.

Suppose I know or truly believe that what I get you to believe is true. I can, nevertheless, deceive you. I know that your friend is dishonest, but I know that you will not be convinced by the evidence I have, so I invent evidence that convinces you that he is dishonest.[7]

[6] The case I give parallels that given by van Fraassen: "Suppose that a certain bridge is dangerous, and I do not know this, that I really have no evidence that makes it less likely than not, for me, that the bridge is safe. But suppose in addition that I think it would be very good for me if you believed the bridge to be safe and I successfully persuade you to believe this falsehood. Then I have certainly deceived you, although I did not know that the information was false." "The Peculiar Effects of Love and Desire," p. 124.

[7] See Brian McLaughlin, "Exploring the Possibility of Self-Deception in Belief," in *Perspectives on Self-Deception*, ed. Brian McLaughlin and Amelie Oksenberg Rorty (Berkeley: University of California Press, 1988), p. 35. He gives the following case. "Take any Tom, Dick, and Harry. Let Tom be the deceiver, Dick be the one the deception is about, and Harry be the victim. Tom believes that Dick is innocent of a certain

In the last two cases I deceive you into believing something that is true. Let us say here that I deceive you ***into*** believing that *p* in these cases although you are not deceived ***in*** believing that *p*. While it is the case that if *B* is deceived in believing that *p*, then *B*'s belief that *p* must be false, it need not be the case that when *B* has been deceived into believing that *p*, *B*'s belief that *p* must be false.[8]

Suppose we are agreed that claim 2 is true. What follows from the truth of claim 2?

II. WHY IT WOULD BE A MISTAKE TO ASSUME THAT IF CLAIM 2 IS TRUE, CLAIM I MUST BE TRUE

Why would someone believe that if I need not know or truly believe that not-*p* when I deceive you into believing that *p*, then in interpersonal deception the deceiver need not know or truly believe that something he or she intentionally gets the deceived to believe is false? Suppose a manufacturer lies to his customers about the safety of his product. He intentionally gets them to believe that his product is not harmful, when he knows or truly believes that it is. The manufacturer, in deceiving his customers, intentionally gets them to believe a certain proposition, the proposition that such-and-such product is not harmful. It is tempting to believe that this proposition is the relevant something that he intentionally gets the deceived to believe is true, when he knows or truly believes that it is false.

If it can be shown that the deceiver need not know or truly believe

wrong-doing. Harry believes Dick is guilty. Tom is unable to produce evidence that will change Harry's mind. So, diabolical as he is, Tom attempts by deceitful means to get Harry to believe that Dick is innocent. Tom tries to convince Harry by lying about some particularly pertinent matter, Dick's whereabouts on a certain night. Tom thus performs an act of deception by means of which he intends to get Harry to believe that Dick is innocent. Suppose that Tom succeeds: Harry believes the lie and infers that Dick is innocent. Then, Tom will have succeeded in intentionally deceiving Harry into believing that Dick is innocent. Yet Tom himself believed that Dick was innocent when he initiated the deceitful act. So, one can intentionally deceive someone into believing something one believes is true when one initiates the act in question."

8 This distinction between deceiving someone into believing something and someone's being deceived in believing something informs McLaughlin's "Exploring the Possibility of Self-Deception in Belief." If one does not keep this distinction clearly in mind, one might object to my describing myself as deceiving you *into* believing that your friend is dishonest when it is true that he is dishonest.

that this particular proposition – ***the proposition he is deceiving the other into believing*** – is false, then it might look as if the deceiver need not know or truly believe something is false when he deceives the other into believing that the proposition in question is true. That is, the temptation is to assume that the ***something*** that is mentioned in claim 1 ("it need not be the case, when *A* intentionally deceives *B* into believing that *p*, that (a) *A* knows or truly believes that ***something*** is false, and (b) *A* intentionally gets *B* to believe that it is true") ***could only be p***. If the something could only be *p*, then showing that claim 2 was true would be sufficient for showing that claim 1 was true.[9] But, as some philosophers have noted, while the something, *q*, may be *p*, it may also be something else.[10] And if the something can be something other than *p*, then even if it is the case that if I deceived you into believing that *p* I need not know or truly believe that not-*p*, the possibility is still open that if I deceive you into believing that *p*, I must know or truly believe that something (in this case something other than *p*) is false which I intentionally get you to believe is true.

In the cases discussed it is easy to find some proposition, *q*, where *q* is other than *p*, that I knew or truly believed was false, and which I intentionally got you to believe was true. In the first example, I got you to believe that I believed your friend was honest when I knew that I did not believe this. I neither believed that he was honest nor that he

[9] Van Fraassen, after discussing the bridge case (see note 6 above) writes: "Similarly I expect that there can be cases of self-deception in which the person cannot correctly be said to have known or even recognized the truth as the most likely. The main requirement for it to be (self-) deception, as opposed to unintentional (self-) misleading, is that he be culpable of persuading himself by epistemically unfair means or practices" (p. 124). But to show that claim 2 is true, as the bridge example does, is not, I shall argue, to show that claim 1 is true, and hence one cannot on the basis of claim 2 alone rule out as a requirement for (self-) deception getting oneself to believe *something* one knows or truly believes is false. If, however, one has succumbed to the temptation that I am discussing, the temptation to assume that claim 2 is sufficient for showing claim 1 is true, then it would be natural to conclude that the main requirement for self-deception is persuading oneself by epistemically unfair means or practices.

[10] Brian McLaughlin recognizes that the something may be other than *p*. His characterization of other-deception is: "for any *x* and for any *y*, if *x* intentionally deceives *y* into believing or continuing to believe something, *p*, then there is something, *q* (*p* or something else) that (i) is false, that (ii) *x* disbelieves when initiating the deceitful act, and that (iii) *x* intentionally gets or allows *y* to come or to continue to believe." "Exploring the Possibility of Self-Deception in Belief," p. 36.

was dishonest. In the second and third examples, I got you to believe that the means I was using to persuade you of your friend's dishonesty were reliable when I knew they were not.

If the truth of claim 2 does not ensure the truth of claim 1, is claim 1 nonetheless true? While some who recognize that claim 2 is true hold that claim 1 is false,[11] I shall argue that claim 1 is true. It need not be the case that whenever I intentionally deceive you I intentionally get you to believe something is true which I know or truly believe is false.

In the majority of cases in which *A* intentionally deceives *B* into believing that *p*, there does seem to be some proposition that *A* knew or truly believed was false, which *A* intentionally got *B* to believe was true.[12] For example, the proposition might be the proposition *p*; or it might be the proposition that *B* has adequate evidence for *p*; or the proposition that *B* has direct sensory awareness that *p*. However, there are, I believe, some cases where no proposition of the relevant kind seems to be available. If there is nothing in these cases that I intentionally get you to believe is true that I know or truly believe is false, and yet we are prepared to say that I have deceived you, then this suggests that claim 1 is true.

Suppose I know that there is a shy, unpredictable rabbit in your garden. I, however, want to make sure that tomorrow your five-year-old daughter believes that she is seeing a rabbit in her garden, so under cover of darkness I place a lifelike model of a rabbit in a prominent place in your garden. While I am in the garden doing this, the rabbit exhibits great curiosity and comes out of hiding. Although I have only a small flashlight I clearly see it. I retreat. When I call your house the next day and ask to speak to your daughter I am told that she is unable to come to the phone because she is seeing a rabbit in her garden. I hang up not knowing whether your daughter is seeing the real rabbit or the lifelike model, so I do not know whether or not I have deceived your daughter into believing that she is seeing a rabbit in her garden. Let us suppose that your daughter is seeing the lifelike model I placed there and not the real rabbit. Haven't I deceived her into believing that she is seeing a rabbit in her garden even though I did not know whether the proposition I got her to believe – "I am seeing a rabbit in my garden" – was false?

[11] Brian McLaughlin would be one such person, for he believes that the characterization of interpersonal deception he gives (see note 10 above) is correct.

[12] I discuss in detail in "On Deceiving Others" what *q* might be when it is not *p*.

Is there some other proposition I got her to believe was true which I knew or truly believed was false? Even if I intentionally got her to believe that there was a rabbit in her garden – if I intentionally get her to believe that she is seeing a rabbit in her garden, then she believes that there is a rabbit in her garden – and I also intentionally got her to believe that she had direct sensory awareness that there was a rabbit there, then, given that I do not know whether I have deceived her, I do not know, and need not truly believe, that one of these propositions is false.[13] Because I do not know whether I have deceived her, I also do not know, and need not truly believe, that she does not have adequate evidence for believing there is a rabbit there. Moreover, I need not have intentionally gotten her to believe that she has adequate evidence.

If there is some proposition here that I know or truly believe is false that I must intentionally get your daughter to believe is true, then it must be a proposition that I can know or truly believe is false, whether or not I know that I have deceived her. The only propositions that come to mind here, however, are not ones which it is realistic to suppose that your daughter believes. They are the propositions that she is justified, in a very strong sense of "justified," in believing either that she is seeing a rabbit in her garden or that there is a rabbit in her garden. It is a sense of "justification" that is sensitive to a kind of case Alvin Goldman describes.

A man, out driving in the countryside with his son, is identifying objects on the landscape for him. "That's a barn," he says of one object. The man has excellent eyesight and has had a reasonably careful look at the object. He has no doubt that the object he identifies is a barn, and it is. However, although the man does not know this, the district he has just entered is full of papier-mâché facsimiles of barns. The facsimiles are cleverly constructed so that travelers invariably mistake them for barns. Having just entered this district, the man has not yet encountered any facsimiles. He sees a real barn, but if the object on the site were a facsimile, the man would mistake it for a barn.[14]

[13] As the case is described, if I had the belief that one of these propositions is false, the belief would have to be true, but I need not have that belief, because, aware that I do not know, I may suspend judgment.

[14] Alvin Goldman, "Discrimination and Perceptual Knowledge," *Journal of Philosophy*, vol. 73, no. 20 (1976), pp. 771ff.

A person is not justified in the strong sense in question if the person has not ruled out a relevant counterpossibility, even if she is unaware that there is such a counterpossibility. Not all counterpossibilities will be relevant counterpossibilities, for if they were, we would never be able to say of a person that she was justified in this sense in believing anything.[15] In the rabbit example I have introduced a relevant counterpossibility which your daughter has not ruled out. She has not ruled out the possibility that she is seeing a lifelike rabbit model and not the real rabbit.[16] In this sense of "justification" I can know or truly believe that your daughter is not justified in believing either that she is seeing a rabbit in her garden or that there is a rabbit in her garden, whether or not I know I have deceived her.

It would, however, be implausible to think that a five-year-old child would believe that she was justified in this sense in believing either that she was seeing a rabbit in her garden or that there was a rabbit in her garden. So clearly I do not have to be intentionally getting her to believe that she is thus justified.

While in straightforward cases of lying or setting up deceptive appearances there typically is some proposition that I know or truly believe is false that I get you to believe is true, in the rabbit case no such proposition seems available. If none is available, then claim 1 is true. If I intentionally deceive you into believing that *p*, I need not intentionally get you to believe something which I know or truly believe is false.

What, however, are we to conclude if claim 1 is true? We cannot, I argue, conclude that self-deception can without paradox be modeled on interpersonal deception. The truth of claim 1 rules out the doxastic paradox. It also rules out one form of the strategic paradox. It does not, however, rule out another form of strategic paradox.

[15] Whether this notion of a relevant counterpossibility is sustainable in the absence of some criterion for distinguishing relevant counterpossibilities from the larger realm of counterpossibilities is one question; whether a satisfactory criterion is possible is another.

[16] The rabbit example is less good than the barn one, because rabbits move, and thus one could tell if one saw movement whether one was seeing the real rabbit or the model. So let us suppose that the real rabbit remains stationary or alternatively that the lifelike rabbit model can move.

III. WHY IT IS A MISTAKE TO BELIEVE THAT SELF-DECEPTION CAN WITHOUT PARADOX BE MODELED ON OTHER-DECEPTION

One can be tempted by that mistaken belief if one believes that the epistemic requirement on the deceiver which claim 1 rejects is the only possible source of paradox. If that epistemic requirement on the deceiver is dropped, then when self-deception is modeled on other-deception, the self-deceiver is no longer required to believe something which he or she knows or truly believes is false. The paradox of belief or doxastic paradox does not arise. But what about the strategic paradox? If self-deception is modeled on other-deception, then as deceived, I must be taken in by a deceitful strategy that, as deceiver, I know to be deceitful. The deceitful strategy has typically been thought to be the strategy of getting the deceived to believe something the deceiver knows is false. But if the rabbit-facsimile case is a coherent one, then I need not engage in that strategy in other-deception, nor, therefore, need I engage in it in self-deception.

There is, however, a strategy that I believe the interpersonal deceiver is required to pursue. If I deceive you I get you to believe something I want you to believe. But not all non-straightforward ways of getting you to believe something I want you to believe involve deception. If I were to use purely mechanical means, hypnosis or drugs, to induce the belief in you, I need not have deceived you.

But it does seem that if I intentionally deceive you I must get you to believe something I want you to believe in the following way. I introduce into your situation something such that I believe there is a real possibility that that something will cause you to believe that *p*, and I take that something to provide neither adequate evidence for *p* nor direct sensory awareness that *p*. I believe this to be a necessary, but not a sufficient, condition for interpersonal deception.

For example, suppose that I deceive you into believing that a museum is open today by telling you that it is open. My telling you that it is open brings it about that you believe it is open. I take my telling you it is open to provide neither adequate evidence for its being open nor direct sensory awareness that it is open. In the rabbit case, by installing a lifelike model of a rabbit in your garden I cause your five-year-old daughter to believe that she is seeing a rabbit in her garden. I, however, take the presence of a lifelike model of a rabbit in her garden to provide neither adequate evidence for her seeing a rabbit in her garden nor direct sensory awareness that she is seeing a rabbit in her garden. Your daughter would also believe that there is a rabbit in her garden, and I take the presence of a lifelike model of a rabbit to provide neither adequate evidence for there being a rabbit in her garden nor direct sensory awareness that there is a rabbit in her garden. Even in cases where I deceive you into believing *p* by introducing something that would ordinarily be adequate evidence for *p* – e.g., I cause you to believe that the museum is free this particular Sunday, by correctly citing the museum's policy of free admission on Sundays – given that I know that on this particular Sunday there will be an admission charge, I do not take my citing the museum's policy to provide adequate evidence for the museum's being free this particular Sunday.

While I believe the condition under discussion is necessary for interpersonal deception, it is obviously not sufficient. Suppose I want you to believe that allowing women priests would radically alter Catholicism. I know, moreover, that if I cite papal authority for this proposition I will get you to believe it. You also know that I think the papal authority I cite for you is not any evidence at all for the proposition. And you know that I know how you are disposed to react to papal authority and that I am trying to exploit that. While I have introduced into your situation papal authority because I believe there is a real possibility that it will cause you to believe that women priests would radically alter Catholicism, and I take papal authority to provide neither adequate evidence for women priests' radically altering Catholicism, nor direct sensory awareness that this is the case, I have not deceived you into believing that allowing women priests would radically alter Catholicism.[17]

[17] One reason why this might not be a case of deception is that you believe what I want you to believe even though you know what my strategy is. It would be deception only if you would not have believed it if you knew what I was up to. An anonymous reader has suggested to me that a necessary condition for *A* to deceive *B* into believing that *p* might be this:

A intentionally gets B to believe something which B would not believe if B knew about the strategy that A had employed to get B to believe it (including A's beliefs and intentions involved in the strategy). However, the following case would make trouble for this condition; hence this condition cannot be the source for the paradox that I claim remains when

If it is necessary in interpersonal deception for the deceiver to introduce into the deceived's situation something such that the deceiver believes there is a real possibility that that something will cause the deceived to believe that *p*, and the deceiver takes that something to provide neither adequate evidence for *p* nor direct sensory awareness that *p*, then those who wish to model self-deception on other-deception would have a paradox to contend with. Although this condition would not give rise to a doxastic paradox, it would give rise to a strategic paradox. As self-deceiver I must introduce into my situation something such that I believe there is a real possibility that that something will cause me to believe that *p*, and I take that something to provide neither adequate evidence for *p* nor direct sensory awareness that *p*.

The discussion in this chapter is meant to show that several temptations are to be resisted. The first temptation is to overlook the fact that if I deceive you into believing that *p*, I need not know or truly believe that not-*p*. Overlooking this makes it plausible to think that claim 1 is obviously false.

The second temptation is to draw the wrong conclusion when one keeps the indicated first temptation in mind. That is, one is now tempted to believe that the fact that I need not know or truly believe that not-*p* when I deceive you into believing that *p* shows that in interpersonal deception the deceiver need not know or truly believe that something he or she intentionally gets the deceived to believe is false. In other words, it is tempting to believe that the truth of claim 2 is sufficient for the truth of claim 1. Whether claim 1 is true, however, depends not on whether claim 2 is true, but on whether there are any cases of deception in which there is nothing the deceiver intentionally gets the deceived to believe which the deceiver knows or truly believes is false. I suggested that there were such cases.

A third temptation is to believe that if the deceiver does not need to

self-deception is modeled on other-deception. John, who is having an affair with Mary, the wife of his friend James, deceives James into believing that Mary is unfaithful. He does this by getting James to believe that Mary is having an affair with Luke, a notorious womanizer. If James had a complete description of the strategy John uses to get him to believe that Mary is unfaithful, James would not believe that Mary was having an affair with Luke, but he would believe Mary was unfaithful. John would have to reveal that since he knew that James would not believe him if he told him that he was having an affair with Mary, he had to resort to linking Mary with Luke.

know or truly believe something is false which he intentionally gets the deceived to believe is true, then self-deception can, without paradox, be modeled on interpersonal deception. While dropping one epistemic requirement on the deceiver would get rid of the doxastic paradox and one form of the strategic paradox, I argued that another epistemic requirement cannot be dropped. If it cannot, then those who model self-deception on interpersonal deception would have to contend with a strategic paradox.

2

Two models of self-deception

If claim 1 were false, i.e., if deceivers must intentionally get themselves to believe something which they know or truly believe is false, and if one models self-deception on other-deception, then self-deception, as we saw earlier, appears to be doubly paradoxical. It seems to require that if I deceive myself, then:

(a) as deceiver, I must believe of some proposition that it is false, and at the same time, as deceived, believe that it is true, and

(b) as deceived, I must be taken in by a deceitful strategy that, as deceiver, I know to be deceitful.

If, as I argued, claim 1 is true, but deceivers must introduce into the deceived's situation something that the deceiver believes has a real possibility of causing the deceived to believe that *p*, and the deceiver takes that something to provide neither adequate evidence for *p* nor direct sensory awareness that *p*, then while paradox (a) does not arise in self-deception if one models self-deception on other-deception, paradox (b) would arise.

Nearly all who write about self-deception have assumed that claim 1 was false, that the relevant sort of knowledge or true belief was a prerequisite for the intentional deception of another. While this assumption and the seeming paradoxes it engenders in self-deception when self-deception is modeled on other-deception have led some philosophers to doubt the very possibility of self-deception – a doubt which runs counter to a widespread conviction that self-deception is actual and pervasive – they have led many others to seek a resolution of the seeming paradoxes.

We have already seen, in effect, that one attempted resolution is not wholly successful. For even if one were to accept that claim 1 is true, and hence that relevant knowledge or true belief was not a prerequisite for other-deception, modeling self-deception on other-deception would still lead in self-deception to paradox (b).

Recently some philosophers have argued that the model of interpersonal deception is to be rejected as the model for self-deception. Self-deceivers, unlike interpersonal deceivers, do not intentionally get someone to believe something.

Those who reject the interpersonal-deception model do not, however, embrace the model of deception by appearances. For although self-deception can involve being deceived by appearances, deception by appearances is not thought to be a satisfactory model for the core phenomenon of self-deception. In straightforward cases of simple deception by appearances – e.g., I mistake a stump for a person – there **need not be anyone** who either wants, or attempts to bring about, the deception. In self-deception, however, it is thought that the person him- or herself must always be responsible for, and have some interest in, the appearances being deceptive.

If deception by appearances is ruled out as a model for self-deception, and if interspecies deception (e.g., when a fox deceives a person) and the other deceptions found in nature[1] are also ruled out as models for self-deception, then either self-deception is to be modeled on interpersonal deception, despite seeming paradox, or self-deception is a *sui generis* type of deception. I assume here, without argument, that interspecies deception and the indicated deceptions in nature are not suitable models for self-deception, although once my account of self-deception is spelled out, it should be clear why I believe this assumption to be warranted. On that assumption, either self-deception is to be modeled on interpersonal deception, or self-deception is *sui generis*.

Among those who choose the first alternative, who attempt to model self-deception on other-deception, there are some who would, like Freud, maintain that modeling self-deception on other-deception does not, even if claim 1 is false, lead in self-deception to either paradox (a) or (b).[2] Freud argues that while the self-deceiver intentionally gets the deceived to believe some proposition which the

[1] Cf. Loyal Rue, *By the Grace of Guile: The Role of Deception in Natural History and Human Affairs* (Oxford: Oxford University Press, 1994), pp. 109ff., for a discussion of molecular, plant, insect, aquatic, avian, and mammalian (non-human) deceptions.

[2] Cf. Sigmund Freud, "Repression" (1915), *The Ego and the Id* (1923), and "Splitting of the Ego in the Process of Defense" (1938), in *The Standard Edition of the Complete Psychological Works*, ed. James Strachey, Anna Freud, Alix Strachey, and Alan Tyson (London: Hogarth Press and the Institute of Psychoanalysis, 1954–74).

deceiver knows is false, it does not follow that the "I" who believes of some proposition that it is false is the same "I" who believes of that proposition that it is true. Nor is one and the same "I" the knowledgeable dupe.[3]

Others, like Donald Davidson, maintain that modeling self-deception on other-deception would, if claim 1 is false, lead in self-deception to (a) and (b). Davidson, however, believes that (a) and (b) are, nevertheless, non-paradoxically satisfiable.[4] Both Freud's and Davidson's strategies involve some sort of division.[5] Freud divides the self. Davidson partitions the mind.

Freud's position has been widely discussed and criticized. I focus instead on Davidson's position and then consider Mark Johnston's response to it. Johnston claims that Davidson's partitioning, like Freud's dividing, is unnecessary. He believes that once one sees that there can be mental processes that are purposive but not intentional, and sees that it is processes of this sort and not intentional acts that are

[3] I_1, the deceiver, believes that the proposition is false, and I_2, the deceived, believes that the proposition is true. I_1, the knowledgeable part, intentionally, and hence knowingly, keeps his or her misleading strategy hidden from I_2, the dupe, who is taken in by the strategy.

[4] There are also those who, like McLaughlin, for example, hold that modeling self-deception on other-deception, even if claim 1 is false, does not lead in self-deception to either of these two conditions in self-deception, but nevertheless believe that condition (a) is characteristic of self-deception. McLaughlin argues that if we distinguish between accessible and non-accessible belief, then condition (a) is non-paradoxically satisfiable. Cf. "Exploring the Possibility of Self-Deception in Belief," and "Mele's *Irrationality*: A Commentary," *Philosophical Psychology*, vol. 1, no. 2 (1988).

[5] One could, however, without assuming any division, show that the falsity of claim 1 did not lead, when intrapersonal deception is modeled on other deception, in all forms of intrapersonal deception to (a) and (b). In the following case of self-induced deception, a case I discuss later in the text, the deceiver could intentionally get himself to believe something which he knows or truly believes is false while neither (a) nor (b) is satisfied. A person tries to avoid an unpleasant appointment in the future by deliberately writing down a false date in her appointment calendar. She assumes that given her bad memory she will have forgotten that she had done this when the time for the appointment comes. It seems possible that when she comes to believe that the appointment is on such-and-such date (=the wrong date) she has lost her earlier belief that it was not on that date, and she can also have forgotten her deceitful strategy. See Brian McLaughlin's discussion, in "Exploring the Possibility of Self-Deception in Belief," of this case first introduced by Davidson in "Deception and Division." Such a case is not generally regarded as a case of self-deception.

at work in self-deception, one can see why the paradoxes traditionally associated with self-deception would not arise. If Johnston is correct, modeling self-deception on other-deception is a mistake.

In Davidson and Johnston we thus have two competing models of self-deception. One model makes it analogous to other-deception, the other makes it a *sui generis* form of deception.

I. SELF-DECEPTION AND DIVISION

In this section I summarize what I take to be the essential components of Davidson's view.[6] I go on to discuss some general features of the view before focusing on what I take to be its most important, but most controversial, component.

Davidson believes that the self-deceiver arrives at his self-deceived state via a process or sequence of steps. That is, a person, *A*, deceives himself with respect to some proposition, *p*,[7] if

1. *A* judges that the totality of the evidence available to him supports a belief in not-*p*. (*A* "has evidence on the basis of which he believes" that not-*p* "is more apt to be true" than *p*.)[8]
2. *A* believes that not-*p*. (Or *A* is inclined to believe that, or thinks that, or thinks that he ought rationally to think that, not-*p*.)
3. Believing (or whatever) that not-*p* gives rise in *A* to some unsettling[9] feeling, emotion, or state. In a typical case believing that not-*p* may cause *A* pain.
4. *A*, given 3, has a motive (an "evaluative reason") for making it the case that he believes that *p*.

[6] See "Deception and Division." All quotations in the discussion that follows are taken from this article.

[7] Davidson says he is interested in one sort of self-deception and thus leaves open the possibility that there are other sorts. He also talks about stronger and weaker cases of the self-deception kind that interests him, although his primary interest is in the strongest case of this kind.

[8] See "Deception and Division," p. 88. While Davidson talks of the self-deceptive belief that not-*p*, I talk throughout the book of the self-deceptive belief that *p*. In the quotation cited he would therefore speak of evidence on the basis of which one believes that *p* is more apt to be true than not-*p*.

[9] "Unsettling" is a word I use, for, as we shall see, Davidson believes that the motive in some cases of self-deception may involve something other than wishful thought, and "unsettling" is intended to be broad enough to include these cases.

5. *A* intentionally does *x*, *y*, and *z*, things he believes will promote the belief that *p* in himself. The actions involved may include, for example, an intentional directing of attention away from the evidence in favor of not-*p*, or seeking, favoring, or emphasizing evidence for the falsity of not-*p* or actively searching for evidence for *p*.[10]
6. *A* believes that *p*.
7. In order to believe that *p*, however, *A* must violate the Requirement of Total Evidence (RTE) – one of the norms of rationality.

RTE demands that a person give credence, when confronted by mutually exclusive propositions, to the proposition that is best supported by all the person's available evidence. The proposition, however, that is best supported by *A*'s evidence is not-*p*. But *A*'s desire to avoid what RTE calls for causes him to wall off, or neglect, RTE and his belief (or whatever) that not-*p*, thus enabling him to believe that *p*. When *A* is self-deceived, he thus believes that not-*p* and he believes that *p*, although he never conjoins the two beliefs, for he has created a boundary between them. The contradictory beliefs are located in separate territories of the mind.

8. Given 1–7, *A* is guilty of self-induced Weakness of the Warrant (WW).

WW is a cognitive error which occurs when a reasoner, having evidence both for and against a proposition, judges that relative to all his evidence, the proposition is more probable than not, yet he does not accept the proposition, or the strength of his belief in the proposition is less than the strength of his belief in the negation of the proposition.

The crucial, and the most difficult to understand, feature of Davidson's account is the walling off or neglecting of RTE. Before discussing that, I want to mention three other features of the account. First, Davidson believes that the self-deceiver's motive or evaluative reason is not always a desire that *p*. Second, Davidson's self-deceiver, while intentionally deceiving himself, does not lie to himself; third, when he is self-deceived, he is not aware that he has intentionally deceived himself. A discussion of the third feature will lead to a discussion of walling off.

[10] "Deception and Division," p. 88.

(1) Davidson suggests that in some but not in all cases of self-deception the self-deceiver's motive springs from the fact that the agent wishes that the proposition he gets himself to believe were true, or fears that it might not be true. A self-deceiver may be motivated by a desire to believe what he wishes were the case, and this may be what self-deception typically involves, if, as Davidson suggests, self-deception "typically relieves a person of painful thoughts the causes of which are beyond his or her control."[11] However, Davidson believes there are other possibilities – not all cases of self-deception involve wishful thinking. The jealous person who finds "evidence" which confirms his worst suspicions, the person who wishes privacy but thinks he sees a person behind every curtain, the pessimist who believes what he wishes were not the case are the examples he gives. Whereas in wishful thinking the belief induced is always welcome, the induced belief in self-deception need not be welcome. "The thought bred by self-deception," as these cases are meant to illustrate, may, he says, "be painful."[12] In light of such examples he concludes that "it is hard to say what the relation must be between the motive someone has who deceives himself and the specific alteration in belief he works in himself."[13] He is quick to point out, however, that the relation cannot be accidental, for it is not self-deception simply to do something intentionally, say, read a book, and as a result to be deceived (be taken in by the author's intentionally false statements).

(2) While Davidson believes that self-deceiving and lying both involve "intentional behaviour which aims to produce a belief the agent does not, when he institutes the behaviour, share,"[14] lying, since it is a special kind of deceit, requires a special intention. The liar must intend to keep hidden from his hearer his intention of representing himself as believing what he does not believe.[15] To Davidson "[i]t does not seem possible that this precise form of deceit could be practised on oneself, since it would require doing something with the intention that that very intention should not be recognized by the

[11] Ibid., p. 79. [12] Ibid., p. 87. [13] Ibid. [14] Ibid.

[15] Davidson suggests that in order for *A* to lie to *B*, (1) *A* must intend to represent himself to *B* as believing what he does not (*A* may assert what he does not believe or *A* may say what he believes in a manner or in circumstances such that *B* takes him to believe the reverse of what he says) and (2) *A* must intend to keep this intention hidden (p. 88). *A*'s lie is *successful*, however, only if *A*'s intention to deceive *B* in this way is realized.

intender."[16] Lying to oneself, therefore, seems to require a self-defeating intention.

In a footnote Davidson acknowledges that one can intend to hide a present intention from one's future self.[17] He cites the person who tries to avoid an unpleasant engagement in the future by deliberately writing down a wrong date in his appointment book, counting on his bad memory to make him forget the deed before the time comes. If the intention to hide one's current intention (of representing oneself as believing what one does not) from one's future self were sufficient for lying to oneself, then it would seem possible for one to practice this form of deceit on oneself. We need not, however, decide here whether the person in the appointment example could be lying to himself, for even if he could, he is not, in Davidson's view, a pure self-deceiver. What this person does is abandon his original belief that the appointment is not on the date he writes down before he believes that it is on that date. Davidson's self-deceiver, however, is not allowed to abandon his original belief.

To intend, and to carry out successfully, a deception of oneself, as one does in the appointment example, is not sufficient for being a self-deceiver in the requisite sense. As Brian McLaughlin puts it, intentionally self-induced deception, of which the appointment case is an example, is not the same as self-deception.[18] For Davidson, what is needed in self-deception, but is not needed in self-induced deception, is that the intention that produces the intended belief sustains it, that is, the originating intention remains causally efficacious. For it to remain so, one must not forget that one believes that not-*p* (or that one thinks that one has better evidence for not-*p* than for *p*) and that one intends to try to promote the belief that *p* in oneself when one believes that not-*p* (or believes that the totality of one's evidence favors not-*p*).

(3) The Davidsonian self-deceiver, since he does not lie to himself, is not required to have the intention of keeping a certain intention of his hidden from himself. He must, however, intentionally deceive himself without realizing that he has done this. The successful self-deceiver is not aware of having intentionally deceived himself because he has, in the course of the deceiving process, effected a division that

[16] "Deception and Division," p. 88. [17] Ibid., no. 5.

[18] See "Exploring the Possibility of Self-Deception in Belief."

keeps certain of his propositional attitudes – e.g., his judgment that his evidence favors not-*p*, his belief that not-*p*, his belief that he should give credence to the proposition that is best supported by all his available evidence – segregated from other attitudes of his. The Davidsonian self-deceived person does not lack the information he needs to realize what he has done – the information he needs for this realization is, in some sense, available to him, for he can be conscious of each item that he needs. What he lacks is a simultaneous awareness of all the relevant items he needs, for this is just what the segregation prevents. The successful self-deceiver fails to realize, when (or at the same time as) he believes that *p*, that he continues to believe that not-*p* and that not-*p* is warranted by all his reasons. The territory in which his belief that not-*p* resides is not closed to consciousness, but since he cannot be aware that he still believes not-*p* when he believes that *p*, he does not see that any deception was involved in his coming to believe that *p*.

A certain sort of mental division is thus crucial to Davidson's position. But exactly how is this division effected? There is, I believe, no easy answer to this question, for there is no easy answer to the question of what walling off involves.

Davidson tells us that one of the steps in the sequence of steps via which the self-deceiver arrives at his self-deceived state is irrational. It involves a mental cause which is not a reason for the mental state it causes. The irrational step consists in drawing a boundary that walls off the troublesome propositional attitudes, including the Requirement of Total Evidence, from the rest of the mind. The isolation of RTE has a cause –

> the desire to avoid accepting what the requirement counsels. But this cannot be a *reason* for neglecting the requirement. Nothing can be viewed as a good reason for failing to reason according to one's best standards of rationality.[19]

Davidson thus claims that what causes the neglect of RTE, what causes its walling off – the desire to avoid accepting what RTE counsels – is not a reason for neglecting RTE. How should we understand this claim?

What he says suggests that the desire cannot be a *good reason*, given

[19] "Deception and Division," p. 92.

one's norms of rationality, for performing the activity in question. The activity in question is alternatively described as walling off the requirement or neglecting the requirement. I take it that neglect and walling off are not in this context distinct activities but more or less interchangeable descriptions of a single activity.

Davidson, however, also says that the desire cannot be **a** reason, and this suggests that he might mean something in addition to its not being a **good** reason. What might he mean here?

It seems clear that the self-deceiver, as characterized by Davidson, does not neglect RTE by accident, that his walling it off is not a chance occurrence. The step in the sequence in which it occurs, says Davidson, is an irrational step.

On Davidson's account, if the walling off of RTE were an action, something that the self-deceiver did, rather than something that happened to him, it would be intentional under some description. Suppose, as Davidson acknowledges, the self-deceiver has a pro attitude toward avoiding (he desires to avoid) what RTE counsels. Is there a belief that by doing such-and-such (= walling off) he will avoid what RTE counsels, a belief which, together with this desire, not only gives him a reason for wanting to wall off (to neglect) RTE but is his reason for walling off? The answer depends upon whether walling off is an action intentional under the description "walling off."

To wall off intentionally would seem not to require that one wall off at will, something it seems clear that one could not do. While there are many things people cannot do at will – things they must do by doing something – these things are nevertheless intentionally done.[20] For example, I intentionally get your attention by waving my arms. I desire to get your attention, I believe that by waving my arms I'll get your attention, so I wave my arms. Is walling off like getting your attention?

[20] People frequently arrange things in order to obtain effects they cannot produce at will. One knows that if one takes another drink one will no longer worry about driving home safely even though one cannot at will stop oneself from worrying about driving home safely. One cannot stop being angry at will, but one can break a glass one knows one will have to pick up in order to avoid injury to the cat, knowing further that by the time one has finished this painstaking task, one's anger will have dissipated. There are other cases where one can intentionally do something either *directly* or *by* doing something. One can, for example, intentionally raise one's arm directly, or one can raise it by lifting, with one's other arm, the sling the arm one wishes to raise is in.

If the walling off in self-deception is done intentionally, then it must be done by doing things like directing one's attention to positive evidence for *p* or to evidence against not-*p*.[21] Intentionally doing these sorts of thing would be intentionally walling off, if doing these things were the same action as walling off. While it may be plausible to think of my waving my arms and my getting your attention as the same action, I believe it is not plausible to think of directing one's attention to positive evidence for *p*, say, and walling off as the same action. If it is not, then walling off RTE is not something one intentionally does. It is clear that focusing on positive evidence for *p*, or on evidence against not-*p*, are not problematic things to do, whereas the walling off a self-deceiver is said to do is problematic. While this by itself would not show that doing these things is not the same as walling off, given that it seems possible that an action could be problematic under one description, but not under another,[22] it nonetheless seems likely that doing any of these things is not an instance of walling off. If it is not, then one would not have intentionally walled off. There would be no reason that was one's reason for walling off.

If any description which one came up with in this area – seeking positive evidence for *p*, seeking evidence against not-*p* – is not a description under which walling off is intentional – if I do not intentionally wall off – my walling off would not be caused, non-deviantly, by something which is a reason for it. If walling off were not like intentionally calling attention to oneself, because not done intentionally, then there is no reason – no belief–desire pair which rationalizes the walling off – as well as no good reason why the person walled off. What, however, could walling off be like?

I suggest that walling off is most plausibly compared with forgetting, which is neither intentional nor an action. One can intentionally do things that result in one's forgetting, and one can do those things because one believes that forgetting will result, without forgetting being either intentional or an action. I want to forget to do something, and I know that if I do not write down what it is that I am to do, I will forget it, so I intentionally do not write it down.

21 I am concerned with what must be realistically done. Taking a pill, hypnosis, etc. are not realistic options here.

22 What I say here depends upon how strong "problematic" is; if it is strong enough, then the problematic description doesn't apply to the action. For example, rubbing my left ear is "problematic" under the description "rubbing my right ear."

Let us suppose that by focusing on positive evidence for *p*, a self-deceiver comes to believe that *p* and believes that *p* on the basis of only some of his evidence. If he does this, then he avoids what RTE counsels; RTE is neglected. He intentionally does things, and those things bring it about that RTE is neglected. Suppose that the self-deceiver looks for new evidence in a **conscious** attempt to avoid what RTE calls for, although his seeking new evidence suggests he is not attempting to violate RTE but to conform to it.[23] At some point he must be taken in by the new evidence, something that can happen only if RTE is walled off. Just like the person in the appointment-book case who must forget (not intentionally forget) in order for the deception to succeed, the self-deceiver must do things which bring it about that RTE is walled off, neglected, in order for his deception to succeed.

The person in the appointment-book case, as Dion Scott-Kakures points out, can be said to treat himself as a mechanism.[24] When we treat ourselves as mechanisms, "we can exploit our (rather thin) understanding of the causal structure of our bodies and cognitive architecture to bring about effects we cannot produce at will."[25] The person in the appointment-book case exploits his understanding of how he functions – he knows he will forget what he has written down – in order to bring about a result – not knowing the date of the meeting – that he cannot produce at will. It is also plausible, as Scott-

[23] Contrast this with the self-deceiver who reasons in the following way: I want to discover whether I have overlooked any evidence for *p* or misinterpreted any of the evidence for not-*p*. I believe that by temporarily putting aside my judgment that the totality of my evidence supports not-*p* and my belief (or whatever) that not-*p*, I have a better chance of finding this out. I intentionally put these propositional attitudes aside by intentionally focusing my attention on positive evidence for *p* or trying out new interpretations of the alleged evidence for not-*p*. The self-deceiver could reason in this way at any stage in the process.

The self-deceiver so described is not, however, intentionally neglecting RTE, intentionally walling it off. By focusing on positive evidence for *p*, for example, he may come to believe that *p* and believe that *p* on the basis of only some of his evidence. If he does, then he avoids what RTE counsels; RTE is in a sense neglected. The self-deceiver could agree that it would be irrational to violate RTE, but he does not believe that this is what he is doing. The walling off and neglecting here would be nothing more than the unintentional consequence of this sort of putting aside.

[24] "Self-Deception and Internal Irrationality," p. 41. All the quotations in the discussion that follows are from this article. [25] Ibid.

Kakures suggests, to regard the self-deceiver in the case we are imagining as similarly exploiting his understanding of how he functions – as relying, for example, on his being seduced by salient positive evidence.

> Davidson's description of the process by which the self-deceptive belief is generated makes it hard to see why we do not have a case of treating oneself as a mechanism . . . For the way in which the self-deceiver brings about his deception – by averting his attention from contrary evidence, by seeking evidence for the favored proposition – intimates that the self-deceiver is taken in . . . by the ruse,[26]

just as the person in the appointment case is.

If the walling off and neglecting that Davidson suggests is irrational were the intended consequence of doing these other things, the walling off would not be accidental. The self-deceiver would have set up conditions in which the walling off was likely to occur. It would be the intended, not the unintended, consequence of doing these things.

But while the walling off would not be accidental, it would not be irrational in the way Davidson requires. Davidson wants to account for what he believes is the special sort of irrationality that makes self-deception so *prima facie* troubling. He wants to "identify an incoherence or inconsistency in the thought of the self-deceiver."[27] The Davidsonian self-deceiver does things intentionally with the aim of bringing it about that he believes something, the negation of which he has better reasons to believe. The neglect of his own norm of rationality is the intended consequence of his action. He thus knowingly brings it about that his own norm of rationality is violated. He is unlike the negotiator who, after an all-night session, comes to believe that his union will accept a certain provision in a contract he knew at the start of the session they would not accept. The negotiator does not knowingly violate his own standard of rationality. He does not intentionally set up conditions under which it will be likely that he will neglect his own norm; the neglect is the unintended, not intended, consequence of his all-night negotiations.

But even if the neglect of RTE were the intended, not unintended, consequence of the self-deceiver's actions, this does not show, as Scott-Kakures points out, that the self-deceiver has knowingly

[26] Ibid., p. 42. [27] "Deception and Division," p. 91.

violated his own standard of rationality.[28] We saw that if the self-deception is to succeed, then at some point in the self-deceiving process, the self-deceiver's desire to avoid what RTE counsels must cause RTE to be walled off; relevant information must no longer be present to the self-deceiver. But if the self-deceiver is not aware of the contrary evidence at the time he comes to believe that *p*, then he does not knowingly violate his own norm of rationality. Rather, he is like the person in the appointment-book case who comes to believe that *p* when he no longer has the relevant information about not-*p* at hand. Both would have intentionally done things which exploit what they knew about how they function, in order to come to believe that *p* on the basis of inadequate evidence. Although, according to Davidson, in the self-deceiver's case there is a belief that not-*p* or a belief that one ought to believe that not-*p* still present, the self-deceiver, given the walling off, is no more able knowingly to go against his own norms than is the person in the appointment case. Moreover, once the walling off takes place, the self-deceptive state would be a state in which one believes *p* and believes not-*p*, but one would not realize that one believes both these things. The state of being self-deceived seems no more incoherent or inconsistent in a troubling way than the more ordinary state of believing, but not realizing that one believes, inconsistent things.

Davidson, in his attempt to explain how in self-deception the seemingly paradoxical conditions (a) and (b) could be satisfied, is driven to partition the mind, to postulate a walling off. But if the walling off is something that humans can do, it seems that walling off must be an activity like forgetting. But if walling off is like forgetting, and it is difficult to see what else it could be like, then self-deceivers would not, despite what Davidson claims, knowingly violate their own standard of rationality.

While this suggests that the Davidsonian partitioning is not able to do what Davidson requires of it, Mark Johnston argues that Davidson's partitioning is unnecessary. The paradoxes that partitioning was invoked to explain arise, according to Johnston, from the tendency to "over-rationalize mental processes."[29] Once, he says, one

[28] "Self-Deception and Internal Irrationality," pp. 41ff.

[29] See "Self-Deception and the Nature of the Mind," p. 65. All quotations in the discussion that follows are from this article.

sees that there can be mental processes that are purposive but not intentional, and that it is processes of this sort, and not intentional actions, that are at work in self-deception, one can see why the paradoxes mentioned would not arise.

II. SELF-DECEPTION AND TROPISMS

In the summary of Johnston's position that I give in this section, I highlight the differences that exist between Johnston's and Davidson's accounts of self-deception.

Johnston accuses Davidson of overrationalizing self-deception by assimilating the purposive but not intentional processes involved in it to intentional acts. Davidson supposes that the self-deceiver initiates and directs his acts because he recognizes that they serve some specific interest of his. While Johnston claims the processes involved in self-deception serve some interest of the self-deceiver, the processes are not initiated by the self-deceiver for the sake of this interest or for any other reason. Mental processes which are thus purposive, which serve an interest, but which are not initiated for and from a reason, are subintentional processes.

For Johnston, self-deceptive thought is a species of wishful thought. The self-deceiver adopts his "wishful belief *despite* his recognition at some level that the evidence is to the contrary."[30] However, wishful thinking is not, he argues, an intentional act. It consists rather of "a mental mechanism or tropism by which a desire that *p* and accompanying anxiety that not-*p* set the conditions for the rewarding (because anxiety-reducing) response of coming to believe that *p*."[31] Wishful thinking is an example of what he calls a mental tropism, a non-accidental or lawlike subintentional causal process. In all such processes a natural kind of mental state regularly gives rise to another natural kind of mental state. In self-deception, the self-deceiver's anxious desire that *p* (he desires that *p* and is anxious that not-*p*) causes him to believe (wishfully) that *p*. But obviously the self-deceiver's anxiety will not be reduced if he continues to recognize that the evidence is strongly against *p*. So the self-deceiver's anxious desire that *p* causes him not only to believe that *p* but to repress or cease to consciously acknowledge that the evidence is strongly against not-*p*.

[30] Ibid., p. 75. [31] Ibid., p. 73.

Rationalizing, selectively focusing, evading, overcompensating, and so on make the repression possible. Neither the repressing nor the acquiring of the wishful belief that *p* essentially involves intentional action. Both are tropisms. While the self-deceiver's activities are motivated in that they have a purpose – to relieve his anxiety (and hence the belief, since it reduces anxiety, is always welcome) – they are not done from or for a reason.

According to Johnston, the operation of mental tropisms underlies both rational and non-rational belief change. In rational belief change the belief is caused by a mental state that provides a reason of the right sort (a non-evaluative or cognitive reason) for it. In non-rational belief change, the belief is not caused by a mental state that provides a cognitive reason for it.

III. SELF-DECEPTION: INTENTIONAL OR NONINTENTIONAL?

Johnston and Davidson, as we have seen, fundamentally disagree about the nature of the activity that is involved in self-deception; Johnston opts for non-intentional deception, Davidson for intentional deceit. How is one to choose between these alternative characterizations? One might, for example, assess the characterizations phenomenologically, that is, one might see if one better accords with what the self-deceiver would say he is doing.

While Davidson is aware that his account introduces some conceptual territories that the self-deceiver would not discover in himself by introspection, his account must nevertheless have some phenomenological accountability, since it requires that the self-deceiver intentionally try to promote a belief that *p* in himself, and that he be aware of intending to do this when he is aware that he believes that not-*p*.

It seems unlikely that a self-deceiver typically takes himself to be trying to promote the belief that *p* in himself when he believes not-*p*. What the self-deceiver would most likely admit doing is trying to ascertain what is the case. He believes that his motive is epistemic; what he believes will depend upon what he finds to be the case. Even if the totality of the evidence he had favored not-*p*, a reexamination of the situation might uncover evidence for *p* or against not-*p*. The self-deceiver would, of course, deny that in trying to find out what is the case he rationalizes, etc., but no one supposes that he would admit to this.

Johnston's account fares better phenomenologically than Davidson's in this regard, since it does not demand that the self-deceiver intentionally try to do something which he does not believe he is trying to do. But there is another regard in which Johnston's account fares no better than Davidson's, a regard, moreover, that makes choosing between them unnecessary.

Both Johnston's and Davidson's accounts cannot adequately deal with a familiar kind of self-deception. If, as I argue in the next chapter, these two philosophical models of self-deception are not ultimately satisfactory as general models of the phenomenon, then one need not choose between them.

One must, however, choose between an intentional and a non-intentional account of self-deception. My account, like Johnston's, is a non-intentional one. Self-deception is not subject to whatever epistemic condition other-deception is subject to. Self-deceivers, for example, are not required to introduce into their situation something which they believe has a real possibility of causing them to believe that *p*, and yet take that something to provide neither adequate evidence for *p* nor direct sensory awareness that *p*. In my account, as in Johnston's, self-deceivers must be in a certain affective or conative state – a state of anxious desire. Johnston and I differ, however, about the content of that anxious desire and hence about whether the self-deceptive belief is always wishful.

I also take issue with a point on which Davidson and Johnston agree, for I maintain that self-deceivers need not recognize that the totality of their evidence favors not-*p* when they come to believe, self-deceptively, that *p*. There is, however, agreement among us that self-deceivers do not lie to themselves, nor do they realize that they have deceived themselves. And we agree, moreover, that self-deceivers are partial or biased in coming to their belief that *p*.

3

The need for an alternative model of self-deception

In a familiar enough type of self-deception, the self-deceptive belief seems not to be welcome. A parent deceives herself into believing that she is to blame for her child's death, although the child died of leukemia;[1] a husband deceives himself into believing that his wife is unfaithful; an adolescent deceives herself into believing that she is overweight. Cases of this type, however, pose problems for many of the prominent accounts of self-deception, including those of Davidson and Johnston.

For example, if we apply Davidson's analysis to the case of a husband deceiving himself about his wife's fidelity, a segregated and hence covert belief[2] in his wife's fidelity would be required to sustain causally the man's overt belief in her infidelity. But it seems highly doubtful that the man's belief in her infidelity is causally sustained by a belief in her fidelity.[3] Johnston would seem to require that an anxious desire that his wife be unfaithful be the cause of his believing that she is unfaithful. However, it seems highly doubtful that the man's belief in his wife's infidelity is a wishful belief reducing anxiety about her fidelity.[4]

[1] Martha Knight, "Cognitive and Motivational Bases of Self-Deception: Commentary on Mele's *Irrationality*," *Philosophical Psychology*, vol. 1, no. 2 (1988), pp. 182ff., discusses this case of seemingly unwelcome self-deceptive belief. She also considers the case of a bright young college student who deceives herself into believing that she is less able than she is.

[2] Belief in the strongest case; see Chapter 2 for other possibilities.

[3] Assume here that the husband's belief in her fidelity is welcome and his belief in her infidelity is not welcome.

[4] If Johnston allows that self-deceptive beliefs other than the belief that *p* might arise in the course of coming to believe that *p*, when one anxiously desires that *p*, then a man's belief that his wife is unfaithful could on his account be a self-deceptive belief. As we have seen, "If anxiety that not-*p* produced by recognition of telling evidence for not-*p* is to be reduced, not only must the wishful belief that *p* arise, but the recognition of the evidence

On both Johnston's and Davidson's accounts, moreover, the man would be required to recognize that the totality of his evidence supports fidelity. I argue that it need not be the case that a man in such a situation recognize this and, consequently, the man need not engage in either a walling off of this recognition, as Davidson would require, or in its repression, as Johnston would require.

If, as I claim, Davidson's and Johnston's accounts of self-deception cannot adequately deal with seemingly unwelcome self-deceptive belief, they are not adequate as general accounts of self-deception. While Johnston's account seems intended as a fully general account of self-deception, Davidson acknowledges that he is dealing with one sort of self-deception. But a correct fully general account would be preferable to an incorrect fully general account, and to a partial account. I go on to argue for a certain account that can adequately deal with seemingly unwelcome self-deceptive belief and that can be generalized. I develop the general account in this and subsequent chapters.

While I believe that Johnston is correct in assuming that one cannot understand why people deceive themselves without assuming that they gain something by doing so, and that he is also correct in assuming that the gain always involves **some reduction of anxiety** about the non-satisfaction of their desires,[5] Johnston is not right to assume

as more or less establishing the contrary must also be repressed, i.e., the subject must cease consciously acknowledging it. The strategies by which one ceases consciously to acknowledge that one recognizes the evidence to be against one's wishful belief are manifold. One may selectively reappraise and explain away the evidence (rationalization). One may simply avoid thinking about the touchy subject (evasion). One may focus one's attention on invented reasons for *p* and spring to the advocacy of *p* whenever opportunity presents itself (overcompensation)" ("Self-Deception and the Nature of the Mind," p. 75).

It seems plausible to suppose that in employing some of these strategies, e.g., rationalization and overcompensation, one would come to have a number of false beliefs. If one was willing to count some of these as self-deceptive beliefs, then the belief that one's wife is unfaithful could be a belief that arose as a result of having used one of these strategies of repression. The anxious desire that *p* (and *p* here would not be that my wife is unfaithful but something else) could have as its byproduct the belief in her infidelity. But if Johnston were to allow this, he would either be abandoning his analysis of self-deception or at least making it implicitly much more complicated than it explicitly is.

5 The reduction of one anxiety can lead to other anxieties, sometimes far greater ones. The gain, therefore, is not necessarily an all-things-considered gain, nor is it necessarily beneficial for the person.

that the anxiety that is reduced by a self-deceptive belief that *p* is always the anxiety that not-*p*. In the case at hand, it is not the man's anxiety about his wife's fidelity that is reduced by his believing in her infidelity. The man is not made anxious by her fidelity. Rather, I suggest that some other anxious desire operating here is reduced by his belief in her infidelity.

While I agree with Johnston that self-deceptive belief functions to reduce anxiety, I hold that the relation between self-deceptive belief and anxious desire is more complicated than the Johnston formula allows. On his account the relation between self-deceptive belief and anxious desire is in a certain respect very simple. The self-deceptive belief that *p* reduces the anxiety that not-*p*. Let us call this the one-variable formula for self-deceptive belief, where the one variable is "*p*." I complicate the Johnston formula by introducing a second variable "*q*." Although the self-deceptive belief that *p* may sometimes function to reduce anxiety that not-*p*, it can sometimes function instead to reduce anxiety about some other proposition. I introduce a second variable "*q*" where *q* may be, but need not be, *p*. The self-deceptive belief that *p* can reduce anxiety that not-*q* because the subject believes that if *p* then *q* (or, perhaps, if *p* then probably *q*). That is, on what I call the two-variable formula for self-deceptive belief,[6] the self-deceptive belief that *p*, together with the belief that if *p* then (probably) *q*, reduces anxiety that not-*q*. This formula allows for the relevant conditional (if *p* then *q*)[7] to be itself the result of an arbitrarily long series of conditionals (e.g., if *p* then - - -; if - - - then . . ., if . . . then *q*). This two-variable formula can, I argue, handle all cases of self-deceptive belief.[8]

Mele, whose view is similar to Johnston's with respect to the non-intentionality of self-deception,[9] focuses in self-deception on a rela-

[6] I speak here of the one- and two-variable formulas for self-deceptive belief, but more exactly they are formulas for the relation between self-deceptive belief and anxious desire.

[7] The formula also allows that when $q = p$ the conditional is "if *p* then *p*."

[8] This is not the only formula that would handle all cases of self-deceptive belief, but it is the simplest of the available formulas that would do so. I have opted for it because of its simplicity. In note 19 I discuss a three-variable formula that would also do the job. And in note 24 I show how the three-variable formula would handle a particular case of self-deception.

[9] Mele believes that "the vast majority of cases of self-deception are not cases of intentional deceiving." *Irrationality*, p. 123.

tionship between a desire that *p* and a self-deceptive belief that *p*. However, Mele recognizes that in the case, for example, of a jealous husband who believes that his wife is unfaithful, the motivational work "may be done by a variety of desires."[10] While Mele can thus accommodate a desire that *q*, his account differs in an important respect from both mine and Johnston's. Whereas Mele assigns the pivotal causal role in self-deception to desire, I follow Johnston in assigning that role to **anxious** desire.[11]

Not all desires, of course, are anxiety-linked. A man who desires to pass his driving test or to have a cup of coffee may not be anxious that he will not pass his test or will not have the coffee. While a man who desires to pass a test may believe that he will pass, he need not have deceived himself into believing this.

Let us suppose, however, that a man deceives himself into believing that he will pass his driving test. His belief that *he will* pass the test does not give him the same satisfaction that the belief that *he has* passed the test would give him.[12] But had he been anxious that he would not

[10] Ibid., p. 118. These other desires may include "the elimination of rivals," a suggestion made by Pears, or "certain self-destructive wishes." I discuss Pears' suggestion in note 27.

[11] I disagree with Mele not only with regard to the issue of desire versus anxious desire. Mele gives the following as characteristic and jointly sufficient conditions for a central case of *S*'s entering self-deception in acquiring the belief that *p*:

1. The belief that *p* which *S* acquires is false.
2. *S*'s desiring that *p* leads *S* to manipulate (i.e. to treat inappropriately) a datum or data relevant, or at least seemingly relevant, to the truth value of *p*.
3. This manipulation is a cause of *S*'s acquiring the belief that *p*.
4. If, in the causal chain between desire and manipulation or in that between manipulation and belief acquisition, there are any accidental intermediaries (links), or intermediaries intentionally introduced by another agent, these intermediaries do not make *S* (significantly) less responsible for acquiring the belief that *p* than he would otherwise have been. *Irrationality*, p. 127.

With regard to 2, the subject's desire that *p* can lead "him to fail to appreciate the gravity of some evidence that he has that not-*p*, to misconstrue the import of such evidence, to focus selectively on evidence supportive of *p*, or to fail to locate readily available evidence that not-*p*, while seeking evidence that *p*." Ibid., p. 126.

Later discussion should make clear why I believe these conditions are not sufficient. Not only must anxiety be added, a requirement concerning the self-deceiver's false consciousness is needed.

[12] Johnston makes this point about wishful believing in "Self-Deception and the Nature of the Mind," p. 72. "[T]he belief that is correlated with or brings the good news of winning is the belief that one *has* won, whereas the wishful belief correlated with the desire to win

pass, his belief that he will pass would function to reduce his anxiety about not passing. This suggests that when self-deceivers deceive themselves into believing that some future event will occur, their self-deceptive beliefs function to reduce their anxiety about the non-occurrence of that event. I try to show that self-deceptive belief *always* functions to reduce a self-deceiver's anxiety, whether the self-deceptive belief is about what will occur, what has occurred, or what is occurring.

In the case at hand it is, moreover, difficult to see what function the man's belief that he will pass his driving test would perform if he had not been anxious about passing; its presence would appear to be mysterious, superfluous, inefficient. But self-deception is not a gratuitous, useless process. As Johnston points out, not only does a creature do better in certain environments by monitoring its desires and rationally exploiting means to their satisfaction, such a creature also "does better in other ways if its frequent and debilitating anxieties that its desires will not be satisfied are regularly dealt with by doses of hopeful belief."[13]

To "have an anxious desire that something" as I shall use the expression throughout is to have a specific complex sort of propositional attitude toward that something.[14] A person has an anxious desire that *q*, i.e., that it be the case that *q*, just in case the person both desires that *q* and is anxious that it is not the case that *q*.[15]

is typically anticipatory. It is the belief that one *will* win." "A future-tensed belief can reduce anxiety about the future. If this is the relevant role of anticipatory wishful thought – the reduction of anxiety about a desired outcome – then we should expect anticipatory wishful thought in the presence of the desire that *p* coupled with the fear that not-*p*."

13 Ibid., p. 89. I shall argue that not all self-deceptive belief is wishful, as Johnston supposes. If self-deception were selected for in evolution, that self-deceptive belief functions to reduce anxiety could explain why.

14 The expressions "anxious that . . .," "anxious desire that . . .," "desire that . . .," "belief that . . ." are used in the philosophical literature to indicate propositional attitudes. While the expressions are technical expressions, they can be reexpressed in ordinary language terms.

15 *A* can be aware or unaware of having an anxious desire that *q*. *A* can, for example, be aware of his anxious desire to obtain (that he obtain) a new car but unaware of his anxious desire to dominate discussions. Although what I go on to say about anxious desires may hold true of anxious desires that *q* of which *A* is unaware, the discussion will focus on anxious desire that *q* of which *A* is aware.

A's anxious desire that something can also be either real – e.g., it is the case that *A* anx-

There is, however, a certain redundancy in the phrase "anxious desire," for being anxious that not-*q* requires desiring that *q*.[16] When a person is anxious that not-*q*, the person (1) **is uncertain whether *q* or not-*q*** and (2) **desires that *q***.[17] So a simpler analysis is also correct: one has an anxious desire that *q* just in case one is anxious that not-*q*. But the redundant analysis has the advantage of making explicit the desire that enters into anxious desire.

When the two-variable formula for self-deceptive belief speaks of *q*, the *q* of which it speaks must be understood according to a certain important restriction: while the person desires that *q*, ***the person desires that q for its own sake*** and not for the sake of something else to which the person takes *q* to be importantly related. For example, suppose a woman anxiously desires that her husband be faithful. To represent this situation in terms of the two-variable formula is to take it as a given that the woman desires for its own sake that her husband be faithful. Suppose, however, the woman desires that her husband be faithful "only because she wants it to be true that he loves her and believes that love entails fidelity."[18] If we assume that she desires for its own sake that her husband love her, then we would represent that desire and not the desire that he be faithful by means of *q*. The anxious

iously desires that he obtain a new car – or merely apparent, e.g., *A* anxiously desires to eat (that he eat) the grapes on his plate. His desire to eat them depends upon his mistaken belief that they are sweet. However, if *A* had an accurate description of the grapes, if he knew how sour they were, he would no longer have the desire to eat them. *A*'s anxious desire that something is a merely apparent anxious desire if the desire essential to it would be extinguished if *A* had an accurate description of that something. Though anxious desires can be distinguished in this way, this distinction will play no significant role in the discussion.

[16] Q can be that someone have or not have something, or that someone had (or did not have) or will have (or will not have) something; that someone be or not be some type of person, e.g., generous, easygoing, manipulative; that someone perform or not perform some action, e.g., fly on a space shuttle, play real tennis; that some state of affairs be or not be the case, e.g., that the Gulf War be a short war, that Smith get promoted.

[17] Robert Gordon, *The Structure of Emotions* (Cambridge: Cambridge University Press, 1987), p. 68. In his discussion of fearing that, Gordon claims that if *S* fears that *p*, "then *S* is neither certain that *p* nor certain that not-*p*" and "*S* cares whether or not *p* . . . *S* wishes it not to be the case that *p*." Gordon's analysis of fearing that served as a model for my analysis of anxiety that, although my account diverges from his at a number of points.

[18] The example is Mele's. He is using it to illustrate that something may "be wanted either for its own sake or for the sake of something else to which he takes it to be importantly related." *Irrationality,* p. 125.

desire that *q* in the two-variable formula has to be the bedrock desire.[19]

In cases of self-deception the person must believe that it is at least possible that not-*q*. This uncertainty about whether *q* or not-*q* can be the result of a suspicion that not-*q*, or it can be the result of some stronger cognitive attitude. It is an uncertainty, moreover, that is not in one's power to resolve by, for example, making a decision.

Some philosophers have, as we have seen, held in effect that in paradigmatic cases of self-deception the person must believe that not-*q* (Davidson), or the person must at least recognize that the evidence is telling against *q* (Johnston).[20] I argue that such stronger cognitive attitudes are not essential for central cases of self-deception.[21]

[19] If one wants to focus on an anxious desire that *q* where the person does not desire that *q* for its own sake but for the sake of something else to which the person takes *q* to be importantly related, then a third variable, "*s*," must be introduced. (I use "*s*" for that variable and not "*r*" to avoid confusing this with the "*r*" that I shall use in the main discussion.) In the three-variable formula the variable "*s*" designates the something for the sake of which the person desires that *q*. One can think of this as the reason for which the person desires that *q*.

The reason, *s*, for desiring that *q* will often consist of a belief/desire pair that takes a certain form. The person believes that if not-*q* is the case, then some desire that the person has, the desire that not-*s*, could not be satisfied. There may, of course, be more than one desire that could not be satisfied if not-*q* were the case, that is, *s* may be replaced by s_1, s_2, etc. There may also be more than one anxious desire; *q* may be replaced by q_1, q_2, etc. Anxious desires may be interrelated.

In cases where there is a hierarchy of reasons why one cares whether *q*, the three-variable formula represents *s* as the deepest reason, the reason which is the starting point for all the anxiety. Q is the anxiety immediately behind *p*. Intermediary reasons $q^\star$, $q^{\star\star}$, etc. are accommodated in implicit conditionals between *q* and *s*. That is, whatever level of anxiety you want to accommodate, make the deepest level the content of *s*, and all the intermediary anxieties are to be included in the chain from *q* to not-*s*. The implicit conditionals could be expressed, but this would lead to formulas of indefinitely many variables, and nothing that would be of essential concern for understanding the structure of self-deception would be revealed in such an expansion.

The three-variable formula attends to the complexity that I argue is associated with cases of self-deception as an artefact of the formula. The two-variable formula handles the complexity as a formula-independent fact.

[20] In the cases where the anxious desire that *q* is an anxious desire that *p*, i.e., where $q = p$, the anxiety that not-*q* would derive from the belief that not-*p* or from the recognition that the evidence against *p* was telling.

[21] Mele also believes that the self-deceiver need not recognize that the totality of his evidence favors not-*p*, for although he says that "the self-deceived person, again due to

When the person is uncertain whether not-q, the person will typically have some reason, r, which is responsible for the uncertainty. The person believes, for example, that if r then not-q (or if r then probably not-q or if r then possibly not-q).[22] We are now in a position to see how the two-variable formula handles cases of seemingly unwelcome self-deceptive belief. Suppose a husband deceives himself into believing that his wife is unfaithful. If we assume that he is not made anxious by her fidelity, what anxiety might be at work? Different anxieties can, of course, be at work in different circumstances. For example,

Scenario 1. John's long-time friend George agrees to do something when asked by John's wife Mary, but had refused to do it when asked by John. John, taken aback by George's refusal of his request, wonders why Mary has more influence with George than he has. Could it be that George has a greater regard for Mary than he does for him? John, who cares about George's regard, begins thinking about Mary and George's relationship. Have not Mary and George been rather attentive to one another lately? Indeed, as he reflects upon their closeness he begins to suspect, and ultimately to believe, that they are in fact having an affair. John, by self-deceptively believing that his wife has been unfaithful, avoids concluding, as he otherwise might have concluded, that Mary's greater influence with George is a reflection of George's having higher regard for Mary than for John. For if, as John now believes, Mary's influence with George is illicit, then such influence does not reflect higher regard. John's self-deceptive belief would not be an expression of a wish. Rather it would provide John with an alternative explanation of why George agrees to do something at Mary's request but not at his.[23]

In this scenario the respective values for "p" and "q" are:

p = Mary is unfaithful.

q = George does not have a higher regard for Mary than he does for John.

desire, typically *believes* against his 'better evidence,'" he immediately adds "**or against better evidence he would have had, or could easily have acquired,** if it were not for the desire in question." *Irrationality*, p. 136.

22 The relevant conditional (if r then not-q) may itself be the result of an arbitrarily long series of conditionals (e.g., if r then $r^\star$, if $r^\star$ then . . ., if . . ., then not-q).

23 In Shakespeare's *The Winter's Tale*, Leontes deceives himself into believing that his wife, Hermione, has been unfaithful with his childhood friend Polixenes. I am modeling my three scenarios on what I would take to be plausible interpretations of that play.

John is uncertain whether George has a higher regard for Mary than he does for John, because he believes that if *r* (*r* = Mary has more influence with George than he has), then it is possible that George has a higher regard for Mary than he does for John. (If *r* then possibly not-*q*.) George desires for its own sake that George not have a higher regard for Mary than for him. By believing that *p*, Mary is unfaithful, John can believe that *q*, George does not have a higher regard for Mary than for him. If Mary is unfaithful, then although Mary's has greater influence with George than John, it does not follow from Mary's having greater influence with George that George has a higher regard for Mary than for him, since the influence she has with him is illicit influence. The self-deceptive belief that *p*, that Mary is unfaithful, enables John to believe that it is more nearly likely that his anxious desire that *q*, that George does not have a higher regard for Mary than for him, is satisfied.[24] A fact which looked like a sufficient condition for not-*q*, for George's having a higher regard for Mary than for him, has been shown not to be a sufficient condition, and other sufficient conditions are not in the offing.[25]

John's belief in Mary's infidelity is not causally sustained by a belief in her fidelity. Nor is his belief in her infidelity generated by anxiety about her fidelity; the belief that she is unfaithful is not a wishful belief. Moreover, given that George's self-deceptive belief is distanced from the object of his anxiety – John will not see his belief as functioning to reduce that anxiety – there will be less chance of the self-deceptive belief being undermined by that anxiety. The self-

[24] We could represent scenario 1 on the three-variable formula:
The three variables would be:
p = Mary is unfaithful;
q = Mary does not have more influence with George than he does;
s = George has a higher regard for Mary than he does for him.
On the three-variable formula, John's anxious desire that *q* (Mary does not have more influence with George than he does) gives rise to the self-deceptive belief that *p* (Mary is unfaithful) because believing that *p* allows him to believe that, even though not-*q* (Mary does have more influence with George than he does), it does not follow that (if not-*q* then *s*). That is, it does not follow that if Mary has has more influence with George than he does, then George has a higher regard for Mary than he does for him. He is, therefore, able to believe that not-*s* (George does not have a higher regard for Mary than he does for him).

[25] Schematically, if *p* is the case, then *r*; but even if *r* is the case, it is not the case that (if *r* then not-*q*); therefore, probably *q*.

deceptive belief can be sustained epistemically without bringing John's attention too close to the troublesome area. John's self-deceptive belief would, moreover, give John a reason for taking action against his wife and friend, action in which his anger at George's slight or his jealousy of his wife's influence with George could be expressed.

Although John's belief that Mary has gotten her influence by fraudulent means allows John to believe that his desire that George not have a higher regard for his wife than he does for him is satisfied, this does not ensure that John's desire that his wife not be held in higher regard than he is *is* satisfied. Someone's believing that the conditional – if Mary has more influence with George than I have, then George has a higher regard for Mary than he does for me – is false does not, of course, make the conditional false.[26] Whether or not the conditional is false, John's self-deceptive belief that *p* functions to reduce his anxiety that not-*q* even if the desire that *q* is not satisfied. One's anxiety about *q* is directly affected by one's beliefs, not by reality outside one's beliefs. One's anxiety can be relieved if one believes, mistakenly, that *q*.

John's anxiety about Mary's being held in higher regard by George than he is causes him to believe in her infidelity. It is true that prior to having this anxious desire he believed that she was faithful, that George was loyal. But this does not mean that he therefore intentionally gets himself to believe in her infidelity when he is aware of her fidelity, nor that he simultaneously believes that she is faithful and unfaithful, things he would have to be doing on some accounts of self-deception.

There are of course other possible explanations for why a man would deceive himself into believing that his wife was unfaithful. For example,

Scenario 2. I have described the husband, John, as being anxious about his wife's, Mary's, influence with his friend George, an anxiety that is responsible for John's belief about her infidelity. But one might suppose that whatever anxiety a husband might feel about that is slight in comparison to the anxiety that his belief in her infidelity would cause him. Would John trade his lesser anxiety for a greater one? While people do this, might it not be the case that John is not anxious

[26] And even if this conditional is false, it gives only one sufficient condition of what the husband wants not to be so; another sufficient condition might still be satisfied.

at all about higher regard? The second scenario suggests that John is not jealous of his wife's influence with George; rather he is jealous about Mary's attentions to George. That George agrees at Mary's request and not his strikes him as significant because he is *already* suspicious of the two of them.

Let us see why, even on the assumption that John is jealous of Mary's attentions to George, his belief in her infidelity could nevertheless function to reduce some anxiety of his. A jealous person feels distress or anger when he sees someone else getting the attention he feels he alone deserves. A jealous person also typically tries to justify his response. Suppose John anxiously desires that he not be to blame for having these feelings of anger, distress, and jealousy which are aroused in him by Mary's attentions to George. He believes that if these feelings are not justified he is to blame for having them. And he is unsure whether the evidence justifies his having these feelings. His belief that his wife and friend are having an affair could function to reduce his anxiety, for he could then believe that his feelings of anger, distress, and jealousy are the result of their illicit behavior and therefore not the result of some failing in him. He is not to blame for having these feelings.

In this scenario,

p = Mary is unfaithful.

q = I am not to blame for having the feelings of anger, distress, and jealousy that I have toward Mary and George.

John is uncertain whether he is to blame for having the feelings he has, because he is uncertain whether *r* (*r* = I am not justified in having the feelings of anger, distress, and jealousy that I have toward Mary and George). He believes that if *r* then not-*q*. By believing that Mary is unfaithful, he can believe that he is justified in having those feelings, and hence that he is not to blame for having those feelings. (By believing that *p*, he can believe that not-*r*, and if not-*r* then [probably] *q*.)

Scenario 3. Assume that the husband, John, is jealous of his wife's attention to his friend as in scenario 2. John anxiously desires that he have sole possession of Mary's affections, but since he suspects that she may be sharing those affections with George, he is uncertain whether he has sole possession. By believing that Mary is unfaithful, he believes that George is sharing Mary's affection. But this allows him to take steps to eliminate George as a rival, and thus to believe that he can again have sole possession of Mary's affections.

In this scenario,
p = Mary is unfaithful.
q = I have sole possession of Mary's affections.

John is anxious that he does not have sole possession of Mary's affections because he suspects that r (r = George is sharing Mary's affections). By believing that p, Mary is unfaithful, George believes that r. But believing r motivates him to take steps to put an end to what he believes, mistakenly, is George's sharing of Mary's affections. He believes that if his steps are successful then not-r will be the case, and hence he can believe that q.[27]

The two-variable formula is not dependent upon a particular scenario being the correct one. Whatever the source of the husband's anxiety, the claim is that there must be some perceived gain for him in

[27] In *Motivated Irrationality*, Pears discusses cases of self-deception in which the self-deceptive beliefs, caused by fear or jealousy, are not wishful. One of his cases is not unlike the case I have been discussing. He believes that emotions like fear or jealousy "often lead people to form intrinsically unpleasant beliefs against the promptings of reason" (p. 42). He believes people form such beliefs because these beliefs help them in obtaining some ulterior goal. "In the case of fear we may conjecture that the ulterior goal is avoiding the danger, and that it is best achieved by exaggerating it and so making quite sure of taking the necessary steps. Similarly, we may say that the exaggerated speculations of jealousy, which are intrinsically unpleasant, are the best way of making sure of eliminating all rivals. In both cases the belief is a kind of bitter medicine" (pp. 42–3).

When we, in such situations, have an ulterior goal, we do not intentionally have to get ourselves to do things which will allow us to achieve those goals. Rather where there is a wish for an ulterior goal, for safety or the elimination of a rival, "nature takes over at this point and sets up an emotional programme that ensures its achievement. [Nature has simply programmed us to react in exaggerated stereotypical ways in order to achieve a desirable ulterior goal.] The plan is nature's and not the person's, and that is why the formation of the intrinsically unpleasant belief is not felt to be the object of the wish" (p. 44). Presumably the desire in question is no mere desire. Simply desiring to eliminate rivals would not itself lead one to believe that more people were one's rivals than actually were. But an anxious desire to eliminate rivals, or to avoid danger, might give rise to a self-deceptive belief that so-and-so is a genuine rival or that such-and-such poses a real threat. A man may anxiously desire to eliminate all possible rivals. By believing that someone, *S*, is a rival he is able to try to eliminate him. Although the man need not want that someone to be his rival *qua* "*S* is my rival" he does want to eliminate any potential rival. Believing *S* is a rival allows him to try to eliminate him and thereby to believe that he is eliminating a rival. I shall argue that nature is not, however, the responsible party, the man is, although it is not part of the man's plan to get himself to believe that *S* is a rival.

believing, self-deceptively, that his wife has been unfaithful. The gain involves at a minimum the reduction of anxiety.[28]

While my analysis of self-deception is not dependent upon any particular anxious desire being the correct one,[29] I have not yet explained

[28] It could happen that while one was no longer anxious that something was the case, the desire satisfaction that one anticipated occurring does not occur. The perceived gain in such a situation would be small although the anticipated gain had not been. I discuss a case of this sort in Chapter 4.

[29] I am assuming that some anxious desire or other must always be present in self-deception. But this assumption can be challenged from two quite different directions.

Direction 1. The husband in any of the scenarios I presented was jealous of his wife, either of his wife's influence with his friend, as in scenario 1, or of her attentions to his friend, as in scenarios 2 and 3. But it could be argued that for madly jealous people there need not be an advantage or even any perceived advantage in their believing that their worst suspicions are confirmed. Rather than any reduction in anxiety, the husband's jealousy-induced belief could cause him nothing but continual suffering. Why in such a case should we suppose that the self-deceptive belief functions to reduce any anxiety? Would it not be more plausible to see the self-deceptive belief there as an example of compulsive or pathological or obsessive thought? That is, why not view the husband as analogous to, say, Medea? She does things against her own best judgment because of some compulsive passion; the husband believes in his wife's infidelity against his own sense of epistemic rationality because of some compulsive thought. (I am grateful to Richard Moran for making me aware of this sort of challenge.)

The claim from direction 1 is that anxious desire is not a necessary condition of self-deception. In some cases of self-deceptive belief, a compulsive belief replaces it. But construing some self-deceptive belief as a kind of compulsive belief makes that self-deceptive belief a more problematic kind of belief than (as I try to show) self-deceptive belief ever is. The cases of self-deceptive belief that I go on to discuss will illustrate why I believe that a self-deceptive belief is always other than a compulsive belief, i.e., why a self-deceptive belief always involves anxious desire.

Self-deceptive belief is, I contend, neither compulsive belief nor intentional belief. Rather, like ordinary non-self-deceptive belief, self-deceptive belief occupies middle ground. While wishful belief also occupies middle ground, I show in the remainder of the chapter why self-deceptive belief is not to be identified with it.

Direction 2. The first objection assumed that some self-deceptive belief could be redescribed without loss in terms of compulsive belief. The second objection suggests that there may be unmotivated self-deceptive belief.

Martha Knight, in her discussion of a case of seemingly unwelcome self-deceptive belief, where the motivating desire that operates would seem to be a desire other than a desire that *p*, points out that "what is problematic in any given case of this type is that specification of the motivating [anxious] desire will almost always be *post hoc* and subject to circular reasoning. Further, when numerous plausible [anxious] desires are proffered, *post hoc*, to explain self-deception, there is often no clear way to determine which

why, given this or that anxious desire, the self-deceiver comes to have one anxiety-reducing belief in particular. Presumably other beliefs could also reduce the self-deceiver's anxiety, beliefs, moreover, that might be less unwelcome than a belief in one's spouse's infidelity. Why doesn't the husband believe, for example, that his friend was merely being polite to his wife, that he complied with her request, despite his reluctance, for fear of offending her by a refusal? Since he and the husband were such close friends, he assumed the husband would understand his fear and reluctance and hence understand why he had refused the husband's request but had not refused hers. Surely believing this would allow the husband to believe that his friend did not hold his wife in higher regard than he did him.

While it is necessary in self-deception that there be an anxiety-reducing belief that the self-deceiver acquires, there is no anxiety-reducing belief such that it is necessary that the self-deceiver acquire it. That the self-deceiver acquires the particular belief that he does depends upon further facts about him and the world. A similar point can be made about picking a cherry out of a bowl. That I pick the particular cherry that I do depends upon further facts about me and the world.

Whether a particular belief reduces anxiety in a person depends upon that person's total package of beliefs, desires, anxieties, hopes,

description of the person's motivation is more appropriate" ("Cognitive and Motivational Bases of Self-Deception," pp. 182–3). Knight is responding to Mele's account of self-deception, but her challenge to him is also a challenge to me. I have added "anxious" to her text to indicate that challenge.

While in a later chapter I shall try to show why unmotivated but faulty belief formation does not constitute self-deception, Knight's charges (1) that the positing of any particular anxious desire is *post hoc* and subject to circular reasoning and (2) that there is no way of choosing between any number of plausible *post hoc* positings, need to be addressed here.

If we want to explain why a person does something, we look to what may be causing him or her to do it. That we posit after the fact possible causes to fit the particular case does not commit us to circularity. Knight herself posits as cause the self-deceivers' failure to exercise control over their perceptual/cognitive processes, control they had the capacity to exercise. While she therefore is not faced with the difficulty of deciding among different plausible anxious desires, the fact that it is difficult to decide which anxious desire or desires are operating is no reason to believe that no anxious desire is operating. Only further attention to the details of the specific case would reveal whether one or another of the anxious desires posited is more nearly correct.

etc. as well as upon facts about the world. A husband, for example, who believed that his friend was not attracted to women sexually would not explain his wife's greater influence with the friend in terms of sexual influence. A man who was not jealous of his wife's attentions to other men might also not be tempted to explain her greater influence with other men in terms of her sexual intimacy with them.

While I appeal to the total complex situation of the self-deceiver in order to explain why he comes to have the particular belief that he does, some might find an appeal to ambivalence tempting here. That is, if in cases of seemingly unwelcome self-deceptive belief that *p*, the self-deceiver always has a desire that *p* in addition to a desire that not-*p*, then having the desire that *p* could help explain why the self-deceiver acquires the particular anxiety-reducing belief that he does.

I suggested earlier that it was unlikely that in cases of seemingly unwelcome self-deceptive belief the self-deceiver *anxiously* desired that *p*. Rather it was more probable that he desired that not-*p*, for the belief that *p* was seemingly *unwelcome*. For example, recall the husband in scenario 1. He was not anxious that his wife was faithful, and so did not anxiously desire that she be unfaithful. Presumably he would deny that he wanted her to be unfaithful; he would insist that he desired her fidelity.

But it seems possible that a person could be ambivalent about something – he could desire that *not-p* and he could desire that *p* – even if the person sincerely denied being ambivalent. Suppose the husband did desire that his wife be faithful; might he also not desire that she be unfaithful? After all, believing that she is unfaithful gets the husband something he wants.

If we allow that a person's non-recognition or even repudiation of ambivalence is compatible with that person's nonetheless being ambivalent, then despite the husband's denial of his desiring her infidelity, could not the husband nevertheless desire her infidelity? The husband wants the situation to be one which would allow him to retain his belief in his higher standing with his friend, and his wife's being unfaithful to him with his friend would allow this. But if a person wants something – that he be held in higher regard – and he recognizes that if his wife is unfaithful he can still be held in higher regard, isn't there a good chance that the person, in some sense, or to some degree, wants the something which is his wife's infidelity?

If one supposes that the husband did in some sense, or to some degree, want the something which is his wife's infidelity, it would not follow that he wants the something which is her infidelity *qua* infidelity, that is, what would not follow is that he wants her infidelity in virtue of its being her infidelity. A specification of a desire's content can function merely as an identifying description of the desire's content – the description simply picks out something I want by a description that fits it or, perhaps, a description that I suppose fits it. It does not follow that I want the thing picked out by that description *because* it satisfies that description. A specification of a desire's content can also function both as an identifying and as a desirability-characterizing or ground-giving description. If the description functions in both these ways, then I want the thing in virtue of its satisfying that description. The husband could, therefore, want the something which is his wife's infidelity, where that specification of his desire performs the identifying function – he could want her infidelity insofar as it is something that allows him to believe that his friend holds him in higher regard – while not wanting her infidelity if "her infidelity" is supposed to perform both the identifying and the desirability-characterizing function. That is, the husband does not want her infidelity in virtue of its being her infidelity. What the husband wants, where the specification of the content of his want gives a desirability characterization, is something to be the case that will allow him to believe that he is held in higher regard. But this, of course, leaves open the possibility that the husband is ambivalent about his wife's infidelity – he could want her to be unfaithful because that will allow him to believe in his friend's higher regard; he could want her not to be unfaithful because infidelity is a betrayal.

Let us suppose that the raw material for a *prima facie* desire for his wife's infidelity exists in the husband, where we understand that "her infidelity" provides only an identifying characterization of the content of the husband's desire. The raw material in question consists of various relevant beliefs and desires. The husband links greater influence with higher regard, i.e., he believes that normally the influence another has on us increases with our regard for that person. He believes also that a person's influence on us can derive from a sexual relationship we have with the person even when our regard for that person is not high. He desires for its own sake that he be held in higher regard than his wife, and knows that he desires this. This collection of propositional attitudes is, in context, the raw material out of which a recognition on the husband's part of a link between fidelity and higher regard *might* arise, i.e., a recognition that his wife's infidelity would improve the chances that he still has what he wants, namely, his friend's higher regard.

Whether this material for a desire for infidelity in the husband does give rise to a desire for infidelity, however, depends upon whether the husband recognizes the link between fidelity and higher regard. If he did recognize this link, he would be aware of what his wife's infidelity could get him. We could then say that he desires that his wife be unfaithful insofar as this will get him something he wants. If the husband came in some such way to be ambivalent, this ambivalence would be one way to explain why the self-deceiver came to have the particular self-deceptive belief that he did.

While I believe that the raw material for a recognition of the link between fidelity and higher regard is a part of the causal background in the case under discussion, perhaps an indispensable part, the possibility exists that the husband does not put these materials together, that he does not recognize the link between fidelity and higher regard. If he is not aware of what his wife's infidelity would get him, he would not have a *prima facie* desire that she be unfaithful. He would not be ambivalent. A complex causal non-intentional process could nevertheless be occurring in the absence of such recognition, a process which led to his believing that his wife is unfaithful.

The causal story one tells about self-deception is complex. The particular self-deceptive belief one comes to depends upon a large number of factors, but a recognition of what one gets by believing that *p* is not an essential factor.[30]

I believe that it is doubtful that self-deceivers are in cases of seem-

[30] If we postulate ambivalence in all cases of seemingly unwelcome belief, then on Davidson's account, since the person must intentionally deceive himself, the husband in scenario 1 must, in the face of his awareness of the conflict between his desire for his wife's fidelity and his desire for higher regard, choose infidelity over lesser regard. This, however, is something it would be extremely difficult psychologically to do.

On Johnston's account, the husband would have to have an anxious desire that she be unfaithful. But is it plausible on his account to suppose that he is anxious that she is faithful, given that Johnston requires him to recognize that his evidence supports fidelity? If he believed that infidelity was the ***only*** way that he could be held in higher regard and he desired to be held in higher regard, then he might be anxious about her fidelity. But it is unlikely that he believes that infidelity is the only way to be held in higher regard.

ingly unwelcome self-deceptive belief ***always*** ambivalent about *p*; ambivalence does not explain in all such cases why self-deceivers come to the particular self-deceptive belief that they do. I do not, of course, want to deny that a self-deceiver could be ambivalent. Suppose a man anxiously desires to leave his wife and recognizes that if she were unfaithful, he would be able to leave her. He is, however, ambivalent about her being unfaithful, for being unfaithful would be a betrayal. He comes to believe, self-deceptively, that she is unfaithful. In this case the husband recognizes that his wife's infidelity would enable him to leave her.

Such a recognition can make the process of deceiving himself more difficult. In the face of such recognition he must come up with what seem to him to be powerful reasons for believing that she is unfaithful, for he must deny that he believes in her infidelity because of what it allows him to do. When I recognize that I have reason to be partial to a belief that *p*, I must convince myself that my belief that *p* is nonetheless justified.

While I contend that self-deceivers need not in cases of seemingly unwelcome self-deceptive belief be ambivalent, I want now to show why even if they were ambivalent, their self-deceptive beliefs that *p* **need not** be wishful. In order to see why this is the case, we must first see what it is for a belief to be wishful.

Johnston suggests that we regard wishful thinking "as a mental mechanism or tropism by which a desire that *p* and accompanying anxiety that not-*p* set the conditions for the rewarding (because anxiety-reducing) response of coming to believe that *p*."[31] If, in order to be wishful, the content of a belief and the content of the relevant *anxious* desire which gives rise to it both had to be given by the same description, *p*, then showing that the content of a belief is given by the description, *p*, but the content of the relevant *anxious* desire is given by the description, *q*, where *q* is other than *p*, would be sufficient for showing that the belief in question was not wishful. Showing, for example, that a husband believed that his wife was unfaithful (*p*) but anxiously desired that he leave her (*q*) would then be sufficient for showing that his belief in her infidelity was not wishful.[32] I shall

[31] "Self-Deception and the Nature of the Mind," p. 73.

[32] Assume here that while the husband may desire that his wife be unfaithful, he is not anxious that she is faithful, something he would need to be if he had an anxious desire that *p*. He does not, for example, believe that only if she is unfaithful can he leave her.

discuss a case, however, which suggests that a belief that p can be wishful even when the content of the relevant anxious desire is given by the description, q, where q is other than p. This indicates that some other factor is needed if one wants, as I do, to distinguish between wishful beliefs and self-deceptive beliefs. I identify that factor and show that, even if ambivalence is introduced, this factor will allow one to distinguish between beliefs which are wishful and those which are not. We will be in a position to see why, even if there was ambivalence in cases of seemingly unwelcome self-deceptive belief,[33] the self-deceptive belief need not be wishful.

I suggest that in the following case of wishful belief the content of the relevant anxious desire is plausibly given by a description that is other than the description which gives the content of the wishful belief. Suppose that a man, having lost his money in an unwise investment, anxiously desires that his daughter be well provided-for. A few rich bachelors move into his neighborhood, and the father, knowing virtually nothing about these men, comes, in response to their arrival, to believe that his daughter will marry a rich man. In such circumstances it seems uncontroversial to think of the father's belief as wishful. Although we are supposing in these circumstances that the father desires that his daughter marry a rich man, we are not supposing that he is anxious that that she will not marry a rich man. He does not, for example, believe that marrying a rich man is the only way for her to be well provided-for and so is not, in light of that belief, anxious that she marry a rich man. The anxious desire responsible for the wishful belief is an anxious desire that she be well provided-for. Let us assume that this is a possible case, that there are grounds for saying that the parent's relevant anxious desire is that his daughter be well provided-for. The content of the wishful belief and the content of the relevant anxious desire are not given by the same description.

Let us also assume that the father is ambivalent about his daughter marrying a rich man. He wants her to be well provided-for, but he also knows of the deterioration of character that may attend wealth. While not wanting her to marry a rich man *qua* rich man, he wants her to marry a rich man insofar as a rich man will provide well for her.

[33] Although I believe that it is plausible to assume ambivalence only in some cases of seemingly unwelcome self-deceptive belief, even if there were ambivalence in all cases it would not follow that all self-deceptive belief was, therefore, wishful.

Why does it seem natural in these circumstances to think of his belief that she would marry a rich man as wishful? It is natural to assume this because we are, I believe, assuming that although the man is ambivalent, he does not have a stronger felt desire that his daughter not marry a rich man, nor does he lack a desire, all things considered,[34] that his daughter marry a rich man. For if we assume that he has a stronger felt desire that his daughter *not* marry a rich man and he lacks a desire, all things considered, that his daughter marry a rich man,[35] it is no longer reasonable to regard his belief that she would marry a rich man as wishful.[36]

Let us reconsider the ambivalent-husband case, for we are now in a position to see why, even if a husband were ambivalent about his wife's infidelity, his self-deceptive belief in her infidelity need not be wishful. The husband in such a case could, despite his ambivalence, still have a stronger felt desire that she be faithful and lack a desire, all things considered, that she be unfaithful. But if, as we have seen in the parent case, he had this stronger felt desire and lacked this kind of all-things-considered desire, then his belief in her infidelity would no longer be wishful.[37]

[34] Roughly, a person has a desire, all things considered, that *p* if the person, aware of certain pros and cons, reflects on these, and taking them all into consideration desires on that basis that *p*.

[35] If one lacks a desire, all things considered, that *p*, then one might still, for example, desire that *p*, or one might desire, all things considered, that not-*p*.

[36] Kit Fine convinced me that a belief that *p* could, however, be wishful belief if the believer had a stronger felt desire that *p* and nonetheless desired, all things considered, that not-*p*, or if the believer had a stronger felt desire that not-*p* but desired, all things considered, that *p*.

[37] If, on the other hand, he desires, all things considered, that she be unfaithful, or he has a stronger felt desire that she be unfaithful, then his belief that she was unfaithful could be wishful as well as self-deceptive.

It was said of the British Conservative Party's right-wingers, "Even though they hate to lose a seat like Bath, they were not unhappy to see him [Patten] lose." Suppose they anxiously desire not to lose a seat and come to believe that they will not lose the seat. They are ambivalent about losing the seat; they desire for its own sake not to lose the seat; they desire to lose the seat insofar as it means that Patten will be ousted. If they desired, all things considered, that they lose the seat and had no stronger felt desire that they not lose the seat, their belief could not be wishful. If, on the other hand, they desired, all things considered, that they win the seat, their belief could be wishful. If I want a raise and know that if Nigel gets to be dean I'll get a raise, I might nonetheless be ambivalent about whether I want Nigel to be dean if I think, for example, that Nigel is a scoundrel.

What shows that self-deceptive belief cannot be assimilated to wishful belief is the fact that in wishful belief that *p*, *the believer cannot have a stronger felt desire that not-p and lack a desire, all things considered, that p,* while in possible cases of self-deceptive belief *that p, the believer does have a stronger felt desire that not-p and lacks a desire, all things considered, that p.* Some cases of self-deceptive belief are not, therefore, cases of wishful belief.[38]

While this factor explains why not all self-deceptive belief is wishful, it leaves open the question whether all wishful belief is self-deceptive. There is, of course, a simple answer to this question if we understand a self-deceptive belief to be a belief the believer is self-deceived in believing. For then a self-deceptive belief must be false, while a wishful belief need not be.[39] But if, as I believe, a person can self-deceive himself into believing something true, the question that remains to be answered is whether the process of wishfully believing is always a process of self-deceiving. And that must wait until we know what the self-deceiving process is.

Let us now turn to the standard type of self-deception, the self-deception in which the self-deceptive belief is welcome. I argue that my account deals with this type of case better than Davidson's, Johnston's, or Mele's, although, since I have not yet presented my account in full, not all the ways in which it does so will be evident in this chapter.

If I desire, all things considered, that Nigel not get to be dean and have no stronger felt desire that he get to be dean but, given my anxious desire to get a raise, believe that Nigel will be dean, my belief that Nigel will be dean may be self-deceptive, but it cannot be wishful.

[38] If the husband in scenario 1 were ambivalent, it is not difficult to imagine him as *having a stronger felt desire that his wife be faithful, and lacking a desire, all things considered, that she be unfaithful.*

[39] As Mele points out, the term "wishful thinking" may be used in a variety of ways. In the way I am using it, "wishful thinking" is not equivalent to "wishful false believing."

Suppose however, one accepts "the stipulation that what the wishful thinker wishfully 'does' is to believe falsely that *p*" and also accepts that the wishful thinker does not have good grounds for thinking that the believed proposition is false, then, says Mele, wishful thinking may be a species of self-deception; "it may just be that wishful thinking is a form of self-deception in which, owing to some desire-influenced behavior of an appropriate sort, the self-deceiver lacks good grounds for rejecting the proposition that he is self-deceived in believing." *Irrationality*, p. 135. In Chapter 7 I discuss whether all wishful belief is self-deceptive.

To capture the richness of contexts in which welcome self-deceptive belief occurs, I shall use a fairly well-developed literary example. Monsieur Legrandin, a minor character in Proust's *Swann's Way*, anxiously desires not to be thought a snob. (Q = he is not thought a snob.) He attends church in the company of an aristocratic lady and instead of openly acknowledging his middle-class friends after the service, he first "fixed his eyes . . . on so distant a point of the horizon that he could not see us, and so had not to acknowledge our presence."[40] When they reencounter him moments later in circumstances in which he cannot fix his eyes in this way, he gave them "out of the corner of his blue eye, a little sign, which began and ended, so to speak, inside his eyelids, and as it did not involve the least movement of his facial muscles, managed to pass quite unperceived by the lady."[41] Legrandin is aware that he does not openly acknowledge his middle-class friends when in the presence of members of the upper class, and that such failure to acknowledge them could be a reason to think him a snob. He is uncertain whether not-q (not-q = he is thought a snob) for several reasons.[42] He knows that r (r = he does not openly acknowledge his middle-class friends when in the presence of members of the upper class). And he believes that if r then he might be thought a snob. He also knows that r_1 (r_1 = he associates with members of the upper class), and that this association may lead his middle-class friends to think him a snob.

In this case his anxious desire that q is an anxious desire that p. However, his anxious desire that q gives rise not merely to his belief that p, where $q = p$, it gives rise to a number of other beliefs. Where there is more than one self-deceptive belief that an anxious desire gives rise to, p is replaced by p_1, p_2, . . . Several self-deceptive beliefs – that p_1, that p_2, etc. – may function to reduce an anxiety that not-q.

Legrandin's anxious desire that he not be thought a snob causes him to believe, for example, that p_1 – he associates with the aristocracy because of their grace, virtue, intellect – when the facts belie this.[43] (He made it a habit never to visit "a duchess as such." Instead, "his

[40] Marcel Proust, *Swann's Way*, translated by C. K. Moncrief (New York: Vintage, 1970), p. 96. [41] Ibid.

[42] Where there is more than one reason, r is replaced by r_1, r_2, and so on. Where there is more than one anxious desire, q is replaced by q_1, q_2, and so on.

[43] As we shall see in later chapters, his anxious desire causes him to be biased in acquiring his self-deceptive beliefs.

imagination" made the duchess appear in his eyes "endowed with all the graces. He would be drawn towards the duchess, assuring himself the while that he was yielding to the attractions of her mind, and her other virtues.")[44]

One very common form of self-deceptive belief involves believing that one's motive for doing something is other than one's real motive. The motive one attributes to oneself is a motive that is generally considered to be nobler than one's real motive. Not only does Legrandin attribute to himself noble motives for his visits to members of the upper class, motives "which the vile race of snobs could never understand,"[45] he attributes noble motives to his failure to openly acknowledge his middle-class friends when in the company of the upper class. He believes that p_2 – his wink is a truer form of acknowledgement. As Proust describes it,

> striving to compensate by the intensity of his feelings for the somewhat restricted field in which they had to find expression, he made that blue chink, which was set apart for us, sparkle with all the animation of cordiality, which went far beyond mere playfulness, and almost touched the border-line of roguery; he subtilised the refinements of good-fellowship into a wink of connivance, a hint, a hidden meaning, a secret understanding, all the mysteries of complicity in a plot, and finally exalted his assurances of friendship to the level of protestations of affection, even of a declaration of love, lighting up for us, and for us alone, with a secret languid flame invisible to the great lady upon his other side, an enamoured pupil in a countenance of ice.[46]

Legrandin believes that p_3 – he does not snub his friends – and that p_4 – his wink of complicity shows that he is merely trying to avoid embarrassing the lady. He fails to see that he is trying to avoid embarrassing himself. He was so much afraid, when in the company of the upper class, "of incurring their displeasure that he would never dare to let them see that he numbered, as well, among his friends middle-class people."[47] He thus fails to count his demeaning wink, his avidness to associate with the upper class, his obsequious behavior in relation to them, as good reasons for their thinking him a snob. With that wink, together with the reasons he gives himself for associating with the upper class, he succeeds in not thinking himself a snob. He believes,

[44] *Swann's Way*, p. 99. [45] Ibid. [46] Ibid., p. 96. [47] Ibid., p. 98.

moreover, that his friends have no good reason to think him one. He believes, self-deceptively, that since there is no good reason to think him a snob, he is not thought a snob. (By believing that p_1, p_2, p_3, p_4, he can believe that both conditionals – if r then not-q and if r_1 then not-q – are false, and therefore he can believe that q, and since $q = p$, he can believe that p.)

Legrandin's anxiety is relieved. However, his desire that he not be thought a snob is not satisfied. While he does not think himself a snob, others do think him one.

While Legrandin's anxious desire that q is an anxious desire that p, Legrandin does not start out believing that he is thought a snob, or that there is telling evidence for thinking him to be a snob, and then intentionally try to get himself to believe that he is not thought a snob. He is uncertain whether he will be thought a snob, because he recognizes that some of his behavior might be reason for thinking him a snob. His anxiety is relieved when he believes that this behavior is not in fact good reason for thinking him one. The stronger cognitive attitudes required by Davidson or Johnston, a belief that not-q, or a recognition that the evidence is telling against q, are not essential for central cases of self-deception. While Mele does not require these stronger cognitive attitudes either, he does not require, as I do, that the motivational work be done by anxiety.

The way I sort out anxious desires in the cases I have dealt with is not the only way of so sorting them. We saw that one could sort them out differently in the husband case. One can in the present case also do so. For example, one might focus on Legrandin's anxious desire not to *be* a snob. Just as there can be more than one self-deceptive belief that is relevant, there can be more than one anxious desire. Here a belief that he is not a snob would function to reduce his anxiety. While believing he is not a snob would relieve his anxiety, his desire that he not be a snob would not be satisfied. Self-deceptive beliefs, as we have seen earlier, can function to reduce anxiety without satisfying a relevant desire.

In this case might it not be claimed that Legrandin really knows that he is a snob, since he does all the things that he knows snobs do? But we do things under a description, and the descriptions Legrandin gives himself of what he does need not be accurate or complete descriptions.

In this chapter I have, following Johnston, argued that the function of the self-deception belief that *p* is always to reduce the subject's anxiety, although I have argued that the anxiety in question is not, as Johnston proposed, an anxiety that not-*p* but an anxiety that not-*q*, where "*q*" may be *p* or something else. I have yet to discuss the self-deceptive processes that give rise to the anxiety-reducing self-deceptive belief that *p*, nor have I discussed how these processes also prevent the self-deceiver from recognizing the extent to which the self-deceptive belief that *p* is due to its tendency to reduce anxiety.[48]

Before these issues can be discussed, certain aspects of the relationship between self-deceptive belief and anxious desire need to be clarified. In the next chapter I focus on what is involved in a belief's ***functioning*** to reduce anxiety and what is involved in ***satisfying*** a desire.

[48] While Mele, for example, has much that is useful to say about self-deceptive processes, much more needs to be said about how these processes contribute to what has been called the self-deceiver's false consciousness. Self-deceivers fail to recognize the extent to which their anxious desires influence the formation of their self-deceptive beliefs. While Johnston appeals to repression and Davidson has a division, I show in Chapter 6 that neither a repression nor a division is necessary.

4

Functioning to reduce an anxiety; satisfying a desire

In the preceding chapter I claimed that a self-deceptive belief that *p* functions to reduce the self-deceiver's anxiety that not-*q* and that the anxiety that not-*q* could be reduced without the desire that *q* being satisfied. In this chapter I consider further cases of self-deception, distinguishing those in which the relevant anxiety is reduced and the relevant desire is not satisfied from those in which the relevant anxiety is reduced and the relevant desire is satisfied. Two notions are crucial here: that of a belief functioning to reduce anxiety and that of a desire being satisfied. Let me explain how these notions are to be understood.

A belief's causing an anxiety to be reduced is not sufficient for the belief's functioning to reduce that anxiety. As I use the expression "functions to reduce anxiety," a belief that *p* functions to reduce anxiety that not-*q* when ***(1) the belief that p is caused by the anxious desire that q and (2) the purpose of the occurrence of the belief that p is to reduce anxiety that not-q***. While I thus define "functions to reduce anxiety," I am not claiming thereby to analyze "function" in whatever is its main sense.

According to requirement 2, the having of the belief that *p* is purposive; its purpose is to reduce anxiety that not-*q*. According to requirement 1, the anxious desire plays a causal role in the person's coming to have that belief. In the next chapter I discuss that causal role in detail. I shall argue that self-deceivers' anxious desires cause them to be biased in favor of beliefs that reduce their anxiety. The bias which operates in their acting or thinking or judging or perceiving etc. causes them to believe that *p*. Moreover, I shall contend that self-deceivers' anxious desires do not stand in relation to the behavior and belief that they cause in the way in which people's reasons for acting stand in relation to their actions. Having a self-deceptive belief that *p* is purposive, but it is not the intention of self-deceivers to reduce their anxiety that not-*q* by believing that *p*.

A self-deceptive belief is an effect whose purpose is to alter its cause. Effects in nature whose purpose is to alter their causes are not uncommon. High body temperature in humans causes sweating; the purpose of sweating is to reduce body temperature. Low water level in humans causes thirst sensations. Thirst sensations function to get the affected organism to do things to remedy that condition. It is obvious that only some causal relations are functional relations – heat melts ice but does not function to melt ice.

While many philosophers seem puzzled by functional relations in ways that they are not by other causal relations, causal relations which are functional relations are commonplace, as are causal relations which are not functional relations. The causal connection between anxious desire that *q* and self-deceptive belief that *p* is a causal connection of the first kind.

I appeal to the widely accepted notion of functional explanation, whatever the correct analysis of functional explanation may be. People have self-deceptive beliefs because having self-deceptive beliefs reduces their anxiety. Something (having a self-deceptive belief) which has a certain effect (reducing anxiety) is explained by the fact that it has that effect.[1] When I say that "the purpose of the occurrence of the belief that *p* is to reduce anxiety that not-*q*," I take this to mean that having the belief that *p* occurred because it would (normally) cause the anxiety to be reduced, or, more precisely, to mean that having the belief that *p* occurred because the situation was such that having beliefs like the belief that *p* would (normally) cause anxiety like the anxiety that not-*q* to be reduced.[2]

I rely in this discussion on the strong intuitive contrast between relations that are causal but not functional and those which are causal and functional. That contrast is evident, for example, in the following two cases. In the first case a belief reduces an anxiety without functioning to reduce it; in the second case a belief not only causes the anxiety to be reduced, it functions to reduce that anxiety.

Case 1. A student anxiously desires that she be admitted to a certain college. Her tutors, who have always been reliable, assure her that given her performance on the requisite examinations she will be

[1] G. A. Cohen talks at length about functional explanation in *Karl Marx's Theory of History* (Oxford: Clarendon Press, 1978), chapters 9 and 10, pp. 249–96.

[2] See G. A. Cohen, *History, Labour and Freedom* (Oxford: Clarendon Press, 1988), p. 8.

admitted. She accepts their assurances, and believes that she will be admitted. Although this belief reduces her anxiety, it does not function to reduce her anxiety. Her anxious desire that she be admitted did not cause her to believe that she will be admitted, nor was reducing her anxiety the purpose of her believing that she will be admitted.[3]

> [Case 2. A father says:] I don't care whether a hundred psychologists or a thousand police detectives tell me, I know my daughter did not commit these crimes. The stories we read, we do not believe. Something no one yet knows must have happened. One day the truth will come to light. Who would know her if not her parents – her mother and I? We have been with her all of her life. We ate from the same table.[4]

It is not difficult to imagine that the father anxiously desires that his daughter not be a murderer. Nor is it difficult to imagine that his belief that his daughter did not commit any crime was caused by his anxious desire that she not be a murderer, and has as its purpose the reduction of his anxiety. The father presumably does not in the absence of the relevant anxiety think that other parents' children are not murderers; he does not think that police detectives, psychologists, and journalists always lie to a suspect's parents. It is reasonable to believe that the father's having the belief that his daughter is not a murderer occurred because it would cause his anxiety to be reduced. In case 2, but not in case 1, the belief that reduces anxiety functions to reduce it.

An intuitive contrast also exists between a belief, like the father's, which has been caused by an anxious desire and whose purpose is to reduce that anxiety, and a belief which has been caused by an anxious desire but whose purpose is not to reduce that anxiety.

Case 3. A man anxiously desires that his wife's upcoming operation will be a success. Because of his anxiety about her operation, he is distracted at work and comes to believe that a project will cost more to

[3] Having the belief that she will be admitted did not occur because it would cause her anxiety to be reduced.

Consider another version of case 1, where the anxious desire is a cause of the belief, but, even so, it was not the purpose of the belief to reduce anxiety. The student's anxious desire is a cause of her asking her tutors what her chance is of being admitted. They tell her that she has an excellent chance. She believes accordingly, and the belief reduces anxiety. If she had not asked, she would not have acquired the belief, and if she had not been anxious, she would not have asked.

[4] Melanie Thernstrom, "Diary of a Murder," *New Yorker*, June 3, 1996, p. 70.

complete than it actually will. Although his belief about the project's cost was caused by his anxiety about his wife's operation, the purpose of his belief is not to reduce his anxiety.

That a belief functions to reduce anxiety is to be distinguished from that belief's bringing desire satisfaction. In order for a desire that *q* to be satisfied, *q* must be the case. But *q*'s being the case is not sufficient for desire satisfaction, as I understand desire satisfaction. Not only must *q* be the case, the person whose desire it is must be aware that *q*.[5] One can be aware that *q* if *q* is the case and one believes that *q*.[6]

While a person's desire that *q* cannot be satisfied unless *q*, we have seen that a person's anxiety that not-*q* can be reduced whether or not *q* is the case. A belief that *q*, even if it is mistaken, can reduce anxiety that not-*q*. Legrandin's anxiety about being thought a snob was reduced by his mistaken belief that he was not thought one.

What directly affects one's anxiety is not what is true of the objects of one's anxiety, but what one **believes** is true of them. Believing, falsely, that one is not an alcoholic can relieve one's anxiety about being an alcoholic. And it can be the case that while one is not an alcoholic, one is nonetheless anxious that one is.

While a belief in order to be self-deceptive need not provide desire satisfaction in addition to anxiety reduction, self-deceptive beliefs often enough do provide this. It may not, however, be obvious that a self-deceptive belief, a belief that one is self-deceived in believing, and hence false, can bring desire satisfaction with it. Desire satisfaction occurs when the relevant desire associated with the anxiety is satisfied. If a man anxiously desires not to be an alcoholic, and self-deceptively believes that he is not an alcoholic, his desire that he not be an alcoholic is not satisfied, although his anxiety about his being an alcoholic is reduced.

Non-self-deceptive situations in which people's anxious desires are reduced and their desires associated with their anxieties are satisfied are, of course, commonplace. A woman who depends upon her car for daily transport anxiously desires that her car, which has been stolen, be recovered undamaged. Her anxiety is relieved and her rele-

[5] My notion of desire satisfaction is a technical one and is not to be confused with a more standard notion of desire satisfaction (the notion that John Searle articulates in *Intentionality* [Cambridge: Cambridge University Press, 1983]).

[6] If one was not aware of having a particular belief that *q*, then *q*'s being the case and one's believing that *q* would not be sufficient for one's being aware that *q*.

vant desire is satisfied when the police inform her that her car has been found undamaged. But the woman's belief that her car has been recovered undamaged is not, of course, a self-deceptive one. Her anxious desire that her car be recovered undamaged does not cause her to believe that her car has been recovered undamaged, nor is reducing her anxiety the purpose of her belief that her car has been recovered undamaged. It remains to be seen, therefore, whether a self-deceptive belief that *p*, a belief that is false, can not only relieve anxiety about *q*, but also bring with it desire satisfaction.

I begin by developing a case of anxiety reduction in which there is desire satisfaction. It is a case, moreover, which might be thought to involve self-deception. I show, however, that unless the belief that reduces the anxiety and brings desire satisfaction also functions to reduce that anxiety, the belief in question will not be a self-deceptive one. In the case as I first develop it, the belief does not function to reduce anxiety and would not, therefore, be a self-deceptive belief. However, I show that this case can be modified so that the belief in question functions to reduce the relevant anxiety. If it is, as I suggest, plausible to regard this modified case as a case of self-deception, we would then have a case in which the self-deceptive belief, though false, not only functions to reduce anxiety, it also brings desire satisfaction. I go on to show that bringing desire satisfaction is in fact a common enough phenomenon in self-deception and explore some of the cases in which desire satisfaction is achieved. I contrast these cases with cases in which self-deception brings a belief that one's desire is satisfied but does not bring desire satisfaction.[7]

Clarissa, who is reluctantly taking a form of cortisone prescribed for her asthma, gets severe joint pains. She believes that the asthma medicine causes her joint pains. Although she desires to stop taking the medicine – she believes that if she does not stop, the medicine will cause long-term harm to her body, something she does not want – she is uncertain whether she will stop. Her fear of the medicine's long-term harm is not a reason strong enough to override her reason to take the medicine, namely, her desire to control her asthma. Her belief that the asthma medicine causes her joint pains is a strong enough reason, and she stops taking the medicine. Clarissa anxiously desires that *q*

[7] I discuss an atypical case later in the discussion where the self-deceiver's anxiety is reduced even though the self-deceiver does not believe that his desire that *q* is satisfied.

(the asthma medicine not cause her body long-term harm). She believes that *p* (the asthma medicine causes her joint pains). As a result of believing that *p*, she stops taking the asthma medicine and thus brings it about that *q* (the asthma medicine does not do her body long-term harm). We thus have a situation in which there is anxiety reduction and desire satisfaction. But we need to know more about the case before we can determine whether Clarissa's belief is a self-deceptive one.

Clarissa believes that the asthma medicine causes her joint pains because she believes (1) that her particular medicine can cause joint pains, (2) that she has joint pains, and (3) that no other cause for the pains is likely. She believes (1) because the maker of the drug states that the drug taken orally can have this effect and she believes she is taking the drug orally. However, when Clarissa tells her doctor many months later that she no longer takes the cortisone he prescribed and why she no longer does, he explains that she took the drug by oral inhalation, not orally, and the drug taken in the former way does not cause joint pains. Clarissa reluctantly starts taking the medicine again, but this time she does not get joint pains.

Clarissa's belief that the asthma medicine caused her joint pains was false. Her pains were psychosomatic; the medicine did not cause them. In this case **a belief** that *p* reduces an anxiety that not-*q*, and the desire that *q* is satisfied. Clarissa's anxiety about the medicine causing her body long-term harm was reduced, at least temporarily, and her desire that the medicine not cause harm is satisfied. We have, however, not yet ascertained whether this is a case of a **self-deceptive belief** that *p* ***functioning*** to reduce an anxiety that not-*q*. Is Clarissa self-deceived in believing that the asthma medicine causes her joint pains, or is she only mistaken in believing that it does?

Whether Clarissa is self-deceived or not depends on whether her false belief about the asthma medicine not only reduces her anxiety but also functions to reduce it. If the belief did not so function, we would not ascribe to Clarissa self-deception. Remember that a belief that *p* functions to reduce anxiety that not-*q* when (1) the belief is caused by the anxious desire that *q* and (2) the purpose of the occurrence of the belief is to reduce anxiety that not-*q*.

To take the first requirement: does Clarissa's anxious desire that *q* cause her to believe that *p*? Clarissa arrives at her belief as a result of believing (1), (2), and (3). In the case as described, her belief (1) that her particular medicine can cause joint pains is the result of what seems to be a perfectly natural misunderstanding. Anyone might have assimilated taking the medicine orally with taking it by oral inhalation. Not anyone, of course, would have developed joint pains, but we are now concerned not with why she has joint pains, but with why she believes that her asthma medicine causes them.

It is not, therefore, at all clear so far that (1) her anxious desire that the medicine not cause her body long-term harm causes her to believe that the asthma medicine causes her joint pains, or that (2) the purpose of the occurrence of her belief is to reduce anxiety. It is not clear whether the anxious desire causes the belief, because it is not clear that Clarissa has been partial or biased in acquiring this belief. Such bias or partiality[8] is a feature of this sort of anxious-desire-caused belief. Rather it seems plausible to suppose that the accidental and entirely natural conflation of oral and oral inhalation was the cause of the belief.

But perhaps her belief that the asthma medicine causes her joint pains is nonetheless suspect. Why does she believe (3), that no other cause of the pain is likely? She is aware here of her anxious desire that the medicine not cause her body long-term harm. Is it perfectly reasonable for her to dismiss other causes, given her desire that there not be such causes? Perhaps, if her belief that (1) is in place. Given (1), she has no reason to suspect that any other cause is operative. She reasons that the pains began when she started the medicine, and the medicine has been known to have this effect, so it is likely that the medicine is the cause of the effect in her.

Although it is clear why she believes (2) – that she has joint pains – if it were the case that without her anxious desire that the medicine not cause her body long-term harm she would not have had the joint pains, would she have been biased in coming to her belief that the asthma medicine is the cause of these pains? Let us suppose, however, that her anxious desire that the medicine not cause her body long-term harm is not necessary for her developing joint pains. Suppose that her general susceptibility to medical warnings of this type is such that her belief that the asthma medicine can cause joint pains is sufficient for her to develop joint pains. If this is the case, then while her reasoning might not seem suspect here, it

[8] This feature will, as I said earlier, be discussed in detail in the next chapter.

seems likely that her anxious desire that the medicine not cause long-term harm would have caused her belief acquisition had there been no other cause.

However, given that Clarissa's anxious desire was preempted from a causal role by her convenient and accidental conflation of "orally" with "oral inhalation," one is not, I believe, inclined in this case to ascribe self-deception. What about a case where Clarissa's anxious desire is not causally preempted?

Suppose Clarissa believes (1) that the particular medicine can cause joint pains because she misreads the manufacturer's statement. While the statement says, "There is ***no*** indication that the drug will cause joint pains," she reads it as saying, "There is ***an*** indication that the drug will cause joint pains." If Clarissa has carefully and attentively read the statement, let us suppose that the only plausible explanation for the misreading, a misreading people would not naturally make, is that her wanting it to say this has caused her to read it as saying this and hence to believe that it was saying this. She wants it to say this because she wants a reason to stop taking the medicine. In this case Clarissa's wanting the medicine not to cause her body long-term harm is the reason why she believes that it is causing her joint pains. Her anxious desire has caused her to be biased in acquiring her belief. While in the first case Clarissa's mistake was one a person without the relevant anxious desire could very easily make – her anxious desire was not responsible for the mistake – in the second case, only a person with something like the relevant anxious desire could be assumed to make it.

I have not yet discussed all that is required of a belief if it is to be self-deceptive, but I suggest that Clarissa's belief in the second case is a self-deceptive one. Clarissa's anxious desire that the medicine not cause her long-term harm causes the self-deceptive belief whose purpose it is to reduce her anxiety. Clarissa's self-deceptive belief that her asthma medicine causes her joint pains makes it possible for her desire that the medicine not cause her body long-term harm to be satisfied, for she stops taking the medicine. While Clarissa does not get herself to believe something she knows is false, nor is she aware of contrary evidence, as I argued in the preceding chapter (against what Davidson and Johnston, among others, claimed), neither of these was necessary for self-deception.

The purpose of self-deceptive belief is to reduce anxiety. A self-deceiver gains something by having a self-deceptive belief that *p*, since having that belief reduces the self-deceiver's anxiety that not-*q*. A self-deceiver may also gain something more: she may be able to satisfy her desire that *q*.[9]

I shall in the remainder of this chapter concentrate on the typical ways in which a self-deceptive belief which functions to reduce anxiety effects that reduction. I shall also describe the circumstances in which the self-deceptive belief brings desire satisfaction and the circumstances in which it does not.

There are two typical ways in which a self-deceptive belief achieves its anxiety reduction. In the first way, the self-deceiver believes, as Clarissa did in our latest example, that the ***antecedent*** of the relevant conditional associated with her uncertainty – ***if I don't stop taking the medicine***, the medicine will cause my body long-term harm – ***is false***. In the second way, the self-deceiver believes, as the husband in our earlier case did, that the ***relevant conditional*** associated with his uncertainty – ***if my wife has more influence with my friend, then my friend holds her in higher regard than he does me*** – ***is false***. While considering the various situations that I shall describe which are compatible with these two ways, it would be helpful to keep the following distinctions in mind.

To have an anxious desire that *q* is to be anxious that not-*q* and to desire that *q*. To be anxious that not-*q* is to be uncertain whether *q* or not-*q* and to desire that *q*. There is, moreover, no reason for which the person desires that *q*; the person desires that *q* for its own sake. There is typically some reason, *r*, however, which is the cause of the uncertainty. The person believes that if *r* then not-*q* (or probably or possibly not-*q*).

Given that the function of a self-deceptive belief that *p* is to reduce anxiety that not-*q*, and one is typically anxious that not-*q* because one believes that if *r* then not-*q*, a self-deceptive belief that *p* that allows one to believe not-*r* would address the source of the anxiety. Alternatively, a self-deceptive belief that *p* that allows one to believe that *r* but also to believe that it is not the case that if *r* then not-*q* would also address the source of anxiety. We saw, moreover, that anxiety reduction is possible whether or not the desire that *q* was satisfied. We

9 This is not, of course, to say that having self-deceptive beliefs is beneficial, all things considered. This issue will be discussed in the final chapter.

therefore get the following situations in which a self-deceptive belief that *p* functions to reduce an anxiety that not-*q*. In the discussion that follows I assume that the self-deception has occurred; the self-deceptive belief is in place and anxiety reduction has been effected.

I. The self-deceiver believes the antecedent of the conditional if *r* then not-*q* is false.

The self-deceiver believes that *p*; believes that not-*r*; believes that *q*; and either:

(a) *q* is the case; not-*r* is the case.
(b) *q* is the case; *r* is the case.
(c) not-*q* is the case; not-*r* is the case.
(d) not-*q* is the case: *r* is the case.

II. The self-deceiver believes that the conditional if *r* then not-*q* is false.

The self-deceiver believes that *p*; believes that it is not the case that if *r* then not-*q*; believes that *q*;
and either:

(a) *q* is the case; it is not the case that if *r* then not-*q*.
(b) *q* is the case; it is the case that if *r* then not-*q*.
(c) not-*q* is the case; it is not the case that if *r* then not-*q*.
(d) not-*q* is the case; it is the case that if *r* then not-*q*.

In I(a) and (b) and in II(a) and (b) there is anxiety reduction and desire satisfaction. In I(c) and (d) and in II(c) and (d) no desire is satisfied but there is anxiety reduction. The self-deceiver believes that *q* is the case even though *q* is not the case. Let us look at cases which illustrate these possibilities. The cases I bring up are, I suggest, good test cases; they are representative of actual self-deception.

The second Clarissa case exemplifies situation I(a). Clarissa, when self-deceived, believes that *p*; believes that not-*r*; believes that *q*: *q* and not-*r* are the case. The respective values for *q*, *r*, and *p* are:

q = The medicine will not harm my body.
r = I do not stop taking the medicine.
p = The medicine causes me to have severe joint pains.

There are countless other cases that fit this model. Suppose a man anxiously desires that *q* (his mother will not drive him crazy). His mother's closest friend near whom she had been living has died, and she is currently visiting him. She expresses her strong desire to remain with him. Because of guilt and ambivalence, he is uncertain whether *r* (his mother will live with him). He believes that if *r* (his mother lives with him) then not-*q* (his mother will drive him crazy). He comes to believe, self-deceptively, that *p* (his mother wants to return to her own home) and buys her a plane ticket back. His mother will not live with him, not-*r* is the case, and his desire that *q* (his mother will not drive him crazy) is satisfied.

Or suppose that a man anxiously desires that *q*, I not leave my wife. He is uncertain whether he will leave because he is uncertain whether *r*, she is unfaithful, having seen a woman looking very much like his wife having intimate conversations with Cesar, a notorious womanizer. If his wife is unfaithful, he will leave her. He deceives himself into believing that the woman he has seen with Cesar is not his wife. By believing that *p*, my wife is not having intimate conversations with Cesar, he believes that his wife is faithful. In fact his wife is faithful; the intimate conversations she had with Cesar were not lovers' conversations. The man is not self-deceived in believing that his wife is faithful, he is self-deceived in believing that she is not having intimate conversations with Cesar. Believing the latter allows him to believe that she is faithful, and this belief allows him to satisfy his desire not to leave his wife.[10]

Situation I(b). The self-deceiver believes that *p*; believes that not-*r*; believes that *q*; *q* is the case; *r* is the case.

Heather anxiously desires that she not have to reexamine her relationship with Harold. Her anxiety stems from her uncertainty about Harold's preference – he arranged to have dinner with Hester without consulting Heather – and she believes that if Harold prefers having dinner with Hester rather than with her she will have to reexamine her relationship with him. Heather self-deceptively believes that Hester has put undue pressure on Harold. His having dinner with Hester is, therefore, explained not in terms of a preference on Harold's part for Hester but rather in terms of Hester's pressuring him.

Heather arrives at her belief by giving undue prominence to the fact that Hester has provided Harold with a place to stay and that

[10] Or consider the case of the ambivalent husband discussed in Chapter 3. He anxiously desires to leave his wife. By believing that she is unfaithful he is able to leave her.

Harold feels obligated to her. Heather believes that Hester has not done enough to dispel the sense of obligation Heather knows he feels. Heather, moreover, discounts the facts that Hester assured Harold that he was under no obligation to have dinner with her simply because she had given him a place to stay, that Harold had made independent plans with Hester for dinner, and that he had arranged the visit to Hester's. The following would be the values for *q*, *r*, and *p*:

q = I, Heather, will not have to reexamine my relationship with Harold.

r = Harold prefers having dinner with Hester rather than with me, Heather.

p = Hester puts undue pressure on Harold.[11]

Situation I(c). The self-deceiver believes that *p*; believes that not-*r*; believes that *q*; not-*q* is the case; not-*r* is the case.

Christopher anxiously desires not to decrease his already questionable chances of passing his driving test. He is uncertain whether he will decrease his chances of passing because he is afraid (but not certain) that he will worry about passing, having worried before his last two attempts and believing that worrying will decrease his chances of passing. He discovers reasons for believing that he will pass. He has, he tells himself, taken several lessons since the last failure, discounting the fact that his instructor said disparaging things about his driving ability during these lessons. Because he self-deceptively believes that he will pass, he does not worry about passing, and his anxiety about making his chances of passing worse is relieved. Suppose too that his *not* worrying will make him perform worse on the test than he would have if he worried. Q, *r*, and *p* would in this case have the following values:

[11] Clifford's shipowner in "The Ethics of Belief" (repr. in *Philosophy: Contemporary Perspectives on Perennial Issues*, ed. E. D. Klemke, A. David Kline, and Robert Hollinger, 4th ed. [New York: St. Martin's Press, 1994], pp. 66–71) would also fit this model. The shipowner anxiously desires that *q*, he not go to great expense to overhaul and refit the ship. He is uncertain whether he will have to go to great expense, given that he knows the ship is old, not well built, and often in need of repairs and has done long service. If, however, *r*, the ship is not seaworthy, then he must go to great expense to overhaul and refit the ship. His anxious desire causes him to believe, self-deceptively, that *p*, the ship is seaworthy. Believing this enables him not to go to great expense to overhaul and refit the ship.

q = I, Christopher, not make my chances of passing my driving test worse.

r = I worry about passing my test.

p = I will pass my test.

Situation I(d). The self-deceiver believes that *p*; believes that not-*r*; believes that *q*; not-*q* is the case; *r* is the case.

In *Anna Karenin*, Kitty's mother anxiously desires that she not have to bear the burden of finding her daughter a suitable partner. She is uncertain whether Vronsky will make her daughter a marriage offer – he has not made one, although there have been suitable opportunities – and she believes that if he does not make the offer, she will have to bear the burden of finding her daughter a suitable partner. She believes self-deceptively that Vronsky fears vexing his mother. His not making the offer is explained not in terms of an intention not to make it at all but in terms of a need to consult first with his mother. She believes what she does even though she is aware that the mother would approve the marriage, and that it is strange that he gives no indication that he will make an offer once he consults his mother. Q, *r*, and *p* would have the following values:

q = I shall not have the burden of finding Kitty a suitable husband.

r = Vronsky will not make my daughter Kitty a marriage offer.

p = Vronsky fears vexing his mother.

By believing that *p*, she believes that not-*r*, Vronsky will make Kitty a marriage offer, and therefore she believes that *q*. Not-*q* is the case and *r* is the case.[12]

[12] David Simon, in his book *Homicide: A Year on the Killing Streets* (Boston: Houghton Mifflin, 1991), describes another case that fits this model. Murder suspects sometimes answer police detectives' questions in the interrogation room without having an attorney present. Simon posits that "every last one envisions himself parrying questions with the right combination of alibi and excuse; every last one sees himself coming up with the right words, then crawling out the window to go home and sleep in his own bed . . . the window is as much the suspect's fantasy as the detective's mirage. The effect of the illusion is profound, distorting as it does the natural hostility between hunter and hunted, transforming it until it resembles a relationship more symbiotic than adversarial" (p. 209). The suspect anxiously desires that *q* (he will sleep in his own bed). He is uncertain whether he will sleep in his own bed because he is unsure whether he will get out of jail and believes that if *r*, he doesn't get out of jail, then not-*q*, he will not sleep in his own bed. By believing that *p* (the homicide detective interrogating him is not an enemy) he believes that

Situation II(a). The self-deceiver believes that *p*; believes that it is not the case that if *r* then not-*q*; believes that *q*; *q* is the case; it is not the case that (if *r* then not-*q*).

If we add some details to the first jealous-husband case discussed in Chapter 3, it would fit II(a).

q = My friend does not hold my wife in higher regard than he does me.

r = My wife has more influence with my friend than I have.

p = My wife is unfaithful.

The husband believes that, given that his wife's influence derives from their sexual intimacy, it is not the case that more influence means higher regard. Suppose that the friend does not hold the husband's wife in higher regard than he does the husband and it is not the case that if his wife has more influence with his friend, then the friend holds his wife in higher regard.

Situation II(b). The self-deceiver believes that *p*; believes that it is not the case that if *r* then not-*q*; believes that *q*; *q* is the case; it is the case that if *r* then not-*q*.

Fred is anxious that he will be lonely. He is uncertain whether his friend Fiona will leave him and believes that if she does, then he will be lonely. He deceives himself into believing that Ingrid, a very desirable person, is interested in him. He believes that if Fiona leaves him, given Ingrid's interest in him he will not be lonely. Let us suppose that Fiona will not leave Fred and that Fred will not be lonely but that if she had left him he would be lonely. The respective values of *q*, *r*, and *p* are:

q = I, Fred, will not be lonely.

r = Fiona will leave me.

p = Ingrid is interested in me.

Fred believes that, given that *p*, it is not the case that if *r* then not-*q*. He believes that *q*. Q is the case, and it is the case that if *r* then not-*q*.

Situation II(c). The self-deceiver believes that *p*; believes that it is not the case that if *r* then not-*q*; believes that *q*; not-*q* is the case; it is not the case that if *r* then not-*q*.

not-*r* (he gets out of jail), and he believes that *q* (he will sleep in his own bed); and not-*q* is the case, and *r* is the case. In this case the detective's attempt to deceive the suspect is aided by the suspect's self-deception.

A man is anxious that his chairman judges his colleague to be more talented than he is. He believes that since the chairman accepted an invitation from the colleague, an invitation he believes his chairman would not have accepted from him, his colleague has more influence with the chairman than he does. Imagine that the man comes to believe, self-deceptively, that his colleague is blackmailing the chairman. He believes that the colleague does have more influence but that it is not the result of the chairman's more favorable appraisal of his colleague's talent. Let us suppose that the colleague does not have more influence, the chairman would have accepted a similar invitation from him, and the chairman does believe that his colleague is more talented than he is. Let us also suppose that even if there is no blackmail, it is not the case that if his colleague had more influence, the chairman would judge him to be more talented. The colleague's greater influence could result not from blackmail or the greater-talent judgment, but from his more active participation in departmental affairs. The respective values of q, r, and p are:

q = The chairman does not judge my colleague to be more talented than I.

r = My colleague has more influence with the chairman than I do.

p = My colleague is blackmailing the chairman.

The man believes that, given that p, it is not the case that if r then not-q. He believes that q. Not-q is the case, and it is not the case that if r then not-q.

Situation II(d). The self-deceiver believes that p; believes that it is not the case that if r then not-q; believes that q; not-q is the case; it is the case that if r then not-q.

The Legrandin example fits II(d). The respective values for q, r, and p are:

q = I, Legrandin, am not thought a snob.

r = I did not openly acknowledge my middle-class friends.

p = I am not thought a snob.

In the Legrandin example there is more than one self-deceptive belief at work. For example,

p_1 = My wink was a truer form of acknowledgment.

By believing p_1, he believes that it is not the case that if r then not-q.

He therefore believes that q and hence, since $q = p$, he believes that p. But not-q is the case, and it is the case that if r then not-q.[13]

Although these are the typical ways in which a self-deceptive belief that p functions to reduce an anxiety that not-q, some cases are atypical. For example, consider the case of a man who anxiously desires that he be happy and believes that if r, a particular woman doesn't love him, he will be unhappy. He believes that if only she loved him, he would be happy. He deceives himself into believing that the woman loves him. This belief, however, does not bring the expected happiness. He was mistaken to suppose that because he would not be happy if he thought she did not love him, believing that she does love him would be sufficient for making him happy. He is not happy, nor does he believe that he is. While his anxiety that not-q is reduced – he is no longer anxious that he is unhappy, he knows that he is – his desire that he be happy is not satisfied. This is a case where his believing that he is loved had as its purpose the reduction of anxiety, but believing this gets him less than he supposed it would. While he believes that the antecedent of the relevant conditional – if she doesn't love me, I will be unhappy – is false, he discovers that other factors contribute to his unhappiness. His belief that he is loved occurred because, given his package of beliefs, desires, etc., having such a belief would normally cause his anxiety to be reduced.

There are, of course, easily imagined situations in which having a false belief gets the believer very little. A man anxiously desires that q, he not lose face. He believes that if r, his wife is unfaithful, he will lose face. Suppose he comes to believe, mistakenly, that she is unfaithful. While he would no longer be uncertain about her fidelity, has this false belief functioned to reduce his anxiety that not-q? He does not

[13] In the following case, what situation the case exemplifies will depend upon what sort of self-deceptive belief the person forms. Suppose one anxiously desires to be a good person. Imagine a situation in which someone is uncertain whether he is a good person because he has done something which is considered bad. In such circumstances the person could have any number of self-deceptive beliefs. For example, he might believe that the harm caused by what he did was minimal, or that the person(s) harmed deserved it, or that the people who considered the action bad were themselves corrupt, or that he had not really meant to do it, or that everyone would have done it, and so on. Any of these beliefs could allow him to believe that despite the so-called bad thing he had done, he was nonetheless a good person.

believe that *q* (he has not lost face), for he does not believe that not-*r*, although *q* and not-*r* are the case. His belief in infidelity would not allow him to believe that his desire that he not lose face was satisfied. It would not as in the former case be plausible for him to imagine that this belief could bring desire satisfaction. Given this, it is hard to imagine that his belief in her infidelity functions to reduce his anxiety that he will lose face, that the purpose of the occurrence of the belief is to reduce that anxiety. It becomes plausible to think that a belief that *p* functions to reduce an anxiety that not-*q* only if we can imagine that the having of the belief would normally bring the believer anxiety reduction. Since anxiety that not-*q* consists of uncertainty whether not-*q* and a desire that *q*, we must be able to imagine that having the belief that *p* would, all things being equal, allow the believer to believe that *q*.

While it is not plausible to think that the man's belief in his wife's infidelity functions to reduce his anxiety about losing face, it is possible to imagine circumstances in which his belief in her infidelity would function to reduce some other anxiety. If we imagine that the man is also anxious that his wife may be duping him about her infidelity, then his belief that she is unfaithful would serve his anxious desire that he not be duped by his wife. If the man's belief that *p* is a self-deceptive one, this case would fit situation I(a). The man believes that *p* (his wife is unfaithful); he believes that if *r* (she is unfaithful and he doesn't know it) then not-*q* (she is duping him about her infidelity). He believes that she is unfaithful. He believes that not-*r*. While he believes that she is unfaithful, he believes that he knows that she is. He believes that *q* (she is not duping him). Both *q* and not-*r* are the case, although he is wrong about why they are the case.

In this chapter I have dealt mainly with cases in which a single anxious desire was assumed. But, as we have seen, people can have multiple anxious desires. A man can anxiously desire both that he not lose face and that he not be duped by his wife.

Sometimes a person's anxious desires may pull in opposite directions. Imagine that a professor anxiously desires not to shirk her responsibility to her students. She is uncertain whether she will do so. Because it is snowing, she does not know whether she will attempt the drive to school. If, however, she fails to drive to school, she will miss the last day of classes. She believes that if that happens, she will be shirking her responsibility to her students. However, she also anxiously desires not to have a car accident. She believes that if she attempts to drive, given the hazardous driving conditions she risks having an accident. A self-deceptive belief that the school has been closed could relieve both anxieties. She does not risk having an accident, and she does not shirk her responsibility to her students.

I have argued in this chapter that self-deceptive beliefs that *p* always function to reduce anxiety, and that they sometimes bring desire satisfaction. And I focused on the ways a self-deceptive belief that *p* typically functions to reduce anxiety. A belief that *p* which functions to reduce anxiety that not-*q* is, I said, caused by the anxious desire that *q*. An anxious desire that *q* causes a belief that *p* by causing the person whose anxious desire that *q* it is, to be biased in acquiring his belief that *p*. The person, of course, does not recognize that a bias is operating in his belief-acquisition process, but believes that his belief that *p* is justified. He fails to make a high enough estimate of the role his anxious desire that *q* plays in his coming to believe that *p*. In Chapter 5 I deal with the self-deceiver's bias. Chapter 6 discusses what can be called the self-deceiver's false consciousness, the deceiver's failure to make a high enough estimate of the role his anxious desire plays in the formation of his belief that *p*. Questions about the intentionality, rationality, and morality of self-deception will be considered, respectively, in Chapters 7, 8, and 9.

5

Self-deceptive belief formation: non-intentional biasing

In self-deception people's anxious desires that *q* cause them to be biased in acquiring their beliefs that *p*. In this chapter I discuss a variety of ways in which anxious desires give rise to biases in belief acquisition[1] and the ways in which one can try to resist or prevent or avoid this biasing. While no attempt to resist or prevent or avoid biasing would result in what Hilary Kornblith has called epistemic irresponsibility[2] – we are epistemically irresponsible when we do not do all that we should do to bring it about that we have true beliefs[3] – I take it for granted that even if the charge of epistemic irresponsibility is not always applicable to self-deceivers,[4] the charge of bias is always

[1] The epistemic shortcomings in the belief-acquisition process caused by the believer's partiality for beliefs that reduce anxiety (consider Locke's cases in which there is a "want of will to use the proofs that are within reach") are to be distinguished from those caused, for example, by the sort of natural misunderstanding discussed in the first Clarissa example (Chapter 4), by the lack of opportunity to inquire (consider the headmaster described in Boswell's *Life of Johnson* who "would beat a boy equally for not knowing a thing, as for neglecting to know it. He would ask a boy a question; and if he did not answer it, he would beat him, without considering whether he had an opportunity of knowing how to answer it"), by a natural deficiency in the capacity for inquiry, or by a carelessness or laziness unrelated to any anxious desire.

[2] Hilary Kornblith, "Justified Belief and Epistemically Responsible Action," *Philosophical Review*, vol. 92, no. 1 (January 1983).

[3] Acquiring a belief is not, of course, in typical situations something we do as an action. But we typically acquire beliefs as a result of the things we do. For example, consider how we might come to believe that it is raining or that it will rain. We might look out the window, see, and hence believe that it is raining. Or we might see that the clouds look a certain way, and because we believe that when clouds look a certain way, it will rain, we believe that it will rain. We might recall last evening's weather forecast, and thus believe that it will rain. Or we might ask a friend with an uncanny weather sense whether it will rain and because he says it will, believe that it will rain.

[4] If there were no action the self-deceiver could take which would enable him to prevent or avoid or resist biasing, then the self-deceiver would not be epistemically irresponsible.

applicable. As a result of this bias in the self-deceiver's belief-acquisition process, the self-deceiver's belief that *p* is never justified. A self-deceiver will never have adequate grounds for thinking that his or her belief that *p* is true.[5]

Dispute in the philosophical literature about self-deceptive belief formation is not to any significant extent dispute about whether a bias operates in the belief-formation process. It is generally acknowledged that biasing occurs. There is dispute about whether the biasing is intentional or non-intentional, and about what the source of the biasing is.

While some theories of self-deception, as David Pears points out, insist on the intentional biasing of belief and postulate "a rational subsystem, perhaps a separate centre of agency, insulated in some way from the main system which largely controls a person's life,"[6] to do the biasing, others argue that the

> biassing is sub-intentional: that is to say, it is not planned and is not even the outcome of a plot of which the self-deceiver is unaware. It is the work

[5] For Kornblith, epistemic responsibility is tied to one notion of justification. A person's belief will be justified if "the belief is the product of *epistemically responsible action,* i.e. the product of an action an epistemically responsible agent might have taken." "Justified Belief," p. 34. More precisely, "an agent is justified in his belief that *p* at time *t* as from time *t′* (where *t′* is earlier than *t*) just in case all of the agent's actions between *t′* and *t* which affected the process responsible for the presence of the belief that *p* at *t* were epistemically responsible" (p. 39). This notion of justification, as Kornblith is aware, is "essentially tied to that of action, and equally to the notion of responsibility" (p. 34). Kornblith illustrates the difference between his account of justified belief as belief which is the product of epistemically responsible action, and accounts of justified belief in terms of belief produced by inferences licensed by rules of ideal reasoning or of reliably produced belief or of reliably regulated belief. See "Justified Belief." I do not follow Kornblith in his notion of justification. Justification, as I shall use it, requires the believer to have adequate grounds for thinking that his or her belief is true. While I shall claim that self-deceivers are frequently enough epistemically irresponsible and that their self-deceptive beliefs are not justified, establishing that a person has been epistemically responsible in acquiring a belief is not sufficient for establishing that the belief is justified, in the sense of justification I employ. Kornblith could agree that epistemic responsibility was not sufficient for having adequate grounds for thinking one's belief was true, just as he agrees that it would not be sufficient for the belief's being produced by a reliable process. See pp. 44–5: "Beliefs formed about a population on the basis of a small sample are responsibly arrived at, and thus justified, but they are not formed by a process which tends to produce true beliefs."

[6] David Pears, "Self-Deceptive Belief-Formation," *Synthese*, vol. 89 (1991), p. 393.

of a pre-rational habit of mind, a purposive mental tropism with a quasi-goal [the reduction of anxiety] rather than a genuine goal [truth].[7]

While Davidson and Pears favor intentional biasing, and elaborate their ideas of intentional biasing in terms of some sort of division, Johnston and Mele favor non-intentional biasing. In a recent paper, William Talbott argues that a single coherent self is capable of intentional biasing,[8] and hence no rational subsystem or separate center of agency[9] is needed to do the biasing. I shall argue that the biasing involved in self-deception is non-intentional.

While it is generally agreed that biasing occurs in the self-deceiver's acquisition of his belief that *p*, there is considerable disagreement about the source of the biasing. Johnston suggests that the source is an anxious desire that *p*; Mele, that it is a desire that *p*; Davidson, that it is a belief that, other things being equal, it is better to believe that *p* rather than not-*p*, given that one desires to avoid the unsettling feeling, emotion, or state that believing that not-*p* gives rise to; Talbott, that it is a desire to believe that *p* regardless of whether *p* is true. I maintain that an anxious desire that *q* is the source of the biasing.

In self-deception the input, so to speak – an anxious desire that *q* – always results in an output belief that *p*. This output belief, if it is to be a self-deceptive one, must function to reduce the anxiety that produces it. The resultant self-deceptive belief, however, is arrived at because the person's belief-acquisition process is skewed, **because a bias in favor of beliefs that reduce anxiety is in place.** Perception, memory, imagination, reasoning, etc. can all be distorted by this bias.

In cases of self-deception the biasing caused by an anxious desire that *q* can, therefore, take a number of different forms and can occur at

[7] Ibid., p. 394. [8] "Intentional Self-Deception in a Single Coherent Self."

[9] Pears argues for a separate center of agency, Davidson for a rational subsystem. Pears is, moreover, willing to countenance Johnston's subintentional biasing in simple cases of wishful thinking, but argues that complex cases require subsystems or a separate center of agency.

Pears discusses the objections made to a theory that self-deception is produced by subsystems operating intentionally. They range from claiming that such a theory is incredible – that a drastic hypothesis is not really needed to explain such a commonplace phenomenon as self-deception – to those, like Johnston's, that claim that such a theory is incoherent.

different stages of the belief-acquisition process. A person's anxious desire that *q* can cause him, for example, to misperceive, to misremember, to focus selectively, to see as salient, and to give undue weight to, certain evidence, to disregard or to explain away other evidence, to misinterpret.[10] Mele and others have discussed in some detail the various forms this biasing can take.[11]

When people have an anxious desire that *q*, they are disposed to act and think in ways that will reduce their anxiety that not-*q*. But of course not all ways of reducing anxiety result in biasing or in self-deception. One anxiously desires that it not rain on a day one is wearing new clothes, for one desires not to get them wet. In this situation taking an umbrella might reduce one's anxiety. But suppose one is anxious that it will rain because one believes that if it rains, the picnic, which one's rarely available friend will attend, will be canceled. In situations where the actions people believe they can perform to reduce anxiety are limited, one would expect them to be disposed to be partial to, or biased in favor of,[12] beliefs that reduce this anxiety.[13] But more needs to be said here, for it seems unlikely that a belief that their available actions in the situation are limited will always in situations of anxious desire result in bias and self-deception.

Talbott has argued that the chief obstacle to a non-intentional analysis of the self-deceiver's biasing is that it cannot explain why anxious desires do not always bias believers' cognitive processes and thus give rise to self-deceptive belief.

[10] It can also lead to a pretense that takes in the pretender. Sometimes this may result in self-deception. "Elizabeth was arrogant, but she was not a fool: she knew she was extolled with shallow gestures and flattering lies – but she wanted it done because it elevated her above all others and enforced extreme deference upon those with whom she worked. Courtiers and politicians were drawn into play-acting conspiracies to deceive themselves and the world: they acted out exaggerated versions of what reality was supposed to be, and in doing so came to believe some of it." Christopher Haigh, *Elizabeth I* (London: Longman, 1988), p. 95. See Chapter 7 for a discussion of when cases of being taken in by pretense are cases of self-deception.

[11] See for example, chapter 10 of Mele's *Irrationality*. In this chapter I take it for granted, as do others, that biasing occurs. In Chapter 7 I discuss a few of the difficulties that face anyone who tries to give a systematic explication of the notion of biasing.

[12] I shall use "partial" and "biased" interchangeably.

[13] For another example, consider a person who is anxious that he is an alcoholic. Given how difficult he believes stopping his drinking would be, he may well tend to be partial to beliefs that reduce his anxiety.

> According to all anti-intentionalist accounts such as those of . . . Mele, and Johnston, a strong desire that p . . . or a strong aversion to -p . . . would be expected to give rise to self-deceptive belief, regardless of the content of p. But no such propensity would be favored by natural selection.
>
> Consider for example, the day that, as I later found out, the master cylinder in my car had begun leaking brake fluid. I noticed that my brake pedal could be pushed closer to the floor than usual. This produced in me significant anxiety from the fear that my brakes might be failing. The anxiety increased each time I pressed on the brake pedal, because each time it approached closer to the floor of the car.
>
> Let p = My brakes are functioning well.
>
> Why did my anxiety from the fear that -p not produce the desire for the anxiety-relieving belief that p? . . . Because it was true that I would have been greatly relieved to believe that p; any anti-intentionalist account will be hard-pressed to explain why I exhibited none of the (non-intentional) mechanisms likely to produce the belief that p.[14]

While I believe that people who have anxious desires are in certain circumstances disposed to be partial to, or biased in favor of, beliefs that reduce their anxiety, I do not believe that people self-deceptively believe that *p* **whenever** believing that *p* would tend to reduce some anxiety. It seems both possible and plausible to think that other universal dispositions exist which, in many circumstances, override the universal disposition to be biased in favor of anxiety-reducing beliefs. People are, for example, universally disposed in the face of danger to take action to protect themselves. If I have an anxious desire that my car brakes be in good working order,[15] my desire to protect myself from being injured in a car accident typically overrides my partiality for beliefs that reduce my anxiety. I bring the car in to be checked and serviced rather than deceive myself into believing that my brakes are in good working order. A dictator with enemies who, instead of maintaining vigilance, believed that no one was plotting against him because so believing reduced his anxiety would not last long as a dictator. In many anxiety-producing and potentially life-threatening

[14] Talbott, "Intentional Self-Deception in a Single Coherent Self," pp. 60–1.

[15] Suppose that I believe that the only option available to me is costly and difficult (the repair shop accessible to me is expensive and remote).

situations the universal disposition to protect oneself from harm can reasonably be supposed to override the universal disposition to be partial to anxiety-reducing beliefs, with the result that one acts to prevent the harm rather than believe that the harm is non-existent.

Self-deceivers are always partial to, or biased in favor of, anxiety-reducing beliefs, although, as I shall argue, they are not intentionally partial.[16] Their partiality for such beliefs ensures that their estimates will tend to deviate from the right value in the direction of these beliefs. It may, for example, take less evidence for them to believe something that relieves their anxiety[17] than to believe something which does nothing to relieve it.

Having such a bias ensures that the resultant belief will not be justified; it does not ensure that the resultant belief will be false. For one to be self-deceived in believing something, however, one's belief must be both unjustified and false. And as we shall see in the next chapter, self-deceivers must believe that their belief is both justified and true.

While people with anxious desires are disposed in certain circumstances to be partial to beliefs that reduce their anxiety, people are also disposed to be partial to other sorts of beliefs. Self-deceivers, who are partial to one kind, are likely to be partial to other kinds. That is, they are likely to be partial to beliefs, for example, which are consistent with their views of themselves and the world, or to beliefs which allow them to think well of themselves.

Beliefs which reduce anxiety will frequently be beliefs that allow people not simply to think well of themselves but to think themselves better than they are.[18] For people tend to be biased and prejudiced in

[16] I have been saying, in effect, that everyone in certain situations of anxious desire is disposed to be partial to anxiety-reducing beliefs. Self-deceivers are those of us in whom this disposition to be partial is not overridden, or resisted, or otherwise prevented from operating.

[17] When a person is biased with respect to something, that person is disposed to behave (act, think, judge, . . .) in ways that favor or disfavor that something, and the favoring or disfavoring is unwarranted. If *A* is biased against women, for example, *A* is disposed to believe unfavorable things about them that the circumstances do not warrant. *A* believes that *B*, a woman, cannot, despite her qualifications for the job, do that job. If *A* has a bias for women, he may believe that the woman candidate will do a better job than a male candidate even though the male candidate has much better job qualifications than she.

[18] In a newspaper article on unrequited love, the following explanation is given. "'Most of us think of ourselves as more desirable than others actually see us,' said Dr. Baumeister. 'So people we think of as of equal desirability may not see it the same way.'"

their own favor; to be self-partial. One is self-partial when one is disposed to behave (act, think, judge, . . .) in ways that favor oneself over others, and that are not justified by the circumstances. We are biased in our own favor if our estimates tend to deviate from the right value in ways that favor ourselves. We believe things, for example, that are flattering to ourselves more easily than we believe things unflattering, or more easily than we believe things flattering to others. We are prejudiced in our own favor if we have preconceived ideas about ourselves which typically prevent us from fairly evaluating ourselves. If, for example, we think of ourselves as honest, we may fail to see not only that we lie, but that we lie with a frequency incompatible with honesty.

The self-deceiver, who is always partial to beliefs that serve his anxious desire that *q*, may not in acquiring his belief that *p* do all that he should to ensure that his belief is true, and if he fails in this latter regard, he would be epistemically irresponsible. That is, there are some things that an epistemically responsible agent should do in situations of anxious desire, and there are some things which should be done in advance of such situations, anticipating them. Such an agent should, in particular, try to prevent or avoid or counteract the skewing of his reasoning and other powers by his anxious desires.

It is generally thought that people can, with effort, in some circumstances, resist their biases. People typically learn that being in certain mental states (for example, being angry, grief-stricken, apprehensive) can adversely affect a person's powers of attention, perception, reason, and so on. As a result they learn that, to avoid error, special care must be taken when in these states. People often enough do not take the appropriate care. Taking appropriate care in the context we are concerned with means trying to resist, given one's anxious desire, the skewing of the belief-acquisition process in favor of certain beliefs. If a self-deceiver is epistemically irresponsible, then he does not put up sufficient resistance on a particular occasion, or he has allowed himself to become the kind of person who finds it natural not to resist such skewing. How does one resist such skewing?

A person can, of course, be on the lookout for potential bias. Depending on how the belief was acquired, there would be different things to be on the lookout for. However, it should be noted at the outset that being on the lookout for something – say, for misperceptions – is no guarantee against bias, for a self-deceiver may interpret and apply the precaution to counteract bias in a biased fashion, and, as a result, acquire the unjustified belief that he is compensating for his bias.

While being on the lookout for bias may, therefore, not ensure that a person will not be biased – a point to which I shall later return – being on the lookout for bias may in some cases make it more difficult to be biased. Or, to put the point positively, it may make it possible for one to resist the biasing. For example, in situations in which beliefs are acquired as the result of direct sensory experience, one has a better chance of resisting partiality if one is on the alert for misperceptions. A jealous man "sees," and thus believes, that the woman in the distance embracing a man is his wife. His belief can be self-deceptive, if, for example, the jealous man's anxious desire to blame his wife for his jealousy has caused him to misperceive; the woman in the distance is not his wife. While his misperceiving is not intentional, he could be epistemically irresponsible if he did not consider whether, given his anxious desire that *q*, he is misperceiving. He could be epistemically irresponsible if he assumed without further investigation that his perception is accurate.

We might in some circumstances also hold him responsible for allowing himself to have become the kind of person who does not take adequate precautions against misperceiving in situations in which he has an anxious desire. Doing all that one should to ensure that one's beliefs are true requires one to gather and attend to evidence properly rather than casually,[19] to take steps to correct one's shortcomings in belief acquisition by disciplining one's mental habits, by ridding oneself of bad habits of reasoning. As Kornblith notes, while simple perceptual beliefs are "for the most part arrived at automatically, the agent's actions play a role in the fine tuning of the belief acquisition process. An epistemically responsible agent must be on the uptake for defects in the process, and act to correct for them."[20] While he acknowledges that a "certain amount of accommodation to misleading experience is itself automatic and not the product of free action," he believes that

[19] As Kornblith observes in "Justified Belief and Epistemically Responsible Action," "an agent who reasons perfectly about evidence casually acquired, or who simply refuses to look at evidence not already in his possession is acting in an epistemically irresponsible manner" (p. 35).

[20] Ibid., p. 38.

> there can be no doubt that one can self-consciously instill in oneself a certain circumspection in circumstances where a mistake is likely to occur, such as in emotionally charged situations. Once this circumspection is acquired, more reliable belief acquisition will occur in one automatically, and without any particular action on the agent's part. Nevertheless, the presence of such automatic processes may often be traced to free action designed precisely to result in such processes, and when this is the case, it is to the agent's credit; failure to take such action may be epistemically irresponsible.[21]

Kornblith's point, one with which I agree, is that in determining whether a person has been epistemically responsible we must not simply look at the immediate circumstances in which the belief was acquired – in the case at hand to the man's "seeing" the woman to be his wife – but at events prior to his interaction with the scene perceived. One aspect of the man's epistemic irresponsibility would lie in his casual acceptance of his perception as accurate.

In beliefs acquired on the basis of what is remembered, care must be taken to ensure that what is remembered was the case. One must be on the alert for misremembering. Karenin believes that he never ridiculed but only sympathized with men who he knew had been cuckolded, because he "remembers" this. But he is mistaken; his anxious desire that he not be held in contempt is responsible for his misremembering. Not only had he never sympathized with such men, he "had always plumed himself the more whenever he heard of wives betraying their husbands."[22]

While some beliefs are not arrived at after deliberation and decision, other beliefs are. With regard to some of these latter beliefs, a person is epistemically responsible in acquiring them only if, in his deliberations about what to believe, he imposes on himself something akin to the adversary principle of considering both sides.[23] In the public arena, rational thought has as its ideal an impartial judgment arrived at after hearing non-corrupt representations of opposing sides. Different persons represent the opposing sides, and judgment is

[21] Ibid. [22] Leo Tolstoy, *Anna Karenin* (Penguin Classics, 1986), p. 302.

[23] See Stuart Hampshire, "Justice Is Strife," *Proceedings and Addresses of the American Philosophical Association*, vol. 65, no. 3 (1991), pp. 19–27. I am in this paragraph paraphrasing points he makes in that address. The quotation in the next paragraph appears on p. 22.

rendered by a person independent of either side. In the private sphere, a person, as a rational believer, is sometimes expected to function analogously: to be not only an impartial judge who hears both sides but a non-corrupt representative of first one and then the other side.

Stuart Hampshire points out why it is frequently not possible in solitary investigation to do precisely this. "One cannot," he says, "regularly decide where one event in a mental process ends and another begins, and therefore whether the proper order of events has been followed," an order necessary to ensure that the evidence one considers for each of the sides is genuinely independent. Some approximation to this public procedure is, nevertheless, expected when, for example, a parent is considering whether his son is mentally retarded, a spouse whether his or her partner is faithful, an Aristotelian scholar whether Aristotle wrote a certain work.[24] A person in the special context indicated at the start of the preceding paragraph who fails to try to approximate some standard of impartiality would be epistemically irresponsible. If he failed to try to consider both sides, for example, or failed to try to resist his bias in favor of one side, he would be epistemically irresponsible. However, even if he makes the effort to be impartial, the self-deceiver never succeeds in being impartial. He may, as judge, be partial, or he may, as a representative of one or the other side, be corrupt.

Impartiality, however, is notoriously difficult to come by in matters of concern to the individual. And, as we have seen, the individual has anxious desires about matters that are of concern to him or her. Consider Lear's self-deceptive belief that his daughter Cordelia is deficient in her love for him. On one plausible interpretation of the play, Lear, fearing old age and death, anxiously desires to retain power

[24] It is not clear how much evidence one has to gather in these situations. An Aristotelian scholar, for example, who gives a non-corrupt defense of his belief that Aristotle did not write a certain work is not epistemically irresponsible if he does not, in addition, hunt for all the evidence he could find against his belief. We expect him to look for some evidence against, but it is not clear how much consideration of the other side is needed. Suppose, for example, he does not read another Aristotelian scholar's latest piece upholding the contrary thesis. Whether he is epistemically irresponsible for not doing so depends on further factors – whether, for example, he can anticipate, given what he knows of this other scholar's views, what the other scholar will argue. Obviously one cannot ignore or dismiss non-confirming evidence out of hand if one's defense of a side is to be non-corrupt, but neither is it required that one obtain all the evidence against the side one is defending. I return to a related issue in Chapter 7 when I discuss what biasing is.

after dividing his kingdom among his daughters. He associates losing power with having no status, with being nothing. Cordelia's response to his request for a public declaration of love in exchange for her share of the kingdom is seen as a challenge to his power. He explains her challenge in terms of her lack of love, for such an explanation allows him to meet her challenge with a clear show of power. He withholds from her what he has in his power to give, just as he perceives her withholding from him what she had in her power to give. His evidence for her lack of love is her honest, but not tactful, words, and he dismisses out of hand attempts, like Kent's, to remind him of the evidence against this. Such attempts are themselves seen as challenging his power, and their challenge is met with a show of power.

Lear, like all self-deceivers, is partial to beliefs which reduce his anxiety, and his belief that Cordelia's love for him is deficient is the result of his bias. The evidence he offers in support of this belief is inadequate, as is his handling of evidence in support of the opposing belief.

It may not only be difficult to be impartial in situations we care about, in some situations it may well not be possible to be impartial. While self-deceivers are required, if they are to be epistemically responsible, to try to resist their bias for anxiety-reducing beliefs, some self-deceivers who try to resist their bias nonetheless fail to resist it. And it may not be plausible to regard those who try to resist, but fail, as epistemically irresponsible.[25]

It was reported that Richard Nixon believed that he did nothing wrong in Watergate even after listening to the incriminating tapes. If an anxious desire is powerful enough, it seems possible that it will so bias the person's thinking that all the evidence will only further strengthen the person's belief that his thinking is not biased. In such circumstances, given the power of the anxious desire involved, it is not clear that there is anything that the person could have done that would have prevented the biasing processes from being successful. If there is no action the person failed to take which could have prevented the biasing, it is not clear that the person in such a situation would be epistemically irresponsible.[26] This suggests, as I noted early in this

[25] This of course depends on such things as how hard they tried and why they failed.

[26] Not all the actions that Nixon could have taken to prevent biasing are ones that he should have taken. Consulting a psychiatrist might be one that he should have taken, but considering brain surgery is not. But suppose Nixon had consulted a psychiatrist. Such consultation need not have prevented biasing.

chapter, that one can be partial even if one is not epistemically irresponsible.

We have yet to see why the self-deceiver's biasing is non-intentional. As I understand "intentional," an intentional action is one that is done for a reason that the agent has, a reason which the agent can be non-inferentially aware of, a reason the agent can acknowledge.[27] While a person can be mistaken about his intentions just as he can be mistaken about his beliefs and desires, he can acknowledge, can become non-inferentially aware of, such desires, beliefs, and intentions as he has.

Pears points out that in self-deception there is no contemporary avowal from the self-deceiver of an intention to bias, or any detailed description of the biasing process from the self-deceiver's point of view.[28] Although Pears believes that the biasing can nonetheless be intentional,[29] he acknowledges that, given the lack of a detailed description from the self-deceiver's point of view, "the concept of a self-deceptive basic mental act [of biasing] lacks a feature of the concept of a non-self-deceptive basic mental act, like adding one to nine."[30]

If the self-deceiver's biasing is intentional, and if the self-deceiver, and not, as Pears believes, some subsystem, does the biasing, then the

[27] See Robert Audi, "Acting for Reasons," *Philosophical Review*, vol. 95, no. 4 (October 1986), pp. 511–46. Audi gives an account of acting for reasons and points out that "if intrinsically motivated actions are actions for reasons, then intentional action is equivalent to action for a reason." If it is, then his "account of acting for a reason should serve as an account of intentional action" (p. 544).

It can happen, as in cases of double effect, that actions are ***voluntary*** under certain descriptions although they are not done for reasons under those descriptions. "We must distinguish between the consequences of an action for the sake of which it is undertaken, and the consequences that may arise as predictable and possibly welcome by-products. If we ask an artist what he is doing, he would say, 'trying to get it right,' not 'trying to impress the public,' although he may well know that the public will be impressed if he gets it right." Jon Elster, "Deception and Self-Deception in Stendhal," in *The Multiple Self,* ed. Elster (Cambridge: Cambridge University Press, paperback, reprinted 1988, p. 110). It is not clear to me, however, that these actions are *intentional* under certain descriptions, although they are not done for reasons under those descriptions.

[28] "Self-Deceptive Belief-Formation," pp. 398ff.

[29] Pears believes that the basic biasing action is not the agent's but the subsystem's, and the subsystem does do it under the description "generating the counter-evidential belief preferred by the main system" (p. 401).

[30] Ibid.

self-deceiver must have intentions and reasons of a certain kind. He must, I shall argue, have non-inferentially unrecognizable intentions and reasons.

Non-inferentially unrecognizable intentions and reasons are, to be sure, unrecognized contemporaneously by the person whose intentions they are alleged to be, but they are also intentions and reasons of which the person **cannot become non-inferentially aware**. But while all non-inferentially unrecognizable intentions are unrecognized, not all unrecognized intentions are non-inferentially unrecognizable. If intentions are unrecognized but non-inferentially recognizable, then the person whose intentions they are can acknowledge, can at some time become non-inferentially aware of, them. While I am willing to concede the existence, in that sense, of unrecognized intentions that are non-inferentially recognizable, I am unwilling to concede the existence of unrecognized intentions which are non-inferentially unrecognizable.

Talbott contends that unrecognized intentions or reasons exist. In contrast to what I maintain, he believes that the biasing that occurs in self-deception is intentional, because the self-deceiver has unrecognized intentions and reasons. He shows that unrecognized intentions exist in other areas, and he believes that it is plausible to assume that such intentions exist in self-deception as well. While the unrecognized intentions he points to in areas outside self-deception are not non-inferentially unrecognizable, and hence their existence is not in dispute, I argue that the unrecognized intentions in self-deception cannot be similarly non-inferentially recognizable, and hence that their existence is in dispute.

Let us turn to Talbott's argument. He first establishes the need for unrecognized intentions in self-deception.

> [I]f the fox is to be capable of intentionally biasing his cognitive processes to favor believing that p (that the grapes are sour), the fox must be able to act on an intentional strategy of which he himself is not aware – that is, it must be possible for him to have the intention to favor belief in p (regardless of whether it is true) and for that intention to operate to bias his cognitive process, without the fox's realizing it . . . I claim that this is possible because many of our own mental states, including our beliefs and intentions, are not *transparent* to us – that is, we can be mistaken about them.[31]

[31] "Intentional Self-Deception in a Single Coherent Self," p. 33.

Talbott does not believe that unrecognized intentions are an exotic species of intention, required only by self-deception. He believes that unrecognized intentions are required elsewhere; for example, they are required by a theory of communication like Grice's. Although Talbott concedes that Grice's theory of meaning may be inadequate,[32] he believes that Grice offers a good framework for understanding "*communicative beliefs and intentions* – that is, the beliefs and intentions involved in communication."[33]

Grice claims that quite complex beliefs and intentions are involved in ordinary communication. For example, in ordinary communication, my saying that p is due to a number of complex intentions, including, roughly, the intention that you come to believe that p by way of recognizing that my saying that p indicates that I believe that p, and the intention that you take my believing that p as a reason for you to believe that p. Talbott refers to these intentions as "unconscious" intentions of which the communicant is ignorant. If one believes that there are such intentions involved in ordinary human communication, as Talbott does, then one might have good reasons for supposing that unrecognized intentions exist. If unrecognized intentions exist in ordinary communication, they can exist in self-deception.[34]

Talbott may be right in assuming that Grice's theory of communication gives us a good reason for believing in unrecognized intentions of the kind that are non-inferentially recognizable. I contend that he is not right, however, in thinking that Grice's theory of communication gives us good reason for believing in unrecognized intentions of the kind that are relevant for self-deception, for those intentions, and not communication intentions, are non-inferentially unrecognizable.

Talbott is "sure that people engaged in communication . . . for thousands of years without having any inkling of the complexity of the beliefs and intentions involved. Indeed, for much of that time the

[32] Ibid., pp. 36–7 n. 15. [33] Ibid., p. 37.

[34] Ibid. Talbott says this, for example, on p. 58: "And if the objection is raised that human beings are not capable of such complex intentions, at least not without being aware of them, I think that there are other reasons for thinking that we are – for example, the fact that equally complex "unconscious" beliefs and intentions seem to be involved in communication and other social activity." Cf. also n. 17: "Self-deception seems to me to be another complex activity – actually, less complicated than communication – that we learn how to do without any explicit understanding or awareness of how we do it."

languages employed may have been too primitive to have terms for mental states such as beliefs and intentions. But it is not necessary to be able to *express* one's communicative beliefs and intentions or in any sense to be aware of them, in order to *have* them."[35] The intentions involved in communication are, it is suggested, unrecognized, given that only a small fraction of those who engage in communication could even understand Grice's proposal, much less report the intentions that Grice's proposal implies that communicants have.

But it is not obviously true that most people involved in communication could not understand Grice's proposal, much less report on the intentions involved. While it is true that people might not immediately understand Grice's proposal, it is not obviously false that if it were explained patiently to people, they would understand it. If they understood it, then there is no reason to think that the intentions involved in communication are intentions which people could not acknowledge, or of which they could not become non-inferentially aware.

And Talbott himself admits as much. "In case of communication, a speaker may be unaware of the complex beliefs and intentions involved, but given sufficient time, it ought to be possible to educate her so that she can come to recognize and acknowledge at least some of the complex beliefs and intentions involved."[36] If this is the case, then communication intentions are intentions that are non-inferentially recognizable.

If the existence of unrecognized intentions in communication is to give support to the existence of unrecognized intentions in self-deception, the unrecognized intentions in self-deception must be similarly non-inferentially recognizable. And Talbott tries to muster support for their being so.

Talbott believes that despite the fact that self-deceivers are motivated to deny the existence of these unrecognized intentions, they may nevertheless come to acknowledge their existence. Moreover, there may be ways other than relying on the self-deceiver's avowals that one can use to show that these intentions exist.

> The mechanisms of self-deception (e.g., selectivity of memory, attention, reasoning, and evidence-gathering) can be studied independently of the agent's reports of their working. The various types of selectivity

[35] Ibid., n. 17. [36] Ibid., p. 58.

can also be studied in other contexts not involving self-deception. Also, even if an intentional theory of self-deception would not be supported by an agent's contemporaneous avowals, it could acquire some support by the agent's subsequent avowals.[37]

The self-deceiver might at some later time be offered an explanation of her behavior in which unrecognized intentions play a role, and "she might be inclined to accept that explanation." Talbott admits, however, that "the primary evidence for the theory [of intentional biasing involving unrecognized intentions] would have to come from more subtle experimental strategies than simply asking the subject whether she was intentionally biasing her cognitive processes."[38]

I am dubious about the existence of subtle experimental strategies whose results can, without question begging, be taken to provide support for intentional biasing in self-deception. But more to the present purpose, none of the facts that Talbott appeals to includes the relevant kind of non-inferential awareness that one needs to elicit to establish the existence of unrecognized but non-inferentially recognizable intentions.

A being has intentions or reasons only insofar as that being can (in the full normal range of contexts) ask, and non-inferentially answer, the question "Why?" where this is taken as a request for one's reason for which, or the intention with which, one does or did so-and-so.[39] The intentions that exist in ordinary communication are not non-inferentially unrecognizable intentions (intentions that one cannot become non-inferentially aware of). The intentions can be elicited from their owners with "Why?"; one does not here run into the impasse into which one runs when a similar attempt is made with self-deceivers who repudiate the so-called intentions behind their self-deception.

The requirement given in the preceding paragraph for determining whether a being has intentions or reasons is the basis of the contrast between one's reason for *x*-ing and the reason why someone or something *x*'ed. That requirement can be violated only if one is willing to abandon that contrast. And to abandon that contrast is simply to ignore a very important element of the complexity of the world.

37 Ibid. 38 Ibid.

39 As far as intentions are concerned other questions like "What were you trying to do?" and "Were you trying to *x*?" are also relevant, but I shall focus on "Why?"

A self-deceiver may be inclined, as Talbott points out, to accept an explanation of her past behavior which requires her to acknowledge that biasing occurred in acquiring a particular belief. But what will not be elicited from the self-deceiver, even after prodding, will be the relevant non-inferential responses to "Why?" The self-deceiver never comes to say, "Yes, I intended (or I meant deliberately, or . . .) to do that," but only something like "Yes, that (biasing) must have been what was going on." The words "must have been" reflect acceptance of a conclusion on the basis of inference. Self-deception is in this way crucially unlike communication.

We would, moreover, retract the self-deception verdict as soon as someone changed his response and acknowledged non-inferentially that he had been deliberately ignoring certain evidence, etc., with the intention of generating in himself the belief that such-and-such, e.g., as would be acknowledged by the person in the wrong-date-in-the-appointment-book case if he came to remember what he had done. Because such acknowledgment is possible, this case is not a case of self-deception.

If a necessary condition of the presence of intention is the possibility of the kind of non-inferential response to "Why?" that I have discussed, then that condition is not satisfied in self-deception. But the satisfaction of that condition is necessary for establishing the existence of intentions that, although unrecognized, are non-inferentially recognizable.

One has *intentions* of *any* sort only insofar as they are non-inferentially recognizable. Talbott wants to talk about intentions that are at best *inferentially recognizable*. Talbott is *right* that the *mechanisms* involved in self-deception are at best inferentially recognizable. So whatever mechanisms Talbott is thinking of in connection with "intentional biasing," they are not intentions, and thus they do not make the biasing intentional.

A person might be tempted for other reasons to believe in intentions that are non-inferentially recognizable. Take, for example, young children. Young children, it might be argued, in some sense pursue sophisticated strategies, and such strategies might initially be taken as evidence of their having unrecognized intentions and beliefs that are also not non-inferentially recognizable, given the inability of young children to operate with the "Why?" question. However, in the case of children young enough still to be unable to operate with the "Why?" question, the evidence that these children have unrecognized intentions and reasons is not, I believe, better than the evidence that a spider has unrecognized intentions and reasons.

Someone can, of course, say that young children have unrecognized intentions and beliefs, but I would argue that their saying this is a verbal maneuver, reassigning the extension of "unrecognized intentions and beliefs" from "Why?" users to the whole class of purposive-seeming entities (of which "Why?" users are a subclass). Moreover, as our knowledge of the behavior of "lower" forms of life gets more detailed, it becomes progressively harder to resist ascribing unrecognized reasons and intentions all the way down. That is, it becomes progressively harder to resist ascribing such reasons and intentions to spiders and bacteria as well as to young children.[40]

The debate over whether there exist intentions that are not non-inferentially recognizable, and hence the debate about whether the self-deceiver can intentionally bias his belief-acquisition process, is at bottom, I believe, a debate over whether the contrast between "Why?" users and non-"Why?"-users is interesting and important. I have argued that the self-deceiver cannot be held simply to have unrecognized intentions; because of his inability to avow them non-inferentially, the intentions would have to be non-inferentially unrecognizable (by him). And that is what our standard "Why?" practice calls into question. Anyone who proposes to substitute another practice for that practice owes us an argument.

If our standard "Why?" practice marks an important contrast, then any creature that clearly cannot (yet) operate with that question (be the creature a young child or a spider) lacks intentions. If some philosophers think the contrast is not important and should not be taken to be so, they should explain the reluctance that many of us feel about attributing unrecognized intentions all the way down, or, if

[40] In *By the Grace of Guile*, Rue describes the deceptions that occur all the way down in nature, including those perpetrated by human pathogens (viruses, bacteria, protozoa) to defeat detection by the human immune system (pp. 109ff.). For example, the *E. coli-ki* bacterium coats its surfaces with polymers of sialic acid (self-cells of mammals are similarly surrounded by sialic acid). *E coli-ki* bacteria thus avoid detection by the system that targets invader cells for destruction. Viruses hide the chemical binding site by which they bind and infect nerve cells of the host. The rabies virus binds to protein and gets invited into the cell. Certain protozoa deceive the immune system by carrying a battery of genes for different surface proteins or by carrying a single gene that is prone to mutation.

unrecognized intentions are not to be attributed all the way down, why we should stop at the point at which they favor stopping.

If "intentional" carries with it the implication that I have claimed – i.e., if it requires the agent of an intentional action to do that action for a reason which the agent can be non-inferentially aware of, can non-inferentially acknowledge – then the biasing done by a self-deceiver is non-intentional. I have not, of course, ruled out the possibility that the biasing could be intentional if "intentional" did not carry these implications, i.e., if the agent of an intentional action were not required to do that action for a reason of which he could be non-inferentially aware. I have, however, explained why I am skeptical about the existence of non-inferentially unrecognizable intentions and reasons.

Talbott concedes in his article that the kind of non-intentional biasing that I am advocating is at least possible. He thinks, however, that those of us who advocate unintentional biasing have some explaining to do.

> It is possible to suppose that these very properties (e.g., the desire to believe p regardless of whether it is true) trigger biasing mechanisms without the intervention of any biasing intention on the part of the agent. I have no way of excluding such a possibility in principle. But anyone who would advocate such an account should explain why they are inclined to postulate *two* mechanisms for maximizing expected utility – one intentional and one not . . . Though an unintentional mechanism of Expected Utility maximization is possible in principle, it seems to me much more probable that all of the cases, including self-deception, are intentional, and that they are all cases in which the agent is simply ignorant of and thus unable to report the relevant intentions.[41]

I shall in my response divide Talbott's challenge into two parts. He suggests that it ***seems much more probable that there is only one kind of mechanism*** for maximizing expected utility and that that mechanism is intentional. Rational action is an intentional mechanism for maximizing expected utility. The first part of Talbott's challenge to me is to show that it is even so much as equiprobable that an unintentional mechanism for maximizing expected utility exists also. But to show that it is at least equiprobable that there are two kinds of mechanism

[41] "Intentional Self-Deception in a Single Coherent Self," p. 63.

here, one intentional and one unintentional, would not meet the second part of Talbott's challenge, which is to show that ***it is more likely that there are two mechanisms***.

Concerning the first challenge, there is, I believe, no presumption against a plurality of kinds of mechanism for maximizing expected utility. There appear to be in human beings all sorts of non-intentional physiological and psychological mechanisms which have the tendency to maximize expected utility, coexisting with the intentional mechanism that has that tendency, viz., rational action. Our mechanism for digesting food or the mechanism which brings to our memory things which it is beneficial for us to remember are examples of unintentional mechanisms for maximizing expected utility.

Even if it is no less probable that the mechanism in self-deception is unintentional than that it is intentional, why is it more likely that it is unintentional? It is more likely that it is unintentional because an intentional mechanism cannot account for the special features of self-deception. The self-deceiver, given his inability to avow his supposed intentions non-inferentially, would, I claimed, have to have not simply unrecognized intentions but non-inferentially unrecognizable (by him) intentions. I argued that our standard "Why?" practice calls such supposed intentions into question.

In note 26, Talbott talks about intention ascription to Bayesian agents. What he says here might also be taken to form the basis of an objection to my skepticism about intentional biasing in self-deception. Would not the possibility of unconscious Bayesian intentions establish the possibility of unconscious intentional biasing of the sort that would be a counterexample to my position? I argue that it would not.

Talbott notes that "a Bayesian agent has only one, over-arching intention – to maximize Expected Utility. Thus, whenever I ascribe an intention X to a Bayesian agent (e.g., to bias her cognitive processes in favor of p) I should be understood as simply claiming that X maximizes her Expected Utility."[42]

Bayesian-theory-defined intentions are always just "to maximize Expected Utility." But it seems clear that we can often describe our intentions completely without using Bayesian terms. So it would be reasonable to assume that many Bayesian intentions are, therefore,

[42] Ibid., p. 48.

unconscious. The ascription conditions for Bayesian intentions are, however, different from the ordinary ascription conditions for intentions. My claim is that biasing is not intentional in the ordinary sense of "intentional." So the possibility of unconscious Bayesian intentions does not establish the possibility of unconscious intentional biasing of the sort that would be a counterexample to my position.

In this chapter I have tried to show that purposive anxiety reduction is neither blind nor intentional. The self-deceiver is disposed to be on the lookout for anxiety-reducing beliefs, beliefs that will, for example, allow him to believe that *q*. Although the biasing that occurs which enables the self-deceiver to come to his self-deceptive belief that *p* works non-intentionally, it has as its purpose anxiety reduction, and that purpose ensures that the biasing which occurs is neither random nor haphazard. Furthermore, anxious desire does not automatically trigger biasing and self-deception. What other beliefs and desires, what other dispositions are operating in the agent, will affect when such biasing occurs.[43]

[43] Whether the person has or lacks a certain kind of courage will also affect whether biasing occurs. See Chapter 9.

6

False consciousness

In his book *Self-Deception and Morality*, Mike W. Martin characterizes self-deception as "the purposeful or intentional evasion of fully acknowledging something to oneself."[1] Among the characteristic ways of evasion he gives are keeping oneself willfully ignorant, systematically ignoring something suspected or believed, emotionally detaching oneself from what is happening, self-pretending, and rationalizing. Andre Gombay, reviewing Martin's book, questions whether self-deception is, as Martin suggests, adequately characterized as a complex of such activities. "When a head of state keeps himself in studied ignorance of what his underlings are doing; when (as perhaps he must) he pursues a conscious policy of not becoming emotionally involved in his decisions; do we say that he is fooling himself?" Gombay answers, I believe correctly, "No; we say this only if he also, in some sense sincerely, can deny he is behaving that way." Gombay goes on to say that "It is all right to insist . . . that the self-deceiver acts consciously and deliberately; but not at the cost of omitting the other side – the false consciousness that coexists so precariously with the true."[2]

While I do not agree with Gombay that the self-deceiver's false consciousness coexists, however precariously, with the true, or that the self-deceiver acts consciously and deliberately, if this means that, knowing the truth, the self-deceiver consciously and deliberately gets himself to believe a falsehood, I do agree that the self-deceived's consciousness must be false. In this chapter I focus on this false consciousness.

I offer a characterization of it which I compare with the characterization given by David Sanford. Both Sanford's and my characterizations

[1] (Lawrence: University Press of Kansas, 1986), p. 5.

[2] Andre Gombay's review of Martin's *Self-Deception and Morality* in *Philosophical Review*, vol. 98, no. 3 (July 1988). All the quotes in this paragraph are from p. 444.

see the false consciousness as essentially involving some sort of misapprehension. The self-deceived misapprehends the structure of his attitudes. He takes, as Sanford says, "the having of one attitude to explain the having of another when the true explanation is something else."[3]

While Sanford discusses a misapprehension that emphasizes making an estimate that is too high – that involves an overestimating[4] – I focus on a misapprehension that emphasizes not making an estimate that is high enough. One way of not making such an estimate is by underestimating – by making an estimate that is too low. Another way is by failing to make any estimate at all. I consider both.

While overestimating and underestimating typically go together – given a number of factors that contribute to one's decision to buy a new car, one overestimates the strength of some factors if one underestimates the strength of others – the sorts of overestimating and underestimating I consider are independent of each other. I argue that while the self-deceived's false consciousness sometimes involves an overestimation of the sort Sanford characterizes, it always involves a failure to estimate highly enough of one of the two sorts I characterize.

Since Sanford does not seem to believe that the self-deceived's false consciousness always involves an overestimation, I am not in this chapter challenging what I take to be a conceptual claim made by Sanford. Rather, I am only suggesting that, for whatever reasons, he has not drawn attention to a certain phenomenon, in the region he probes, that is conceptually connected with self-deception. I wish to highlight the sort of misapprehension that I believe is necessary for self-deception, by comparing it with the overestimation he suggests occurs.

What I shall call the lack-of-a-high-enough-estimation condition requires that either the self-deceived underestimate how much his anxious desire that q contributes to his believing that p, or the self-deceived fails to make any estimate at all about the role his anxious desire that q plays in his coming to believe that p.[5] The lack-of-a-

[3] David Sanford, "Self-Deception as Rationalization," in *Perspectives on Self-Deception*, ed. Brian McLaughlin and Amelie Oksenberg Rorty (Berkeley: University of California Press, 1988), p. 169.

[4] As I make clear below, he discusses also another possible sort of misapprehension.

[5] Sanford made me see the need for this second way of satisfying what I now call my lack-of-a-high-enough-estimation condition.

high-enough-estimation condition can be satisfied either by an underestimation or by an absence of estimation.

The underestimation may take importantly different forms. The self-deceived may believe that her anxious desire plays no causal role in the formation of her belief. The person who self-deceptively believes that Hester exerts undue pressure on Harold could, for example, acknowledge her anxious desire that she not have to reexamine her relationship with Harold, yet believe that that anxious desire plays no causal role in her coming to believe this.

The self-deceived may believe that her anxious desire plays a causal role, but that the role is an inessential one. A mother who is self-deceived in believing that her son is not a thief might, for example, believe that her anxious desire that he not be a thief motivates her to seek evidence in support of his innocence. She may further believe that while her anxious desire that he not be a thief plays this motivating role, it is not an essential causal role with respect to her belief in his innocence, for she believes that without this anxious desire she would still have come to believe that he is not a thief.

Alternatively, the self-deceived may believe that the causal role his anxious desire plays is an essential one – he might believe that without pressure from his anxious desire that *q* he would not have come to believe that *p* – but nevertheless underestimate the extent of that causal role. For example, a detective might have an anxious desire that a defendant be innocent – at the trial he sees her for the first time and takes a fancy to her – and this anxious desire that she be innocent might prompt him to look for evidence of her innocence. Suppose his anxious desire not only prompts his search for evidence, but also biases his belief-acquisition process, and he comes to believe that she is innocent when she is not. While he acknowledges that his anxious desire that she be innocent plays an essential causal role in his coming to believe that she is innocent – he would not have come to believe she was innocent without being prompted by this anxious desire to seek evidence – if he is self-deceived in believing that she is innocent, he may nevertheless underestimate the extent of his anxious desire's causal role in the formation of his belief. He may fail, for example, to believe that his anxious desire caused a skewing of his belief-acquisition process.

One can also not make an estimate that is high enough by failing to make an estimate at all. Rather than ***believing that one's anxious desire***

plays no causal or no essential causal role, or plays less of an essential role than it actually does, as one does in underestimation, ***one fails to have a belief either way as to whether one's anxious desire plays a*** causal or an essential causal role. In underestimation one believes something from which a certain denial follows about one's anxious desire doing such-and-such. In failure of estimation one fails to believe something – one does not believe that one's anxious desire does such-and-such. A person may fail to estimate the role of his anxious desire if he is not at the relevant time aware that he has that anxious desire; if, for example, his attention is focused elsewhere than on the anxious desire.[6]

Sanford suggests that two sorts of reason – one he calls an ostensible reason, and one he calls an anticipating reason – are found "[i]n the clearest cases of self-deception of the kind called *rationalization*."[7] Since Sanford also believes that "an element of rationalization is necessary for genuine self-deception,"[8] it seems likely (though not certain) that he believes that one or both of these reasons would be present in any case of self-deception. He characterizes an ostensible reason as follows:

"Generally one's attitude *A* is an ostensible reason for one's attitude *B* when one overestimates how much one's having attitude *A* contributes to the reason for one's having attitude *B*."[9]

He characterizes an anticipating reason as follows:

"One's attitude *A* is an anticipating reason for one's attitude *B* when an essential factor in the final adoption of attitude *A* is that having attitude *A* helps provide what one takes to be an acceptable reason for having attitude *B*."[10]

I want to focus on Sanford's ostensible reason.[11] This reason calls

[6] One can be unaware of an anxious desire one has for other reasons. For example, one may lack a belief as to whether one has this anxious desire, or the anxious desire may not be readily accessible to one.

[7] "Self-Deception as Rationalization," p. 162.

[8] Ibid., p. 167.

[9] Ibid., p. 160. Sanford believes that overestimation can occur when the person takes a reason to support something and it provides no support at all, or when a person takes a reason to play a primary role when it plays "a real but derivative role."

[10] Ibid., pp. 160–1.

[11] Sanford's anticipating reason may itself necessitate a misapprehension. Suppose, for example, that *A* believes that her new car is a bargain only because it provides her with what she takes to be an acceptable reason for taking pleasure in her new car. If one could not acknowledge to oneself that some attitude one has is an anticipating reason for

attention to a familiar kind of overestimation. We frequently take a reason for an attitude to be the real reason for it when the real reason is something else. For example, a husband may believe that he wants to lie to his wife only because he wants to protect her, when his real reason for his wanting to lie to her is his wanting to control her.

Sanford's ostensible reason has the self-deceived misapprehending the structure of his attitudes by overestimating how much having one of his attitudes contributes to the reason for having another. Underestimation, in contrast, has the self-deceived misapprehending the structure of his attitudes by underestimating how much the having of one particular sort of attitude, an anxious desire, contributes to the reason for having another sort of attitude, a belief. While the true explanation for one's having a certain self-deceptive belief that *p* will always involve the causal role one's anxious desire that *q* plays in the formation of one's belief that *p*, the self-deceived will always misapprehend, will always not make a high enough estimate of, the degree to which this anxious desire that *q* contributes to the formation of the belief that *p*. He or she will believe that the belief that *p* is justified; that the belief that *p* is based on evidential beliefs or on direct sensory perception to an extent sufficient for justification. The belief that *p* will not, however, be justified; the anxious desire that *q* causes him or her to be biased in forming his or her belief that *p*. The believer does not have adequate grounds for his or her belief.

It is time to see why a lack of a high enough estimation, but not overestimation, is necessary for being self-deceived. That is, to see why the self-deceived's misapprehension, his false consciousness, always takes the form of a lack of a high enough estimation but only sometimes takes the form of an overestimation.[12] I first argue that

another while the attitude remains to any extent part of one's reason, then when one attitude is an anticipating reason for another, one will misapprehend the structure of one's attitudes. One will not acknowledge that one attitude is an anticipating reason for the other. One could, for example, overestimate how much the attitude which is an anticipating reason for the other attitude contributes to the having of this other attitude. One could underestimate how much one's desire for an acceptable reason for having one attitude contributes to the reason why one has another attitude.

[12] In Sanford's article, it is not always clear that Sanford thinks one can have self-deception without the presence of an ostensible reason, without the overestimation condition being satisfied. It is not entirely clear that the overestimation condition on Sanford's view is not a necessary condition for self-deception. An ostensible reason is independent of an anticipating reason. In the cases he discusses in which the latter but not the former reason

underestimation of the sort I characterize is compatible with overestimation of the sort Sanford characterizes – there are cases of self-deception where both occur. I then look at a case which Sanford believes might be a case of self-deception, but not a clear case, where underestimation, but not overestimation, is present. I suggest that when the case is filled out, it is a clear case of self-deception, and thus shows that overestimation is not necessary for self-deception. The case is not, however, intended to show that underestimation is necessary. Rather it is to show that a lack of a high enough estimate is necessary.

Case I. Agatha is a glutton (people have tactfully tried to tell her that she is one). Being a glutton and liking ice cream, she tries to get as much ice cream as she can. When Agatha is asked, somewhat accusingly, why she wants ice cream – she has already had six that day – she replies that she wants ice cream because she wants something cold. Let us imagine in this case that she anxiously desires to have an acceptable reason for wanting ice cream and that she is self-deceived in believing that she wants ice cream because she wants something cold. In order to have both overestimation and underestimation, we need to specify more than one *A*–*B* pair of attitudes. That is, since it is not possible for a person to overestimate how much the having of one attitude *A* contributes to the reason for having another attitude *B* and at the same time to underestimate how much the having of attitude *A* contributes to the reason for having attitude *B* if all the values of *A* and *B* remain the same, the values of either *A* or *B* or both in underestimation must be different from the values of *A* and *B* in overestimation. Let us give different values of *A* and *B* different designations, e.g., A_1, A_2, and so on. In the case at hand we shall have two attitudes *A* and two attitudes *B*. That is, let

> Attitude A_1 = Agatha wants something cold.
> Attitude B_1 = Agatha wants ice cream.

is present, he either says "it is at best a questionable case of self-deception," or, although he is more inclined to count it as a case of self-deception than some are, he admits "that it is not a clear case." If it is a case, even if it is not a clear case, then the ostensible reason is not necessary. He does not have the same reservations about cases in which the ostensible reason is present but the anticipating reason is not. These can be cases of self-deception, even if they are not the clearest cases.

Attitude A_2 = Agatha anxiously desires that she have an acceptable reason for wanting ice cream. This constitutes Agatha's anxious desire that q.

Attitude B_2 = Agatha believes that her wanting something cold is her reason for wanting ice cream. This constitutes Agatha's belief that p.

Let us look at overestimation first.[13] By believing that she wants ice cream because she wants something cold, attitude B_2, Agatha overestimates how much her having attitude A_1 (wanting something cold) contributes to the reason for her having attitude B_1 (wanting ice cream). She believes, mistakenly, that she has attitude B_1 because she has attitude A_1, when she has attitude B_1 for some other reason. Her attitude A_1 is an ostensible reason for her attitude B_1.

In order to see how underestimation is occurring as well, we must look at attitude A_2, which constitutes her anxious desire that q, and attitude B_2, which constitutes her belief that p.

Attitude A_2 = Agatha anxiously desires to have an acceptable reason for wanting ice cream.

Agatha is uncertain whether she has such a reason, for she is aware both of her passion for ice cream and of her having had six ice creams that day. This anxious desire to have an acceptable reason for wanting ice cream constitutes her having an anxious desire that q.

Her belief that she wants ice cream because she wants something cold (her belief that p) functions to reduce her anxiety about not having an acceptable reason for wanting ice cream. She believes that her desire to have an acceptable reason for wanting ice cream is satisfied: she wanted the ice cream because she wanted something cold.

She fails to see that the desire for something cold could readily be satisfied by the ice water that is, and was, readily available. Her dismissal of this evidence for her not having an acceptable reason for wanting ice cream is an expression of her bias. Her belief that p, her attitude B_2, is not justified. She believes that her anxious desire that she have an acceptable reason for wanting ice cream played no essential causal role

[13] I shall leave open whether an anticipating reason is present in such a case. It would be if Agatha does not want something cold independently of her wanting ice cream. If an essential causal factor in the adoption of one of her attitudes, her wanting something cold, is that it helps provide what she takes to be an acceptable reason for having another attitude, for wanting ice cream, then the first attitude would be an anticipating reason for the second attitude.

in her coming to believe that she wanted ice cream because she wanted something cold. That is, she underestimates how much having attitude A_2, the anxious desire to have an acceptable reason for wanting ice cream, contributes to the reason why she has attitude B_2, the belief that her wanting something cold is the reason why she wants ice cream.

In underestimation, one of the relevant attitudes, A_2, will always consist of an anxious desire; the other attitude, B_2, will be a self-deceptive belief.[14] The attitudes designated A_1 and B_1 in connection with Sanford's overestimation requirement are not similarly limited as to kind. The lack of a high enough estimation required by false consciousness, when satisfied by an underestimation, will always be an underestimation of the influence of the anxious desire on the formation of the self-deceptive belief.

In the case we just looked at, the self-deceptive belief – Agatha believes that her wanting something cold is her reason why she wants ice cream – was a belief in which Agatha overestimated the contribution of one to the other. The belief was also caused by her anxious desire for an acceptable reason for wanting ice cream, and the purpose of the occurrence of the belief was to reduce her anxiety about not having an acceptable reason. She underestimates the degree to which her anxious desire contributes to the formation of her belief because she believes, mistakenly, that her belief is justified.

It is not the case, however, that the self-deceptive belief that *p*, the belief that reduces one's anxiety that not-*q*, is always a belief in which one overestimates the relationship between two attitudes. Nor is it the case that one's anxious desire that *q* is always an anxious desire for an acceptable reason for having an attitude. In the case I look at next, a case in which underestimation, but not overestimation, occurs, the self-deceptive belief that *p* is not a belief in which one overestimates the relationship between two attitudes, nor is the anxious desire that *q* an anxious desire for an acceptable reason for having an attitude.

Case II.

A_3 = I anxiously desire that the dog in my yard be my dog.[15]

[14] This holds true in estimation failure as well.

[15] Frederick Siegler ("An Analysis of Self-Deception," *Nous*, vol. 2 [1968], pp. 147–64) describes such a case which he thinks is not a case of self-deception. It is this case which

B_3 = I believe that the dog in my yard is my dog.

A_4 = I believe that I see that the dog in my yard is mine.

My dog has been missing and my neighbor's dog is a good deal like my dog. I see a dog in my yard, but I am uncertain whether it is my neighbor's dog; if it is, then it isn't mine. When I go into my yard to see whether the dog is mine, I think that I directly perceive that the dog is mine. I am mistaken. Believing that I see that the dog is mine allows me to believe that the dog is mine, and this belief functions to reduce my anxiety that the dog in my yard is not my dog. While my desire that the dog in my yard be my dog is not satisfied by my believing that the dog is mine, I do thereby reduce my anxiety about whether it is mine (at least temporarily). The anxious desire is causally responsible in part for my coming to believe that the dog in my yard is my dog.

I believe that the dog in my yard is my dog because I believe that I directly see that it is my dog. Believing that I see that the dog is mine is my real reason for believing that the dog is mine. I do not overestimate how much the having of attitude A_4, my belief that I see that the dog is mine, contributes to the reason why I have attitude B_3, my belief that the dog in my yard is my dog. Overestimation is not present.

My anxious desire that the dog be mine causes me to be biased in forming my belief that the dog in my yard is my dog. The anxious desire in this case causes me to misperceive the dog as mine. I believe that I see that the dog is mine even though my neighbor's dog, but not my dog, has white markings on his leg fur and the dog I see has such markings. I know, moreover, of this difference between the dogs. I am disposed to see the dog in my yard as my dog and I believe that I do see that he is my dog. Let's suppose I underestimate how much my anxious desire that the dog be mine contributes to the reason why I believe that the dog is mine. I deny that my anxious desire plays any causal role in the formation of my belief that the dog in my yard is my dog; I believe that my belief is justified, for I believe that I directly see that the dog is mine. In this case, while underestimation is present, overestimation is not. If I am in these circumstances self-deceived in

Sanford is "more inclined than Siegler to count . . . as a case of self-deception," although he admits it is not a clear case. I argue that when the case is adequately specified, it becomes a case of self-deception. See "Self-Deception as Rationalization," p. 161.

believing that the dog in my yard is my dog,[16] and I would argue that I am,[17] then overestimation is not necessary for self-deception.

In the case as I have described it, I deny that my anxious desire plays any causal role in the formation of my belief that the dog in my yard is my dog. But it could also be the case that instead of denying this, I could merely fail to believe that my anxious desire plays a causal role in the formation of my belief that the dog in my yard is my dog. That is, I could be mistaken about the dog in my yard without having underestimated my anxious desire. If the situation were thus, there would be neither overestimation nor underestimation but, rather, failure of estimation. Possibilities of this sort suggest that what is necessary in self-deception is not underestimation but, rather, not making an estimate that is high enough. In the situation just imagined that condition would be satisfied.

Let us look at one further case. It is a case where overestimation is present but neither underestimation nor failure of estimation is. This case suggests that the lack-of-a-high-enough-estimation condition is a necessary condition for self-deception, for this case, despite the presence of overestimation, will not be a case of self-deception.

Case III. Agatha has been subjected to subliminal advertising, and solely because of the advertisement she wants ice cream. When she is asked why she wants ice cream she replies, Because I want something cold. Let us suppose that in this case she does want something cold independently of whether she wants ice cream. Let us also suppose that had she not been subjected to the advertising she would not have wanted ice cream, even though she would still have wanted something cold. The relevant belief of Agatha's here is her belief that she wants ice cream only because she wants something cold. She believes

[16] Sanford is tempted to see this case as a case of self-deception because he believes that in such a case an anticipating reason is present. If it were the case, as Sanford suggests, that I believe that I see that the dog is mine because believing that I see that the dog is mine provides me with an acceptable reason for believing that the dog is mine, then an essential causal factor in A_4, my belief that I see that the dog is mine, is that it provides what I take to be an acceptable reason for believing that the dog is mine. Attitude A_4, I believe that I see that the dog is mine, would then be an anticipating reason for attitude B_3, my belief that the dog in my yard is my dog.

[17] This is a case which would satisfy the conditions I specify as individually necessary and jointly sufficient for being self-deceived. I will list these conditions in the next chapter.

that her wanting something cold is the only causal factor in her wanting ice cream. Agatha's belief that p (that she wants ice cream only because she wants something cold) is false.

Overestimation is present in such a case. Let

Attitude A_1 = Agatha wants something cold;
Attitude B_1 = Agatha wants ice cream.

By believing that she wants ice cream because she wants something cold, Agatha overestimates how much her having one attitude (wanting something cold) contributes to the reason for her having another attitude (wanting ice cream). She believes, mistakenly, that she has the second attitude because she has the first, when she has the second attitude for some other reason. Her first attitude is an ostensible reason for her second attitude.

In this case, while there is overestimation, there is not underestimation. There is no underestimation, because Agatha does not have an anxious desire that q. The anxious desire that q that would be relevant here would be one that causes the belief that p, with the purpose of believing that p being to reduce the anxiety that not-q. The plausible candidate for such an anxious desire would be having a reason she could accept for wanting ice cream. While Agatha desires that q – she have a reason she can accept for wanting ice cream – she is not anxious that it is not the case that q, for (let us now add) she has supposed from the outset that she has a reason she can accept for wanting ice cream: all along, she has wanted something cold.

Nor in this case is there the requisite failure of estimation. There is, to be sure, a lack of estimation of the role her anxious desire plays, but this lack occurs not because she has an anxious desire whose effect she fails to estimate, but rather because she has no anxious desire at all to estimate or to fail to estimate.

This case may initially be thought to make trouble for the supposed necessity of the lack-of-a-high-enough-estimation condition, but it does not. In the case as described, although Agatha is mistaken in believing that she wants ice cream because she wants something cold, she is not *self-deceived* in so believing. No anxious desire of the required sort causes her mistaken belief, for she lacks the necessary anxiety. Wanting a reason, she chooses what seems to her the actual one – wanting something cold.

Sanford believes that an element of rationalization is necessary for genuine self-deception. He characterizes rationalization in terms of two kinds of reason, only one of which – the ostensible reason – I have focused on. It is entirely possible, given what I have said in this chapter, that while his ostensible reason – what I have characterized in terms of overestimation – is not individually necessary for self-deception (he acknowledges that his other reason is not individually necessary), one **or** the other of these reasons will be present in any case of self-deception. That is, this chapter leaves open the possibility that Sanford's reasons are disjunctively necessary.

7

Intentional and non-intentional deception of oneself

People can be deceived by appearances, by others, by themselves. If people are deceived in any of these ways, they are deceived in believing something, and consequently they believe something false.

One can be deceived in believing something without there having been any process whose intended outcome was one's state of being deceived. One could, for example, have been deceived by appearances without the appearances having been intentionally used for this effect. Recall the pediatrician who believed that the homeless man was not an affectionate father.

However, when one is deceived in believing something because one was deceived by another person, then, I argued, the deceiver engaged in a deliberate process whose intended outcome was one's state of being deceived. Deceiving another involves an intentional act of deception.

In this chapter I explore the relationship between the process of deceiving oneself into believing something and the state of being self-deceived in believing that something. Several issues will be discussed. One concerns the possibility of intentionally deceiving oneself; of engaging in a deliberate process whose intended outcome is one's own state of being deceived. A second concerns the sufficiency of such a process for the state of being self-deceived. In Chapter 2 we saw that while it is possible to intentionally deceive oneself into believing something, doing so is not sufficient for being self-deceived in believing that something. I discuss Davidson's explanation for this, and offer an alternative. It is a consequence of any non-intentional account of self-deception, such as Johnston's or Mele's or mine, that intentionally deceiving oneself is not necessary for the state of being self-deceived. I consider whether some other process (e.g., a non-intentional deceiving process) is necessary or sufficient for this state, what such a process would consist in, and whether such a process should be called a process of self-deceiving oneself.

The self-deceiving process which I identify, and contend is necessary and sufficient for the state of being self-deceived in believing something,[1] is a non-intentional deceiving process. However, while it is not possible to self-deceive oneself without non-intentionally deceiving oneself, it is possible to inadvertently or unintentionally deceive oneself, and hence to non-intentionally deceive oneself, without self-deceiving oneself. Self-deceiving oneself is not only to be distinguished from intentionally deceiving oneself. Self-deceiving oneself is one form, but not the only form, of non-intentionally deceiving oneself.

I. INTENTIONALLY DECEIVING ONESELF INTO BELIEVING

While some have doubted whether one could engage in a deliberate process whose intended outcome was one's own state of being deceived,[2] we have already seen that it is possible for one to do this. Recall Davidson's example of the man who tries to avoid an unpleasant meeting in the future by writing down the wrong date in his appointment book. While it is generally assumed that for such a process to work, the man must naturally forget what he has done or be caused to forget what he has done by drugs or hypnosis – in Davidson's example the man relied on his bad memory to have forgotten his deed by the time he comes to read the date – such forgetting is not essential. Thomas Cook has shown that even if one remembers that one deliberately set out to get oneself to believe something one thought false, one can, nevertheless, believe that something. One can do this if one's "criteria for evidential warrant" with regard to the relevant belief are altered. One then sees the epistemic condition one was in when one originated the plan as being defective. Although one thought when initiating the process that one's belief (the one to be changed) was warranted, by the time that – as a result of doing what one believes, in Pascalian fashion, will induce belief – one has come to

[1] As we shall see, the self-deceiving process I identify will be necessary, but not sufficient, for the state of being self-deceived in believing that *p*; it will, however, be necessary and sufficient for the state of being self-deceived in believing something.

[2] People have wondered how, if the self-deceiver knows what he is up to, any attempt to deceive himself could succeed.

believe the opposite, one will also have come to believe that one's prior belief (the one to be changed) was unwarranted.

Cook gives the example of a fundamentalist student who, although believing evolutionary theory to be mistaken, deliberately sets out to get himself to believe in evolution. After a course of study at Harvard, the student comes to believe that evolutionary theory is correct. He does not forget what he has done, but he no longer believes that his original belief that evolutionary theory was mistaken was based on evidential support. Rather he believes that "ignorance, social pressure, superstition," and the unjustified credence he gave to the views of his fundamentalist parents and teachers[3] were responsible for his prior belief.

II. INTENTIONALLY DECEIVING ONESELF INTO BELIEVING IS NOT SUFFICIENT FOR BEING SELF-DECEIVED IN BELIEVING

Davidson means his meeting example to show that while a person can intentionally deceive himself into believing something, one's engaging in a deliberate process whose intended outcome is one's own state of being ***deceived*** in believing is not sufficient for one's being ***self-deceived*** in so believing. Davidson explains that what prevents this from being a case of self-deception is that since, when the person sees the entry and believes that the meeting is on such-and-such a day, the person does not judge that the totality of his evidence supports the meeting's not being on that day, the intention that initiates the action that leads to the belief is not the intention that sustains the belief. On Davidson's account, therefore, although the person is deceived, he is not self-deceived.[4]

While I agree with Davidson's conclusion about this example – the man in question would not be self-deceived in believing that the

[3] Thomas Cook, "Deciding to Believe without Self-Deception," *Journal of Philosophy*, vol. 84 (August 1987), pp. 441–6.

[4] Davidson and others believe that it is not enough to have gotten into the state of being deceived in a special way; one must be sustained in that state in a special way in order for it to be a state of self-deception. See also Bela Szabados, "Self-Deception," *Canadian Journal of Philosophy*, vol. 4, no. 1 (1974), p. 54: "[T]o say of someone that he is self-deceived is *not* merely to say that he is in a certain state of mind; ascriptions of self-deceit also involve an appraisal as to how the person in question got into that state of mind and how he sustains himself in it."

meeting was on such-and-such a date – my explanation of why he is not self-deceived differs from Davidson's. Let us assume that the man had an anxious desire to avoid encountering a particular person he believes will attend the meeting. He is anxious that he will encounter that person because he has promised his employer that he would attend the meeting, a promise which carries weight, but he believes that if he attends the meeting, he will encounter that person. He therefore writes down the wrong date for the meeting. He forgets that he has done this and comes to believe that the meeting is on the wrong day. As a result, he misses the meeting and does not encounter the person he wanted to avoid.

He believes, mistakenly, that his belief that the meeting is on such-and-such a day is justified – the date is in his book. He has been epistemically irresponsible in acquiring his belief – he knowingly writes down the wrong date – and his belief that the meeting is on that day is false. His anxious desire, moreover, plays a causal role in the acquisition of his belief. The man is not self-deceived, however, in believing that the meeting is on such-and-such a day, since this belief does not reduce his original occurrence of anxiety.

What reduces that occurrence of anxiety is his belief that ***he will miss the meeting because he will believe it is on the wrong day***. If he misses the meeting, he will not encounter the person he wishes to avoid. This anxiety-reducing belief is true, and he has not deceived himself into believing it, nor has he been biased or epistemically irresponsible in acquiring it. If he is still anxious at a later time to avoid encountering that person, having forgotten what he has done at the earlier time, then that occurrence of anxiety does not cause him to believe that the meeting is on such-and-such a day, although this belief will reduce that occurrence of anxiety, for he will in fact miss the meeting and not encounter the person he wishes to avoid.[5]

[5] That is: *At time t_1 the man's anxious desire that he not encounter a particular person [call this occurrent anxious desire "OAD_1"] causes him to write down in his book the wrong date of a meeting which he believes that particular person will attend. At time t_1 the man's belief that he will miss the meeting relieves his anxiety. OAD_1 is relieved.*

Time passes and memory of what he did at time t_1 fades. *At time t_2, sometime later than t_1, the man has an anxious desire that he not encounter that particular person [call this occurrent anxious desire "OAD_2"]. At time t_2 the man's belief that the meeting is on such-and-such a day relieves his anxiety – OAD_2 is relieved – for he misses the meeting and does not encounter that person.*

We assumed in the above example that there were two occurrences of anxious desire. It could of course happen that by the time the man comes to read his appointment book, he no longer has an anxious desire to avoid encountering that person. Suppose, for example, the person was unexpectedly out of the country. The man's belief that the meeting is on such-and-such a date causes him to miss the meeting. He has deceived himself into believing that the meeting was on this day, but the belief, while being caused by his anxious desire, does not reduce any occurrence of anxiety, for by the time he forms the belief he is no longer anxious. While he has deceived himself into believing that the meeting was on that day, the man is not thereby self-deceived in believing this.

The appointment example shows that intentionally deceiving oneself into believing that *p* is not sufficient for one's being self-deceived in believing that *p*. However, if **intentionally deceiving oneself** were not coextensive with **deceiving oneself**, then the appointment example would leave open the possibility that non-intentionally deceiving oneself was sufficient for the state of being self-deceived in believing something.[6]

The anxious desire at time t_1, OAD_1, causes him to believe at time t_2 that the meeting is on such-and-such a day. The anxious desire at time t_1, OAD_1, is relieved at t_1 by the belief that he will miss the meeting and hence avoid the person. The belief that the meeting is on such-and-such a day relieves his anxious desire at time t_2. OAD_2 is relieved. His desire that he not encounter the person is satisfied. The belief that the meeting is on such-and-such a day is not, however, caused by the anxious desire at time t_2, by OAD_2, but by the anxious desire at time t_1, by OAD_1. The anxiety that causes the belief that reduces a later occurrence of anxiety is not itself reduced by the belief that it causes. In other words the belief that reduces an anxiety at time t_2 was not caused by the same occurrence of anxiety that it relieves. In self-deception, however, it is required that the belief that *p* be caused by the same occurrence of anxiety that it relieves. Since in the case at hand this requirement is not met, the case is not one of self-deception.

6 Johnston, we saw, claimed that deceiving oneself was not an intentional action but a combination of subintentional processes – a process wherein one's anxious desire that *p* generates the belief that *p*, and a process wherein one represses one's recognition that the evidence tells against *p*. Even if it were the case that intentionally deceiving oneself into believing that *p* was not sufficient for being self-deceived in believing that *p*, this would not show that undergoing these subintentional processes was not sufficient.

III. IS NO NON-QUESTION-BEGGINGLY-SPECIFIED PROCESS OF DECEIVING ONESELF INTO BELIEVING SUFFICIENT FOR BEING SELF-DECEIVED IN BELIEVING?

There is an argument that might tempt us into supposing that the process of deceiving oneself into believing something, *whatever that process involved* – be it an intentional act of deceiving oneself, some combination of subintentional processes or . . . – was not sufficient for the state of being self-deceived. The argument would go as follows. Just as it is possible for people to deceive others into believing something that is true, it is possible for people to deceive themselves into believing something that is true. Fingarette cites the person "who on the basis of fear and as an outcome of intellectual fuzziness jumps to the conclusion that he has cancer . . . This belief causes him unbearable distress . . . he proceeds to try . . . to persuade himself that he does not have cancer."[7] If the person can, as Fingarette suggests, deceive himself into believing that he does not have cancer when he does not have it, he cannot be self-deceived (or even deceived) in believing that he does not have it.

What this argument shows, however, is not that the process of deceiving oneself, whatever that process might involve, is not sufficient for a state of self-deception, but only that the process is not sufficient for a particular state of self-deception. That is, if one deceives oneself into believing that *p*, and *p* is true, then one cannot be self-deceived in believing that *p*. But, for all the argument shows, it could still be the case that when one deceives oneself into believing that *p*, and *p* is true, one must be self-deceived in believing some *s* other than *p*. The process of deceiving oneself into believing that *p* could be sufficient for being in a state of self-deception in believing that *s* where *s* need not be (even if it often is) identical with *p*.

IV. SELF-DECEIVING ONESELF

We have thus far established that successful intentional deception of oneself, even if it were sufficient for one's being deceived in believing

[7] Herbert Fingarette, *Self-Deception* (London: Routledge and Kegan Paul, 1969). See also T. S. Champlin, *Reflexive Paradoxes* (London: Routledge, 1988), pp. 17–20.

something, is not sufficient for one's being self-deceived in believing something. It remains to be seen whether some other-than-intentional process of deceiving oneself into believing that *p* is sufficient for one's being self-deceived in believing something.

Let us return to the case of the man who has an anxious desire not to encounter a particular person he believes will be at a meeting. In what circumstances might we say that this man not only has deceived himself into believing, but also is self-deceived in believing, that the meeting was on such-and-such a day?

Suppose that the man does not intentionally write down a date in his appointment book that he knows to be wrong. Rather, not knowing the day, but only the week of the meeting, he looks up the day of the week on which the meeting was held the previous year and without further checking concludes that it will be held on the same day of the week. Had he checked further (and it was easy and non-costly for him to do so) he could have seen that it was rash to assume that it will be held on the same day of the week each year. Suppose the man gets the date wrong and misses the meeting. In such circumstances I suggest the man could have deceived himself into believing that the meeting was on such-and-such a day and could also be self-deceived in believing that it was on that day. Whether he deceives himself and is self-deceived will depend at least upon whether he has some anxious desire, for example, an anxious desire to avoid encountering a particular person, which causes the biasing of his belief-acquisition process and hence causes him to believe, mistakenly, that the meeting was on that day. It also depends upon whether the purpose of his believing that the meeting was on that day is to reduce his anxiety about encountering that person, and whether he fails to make a high enough estimate of the role his anxiety plays in coming to his belief.

What this example, and the examples in previous chapters, are meant to suggest is that people are not self-deceived in believing that *p* because they have intentionally deceived themselves into believing that *p*. In the cases discussed in my examples, the people did not intentionally deceive themselves. They are self-deceived because they have come to believe that *p* in the special way I have been describing in this and preceding chapters.

I have focused in my discussion on cases of *coming to* believe that *p*. In cases where the self-deceptive belief that *p* is a *continuing* belief that at time t was not self-deceptive but is at t_1, what I say about coming to believe that p can be applied to retaining the belief that p.

Those who come to believe that p in the special way I have been describing are deceiving themselves. I call the kind of deceiving oneself that occurs in these cases ***self-deceiving oneself***. "Self-deceiving oneself" is introduced as a technical expression. It is not pleonastic, because "self" serves to exclude intentional deceiving of oneself; intentionally deceiving oneself is one species of deceiving oneself, and self-deceiving oneself is another species of that, a species which leaves one self-deceived. Self-deceiving oneself is an activity that cannot be intentional under that description. One self-deceives oneself in the course of doing other things.

We are now in a position to spell out what self-deceiving oneself involves. The following conditions are offered as individually necessary, and jointly sufficient, conditions for deceiving oneself in the sense required for being self-deceived.

One self-deceives oneself into believing that p, if and only if:

1. One has an anxious desire that q which causes one to be biased in favor of beliefs that reduce one's anxiety that not-q. This bias or partiality operating in one's acting or thinking or judging or perceiving etc. causes[8] one to believe that p.
2. The purpose of one's believing that p is to reduce one's anxiety that not-q.[9]
3. One is not intentionally biased or partial.[10]
4. One fails to make a high enough estimate of the causal role that one's anxious desire that q plays in one's acquiring the belief that p. One believes (wrongly, when condition 1 is met) that one's belief that p is justified.[11]

[8] "Causes" here is to be understood as "causes in the right way."

[9] Given 1 and 2, one's belief that p functions to reduce one's anxiety that not-q. Conditions 1 and 2 repeat two conditions discussed in Chapters 3 and 4, viz., the belief that p is caused by the anxious desire that q, and the purpose of the occurrence of the belief is to reduce anxiety that not-q. From the fact that p functions to reduce an anxiety, it follows that p reduces that anxiety.

[10] I argued in Chapter 5 that the biasing of the belief-acquisition process that occurred in self-deception was non-intentional.

[11] A child can satisfy the conditions, including condition 4, that I have set up for self-deceiving oneself. As soon as a child can understand that one thing can be a reason for another, the child can self-deceive him- or herself. For example, a child, abused by his

There is, I have claimed, a general human propensity in situations where one has an anxious desire that *q* to be partial under certain circumstances to beliefs that reduce this anxiety. While one is disposed in such situations to be epistemically irresponsible in acquiring such beliefs – for example, to fail to check for misperceiving or misremembering, to fail to gather all the relevant evidence – I have shown that even if one does all one can to be epistemically responsible, a bias can nonetheless operate. The self-deceiver fails to resist adequately a partiality to anxiety-reducing beliefs. Because he is partial to anxiety-reducing beliefs, and the belief that *p* is such a belief, he believes that *p*.

Condition 1 describes a certain sort of efficient causation. Condition 2, however, is concerned with a certain sort of final causation. One can take the terminology of condition 2 at face value as some philosophers would do (e.g., Aristotelians), or one can translate it into one's favorite alternative terminology. If one is a reductionist, rather than an eliminativist, with respect to final causality, condition 2 would be intelligible. My analysis would not satisfy the eliminativist, but it is beyond the scope of this discussion to take the eliminativist on.

Just in case all these conditions are satisfied with respect to one person, that person has self-deceived him- or herself into believing that *p*. In cases where the person not only self-deceives himself into believing that *p*, but is self-deceived in believing that *p*, the belief that *p* is false as well as not justified. But there will always be – even in cases where *p*, the belief that one deceives oneself into believing, is true – some belief that will be false which the self-deceiver will believe is true. (A person can self-deceive himself into believing something true, but he cannot be self-deceived (or deceived) in believing something true.) He will, for example, believe that he has adequate evidence for *p* or that he directly perceives that *p* when it is not the case

parents, who anxiously desires that his parents love him, may self-deceive himself into believing that his parents love him. If the child self-deceives himself into believing this, he will believe, at least implicitly, that he has good enough reasons for believing that his parents love him; he will very likely fail to make any estimate, and hence not a high enough estimate, of the role his anxious desire plays in his coming to his belief; his anxious desire will have caused him to be biased in acquiring his belief, a bias he would not believe himself to have; he will not be justified in believing that his parents love him; the purpose of his believing that his parents love him will be to reduce his anxiety that his parents do not love him. I discuss condition 4 in Chapter 6.

that he has such evidence or direct perception. He will believe that his belief about that evidence or perception is true.

This process of self-deceiving oneself into believing that *p*, defined by the four conditions, is necessary for the state of being self-deceived in believing that *p*. It is not, however, sufficient for it. Rather this process is sufficient for the state of being self-deceived in believing something. In this respect, self-deceiving oneself into believing something is analogous to deceiving another into believing something. If I self-deceive myself into believing that *p*, I must be self-deceived in believing something; if I deceive you into believing that *p*, you must be deceived in believing something.

But self-deceiving oneself into believing something is, of course, not analogous to deceiving another into believing something with respect to intentionality. The anxiety-reducing process, defined by the four conditions, that I here identify with self-deceiving oneself, cannot be intentional under any of the descriptions entailed by these conditions.

The self-deceiver is, as condition 1 says, biased or partial in acquiring his belief. The biasing is caused by the anxiety. The biasing may be said to be motivated where "motivated biasing" refers to some sort of causal transaction with some analogies with the causal transaction that is the motivation of actions.[12] Present discussion about self-deception takes this notion of motivated biasing as primitive,[13] explicated by examples rather than analysis. While it would be good to make progress on an analysis, as the discussion that follows should make clear, a systematic explication of the notion of biasing, especially motivated biasing, is a formidable task, a task that is beyond the scope of this book. However, progress about self-deception can, I believe, be increased even in the absence of such a systematic explication.

Consider the following as a first approximation to a characterization of biasing (but *not motivated* biasing): a belief-acquisition process is biased when one (or more) of the following conditions is satisfied.

1. In forming the belief the believer does not consider all the factors that he should consider.

[12] The analogies may include certain sorts of relations between descriptions satisfied by key events and the propositional content of key propositional attitudes belonging to the person around whom a case of action or biasing revolves.

[13] See, for example, Mele's discussion in chapter 10 of *Irrationality*.

2. In forming the belief the believer does not consider appropriately all the factors that he should consider.
3. In forming the belief the believer considers inappropriately factors that he should not consider.[14]

These conditions are, as they stand, obviously vague. They invite charges of triviality or of falsity. One may well ask, What factors should an unbiased believer consider? While I shall not answer this question, I shall indicate a few of the issues that any answer must address.

It seems clear that what factors I *should* consider in coming to a belief will depend on the circumstances I am in. Not all the factors that have bearing on the truth of the belief that I acquire need be factors that I should consider. If I want to know whether the water in a pond is sufficiently pure to sustain fish life, I might base my belief on what I take to be a fair sampling of the pond's water. In such circumstances it is not required that I sample all the water. What is required is that my samples be representative samples. My belief-acquisition process would be biased in such a situation if, for example, I chose to take samples from areas of the pond that I believed would be the least likely to be affected by any pollution, and I based my belief about the pond water's purity on just those samples. It would not be biased simply in virtue of the fact that I did not sample all the water.

If in coming to my belief that a suspect is not guilty I do not consider evidence suggestive of his guilt – I do not, for example, consider that the tool used to force entry was owned by the suspect – my belief-acquisition process need not be biased. Suppose the suspect had successfully disposed of the tool. That the suspect owned the tool that was used to force entry was, therefore, not a factor that was accessible to me. It was not a factor that I should consider, since it was not a factor I could consider.

Suppose that the tool had not been disposed of by the suspect but was in a place that I could find only if I spent vast amounts of time and money searching for it. While it was a fact I could consider, it seems

[14] See Don Adams, "Love and Impartiality," *American Philosophical Quarterly*, vol. 30, no. 3 (July 1993), p. 227: "If you are being partial, then either you have not considered all relevant factors, or you have not considered them properly, or you are taking something into consideration which you ought not consider and which is improperly distorting your view of the situation."

wrong to require that I should consider it if my belief-acquisition process is to be unbiased.

I am in an emergency situation and have to act quickly. I must make a determination of whether a building is safe to enter. I have no time to consider all the factors that in normal circumstances I should consider, but I do the best I can. I am not in this situation obliged to consider factors I would in other circumstances be obliged to consider.

Biasing of the belief-acquisition process is motivated if some desire or anxiety or fear etc. causes (in the right way) one to perform in any of the ways mentioned in the three conditions listed above, assuming that these conditions could be made sufficiently precise and also assuming that one had something useful to say about the "right way" requirement on causing. Suppose, for example, I am anxious to sell a pond to a prosperous trout-fishing enthusiast, and am uncertain whether he will buy it because I do not know whether the pond will sustain a trout population. My anxiety that he buy the pond causes me to collect water samples that would not be considered fair samples. If on the basis of these unrepresentative samples I come to believe that the water is pure enough to sustain trout, my biasing of my belief-acquisition process would be motivated.

Mele provides a number of examples of both motivated and unmotivated biasing. In motivated biasing, for example, a desire that *p* can lead one to treat inappropriately data that are, or seem to be, relevant to the truth value of *p*.[15] A person who wants *p*, for example, (a) can fail to recognize that certain data count against *p*; (b) can take as supporting *p* data which provide support for not-*p*; (c) can fail to focus on data that count against *p*, focusing instead on data suggestive of *p*; (d) can overlook easily obtainable evidence for not-*p*, while rooting out less accessible evidence for *p*.[16] If one does either (a) or (b) one satisfies condition 2 above. If one does (c) one may satisfy conditions 2 or 3. If one does (d) one may satisfy conditions 1 or 3.

Mele, drawing from the psychological literature, also discusses instances of unmotivated (or cold) biasing of the belief-acquisition process. People regularly (i) give disproportionate influence to vivid data (and whether a datum is vivid depends upon such things as the

[15] "What generates the self-deceived person's belief that *p*, on my account, is a desire-influenced manipulation of data that are, or seem to be, relevant to the truth value of *p*." *Irrationality*, p. 128.

[16] Ibid., pp. 125–6.

interests of the person, the concreteness and proximity of the datum); (ii) give disproportionate influence to readily available data; (iii) give disproportionate influence to confirming instances rather than disconfirming instances; (iv) give disproportionate influence to the first explanation which suggests itself.[17] By doing any of these things the person would satisfy one or another of the conditions given.

As Mele points out, it takes little imagination to see that these tendencies toward bias may be exploited in cases of motivated biasing.

> For example, data may be rendered more vivid as a consequence of the apparent support that they offer for a proposition that the subject wishes to be true. And since vivid data are more likely to be recalled, they tend to be more "available." Similarly, motivation, via its influence on vividness, can affect which hypotheses . . . occur to us first.[18]

On my account of self-deception one is biased in favor of beliefs that reduce one's anxiety that not-*q*. The self-deceptive belief that *p* allows one to believe, for example, that not-*r*, therefore *q* (or probably *q*), or to believe that even if *r*, it is not the case that if *r* then not-*q*, and so *q* (or probably *q*). In acquiring the belief that *p*, one may, for example, find data which are suggestive of the falsity of *r*, or of the falsity of the conditional (if *r* then not-*q*), more vivid than data not so suggestive. One may overlook evidence against *p* and root out positive evidence for *p*, one may focus one's attention exclusively on evidence that supports *p*, or one may misinterpret the evidence one has, either by not counting evidence against *p* as evidence against it, or by counting evidence against *p* as evidence for *p*.

There are further interesting questions to explore concerning some of the notions that enter into the statement of my conditions. As we have seen, with regard to the notion of (motivated) biasing in condition 1, one can ask under what conditions a person is biased, and ask for clarification of right way causality. Similarly, one could profitably explore more fully than I have done in Chapter 4 the notion of purpose exploited in condition 2. For example, one can ask for an analysis of functional explanation. But every inquiry has its limits. I draw the boundaries of my inquiry in ways that are customary in present-day discussions of self-deception. Taking the notions of motivated biasing and purpose as primitive, as starting points, enabled me

[17] Ibid., pp. 144–5. [18] Ibid., p. 145.

to explore in more detail and depth certain crucial aspects of the self-deceptive process. For example, assuming that motivated biasing occurs in self-deception, I focused on the kind of motivated biasing that occurs. I showed that it is an anxious desire that *q*, rather than an anxious desire that *p*, or a desire that *p*, or a desire that *q* . . . that links up with the self-deceptive belief that *p*; that the belief that *p* always functions to reduce anxiety;[19] that there are typical ways in which it does this; that the belief that *p* need not be wishful; that it may sometimes bring desire satisfaction. I also showed in Chapter 5 that, as condition 3 reflects, this motivated biasing cannot be an intentional biasing, and that the biasing process not only produces the anxiety-reducing belief that *p*, it also, as condition 4 reflects, prevents the subject from recognizing the extent to which the self-deceptive belief that *p* is due to its tendency to reduce anxiety. Insufficient attention is given to this last feature in Mele's account, and, as I showed in Chapter 6, the self-deceiver's false consciousness can be explained without recourse to either a Davidsonian division or a Johnstonian repression.

Self-deceiving oneself, I have said, occurs in the course of one's doing other things. Among the other things one may be doing is intentionally trying to relieve one's anxiety about *q*. But self-deceiving oneself is not to be identified with the intentional project of relieving anxiety. None of the descriptions that comprise the definition of self-deceiving can be descriptions under which you are doing something intentionally. Intentionally relieving anxiety is intentional under the description "relieving anxiety" and can be intentional

[19] While a successful self-deception results in anxiety reduction, this reduction may be temporary, although long-term reductions are possible as well. For example, if circumstances render it impossible for the self-deceptive belief that *p* to be maintained, then the anxiety the belief was meant to reduce might resurface. Suppose Vronsky's mother comes and Vronsky still does not make Kitty a marriage offer, then Kitty's mother's anxiety which her self-deceptive belief – he does not make the offer because he wants to consult his mother first – was meant to reduce, would recur.

Alternatively, it might be the case that by the time the self-deceptive belief can no longer be maintained, the anxiety that was reduced by this belief is no longer there. E.g., Clarissa comes to believe that the medicine did not cause the joint pains, but the condition for which the medicine was prescribed has corrected itself, so that the medicine is no longer required and she is, therefore, no longer anxious that it will cause her body harm.

The self-deceptive belief that *p* which reduces one anxiety can of course give rise to other anxieties, anxieties that are considerably greater than the original. These in turn might give rise to further self-deceptive behavior.

under different descriptions on different occasions. None of these descriptions on those occasions, however, can be descriptions that go into the definition of self-deceiving oneself.

Self-deceiving oneself may occur in conjunction with the intentional project of relieving anxiety, but it need not. For example, knowingly anxious that I might be in the wrong about a dispute in a shop, I intentionally look for reasons that will minimize any shortcoming in me; the parents of the accused thief intentionally look for evidence of their child's innocence; Clytaemnestra, who anxiously desires to be justified in killing her husband Agamemnon, intentionally seeks reasons for believing she is justified. To intentionally seek reasons or evidence that will relieve one's anxiety, however, is not to self-deceive oneself. Whether these people self-deceive themselves depends upon whether, in the course of their seeking reasons or evidence, they do what is described in the four conditions. That what they do satisfies these conditions is not guaranteed by their intentionally trying to reduce their anxiety.

Nor does it guarantee it. Suppose a man, who anxiously desires not to encounter a person he believes will attend the meeting he is scheduled to attend, tries to resist the partiality to which his anxiety disposes him. He finds out when the meeting is and carefully records the correct date in his appointment book. However, he leaves the appointment book in a place to which he has no access until some time after the meeting (an unoccupied apartment in Berlin, say, that he will not revisit for some months). He cannot remember the date he marked but, having no other way to find out when the meeting is, tries to recall it. He gets the day wrong. Suppose that his epistemic failures – the mislaying of relevant evidence, the failure to remember – were caused by the anxious desire. This man does not intentionally seek to reduce his anxiety, but he too may self-deceive himself, for he may do what the four conditions require. It is only when a person's anxiety reducing takes the form these conditions describe that the person can be said to be self-deceiving himself, to be a self-deceiver. Self-deceiving oneself is a *sui generis* form of deception, distinct from the intentional deception of oneself or of others.

In Chapter 3, I argued that not all self-deceptive belief is wishful, but left open the question whether the process of wishfully believing that *p* is always a process of self-deceiving oneself into believing that *p*. The answer depends upon whether the process of wishfully believing satisfies the four conditions given. If wishful thinking requires, as Johnston suggested, not merely desire but anxious desire, then it might be plausible to think that the process of wishfully believing that *p* would satisfy the four conditions.[20] However, the satisfaction of these four conditions would not be sufficient for being in a state of wishfully believing that *p*. I claimed that to be in such a state one must not have a stronger felt desire that not-*p* and one must not lack a desire, all things considered, that *p*. The satisfaction of these four conditions was also not sufficient for being in a state of being self-deceived in believing that *p*. To be in such a state, *p* must be false. Depending on which, if any, of the latter two conditions, in addition to the four conditions, is satisfied will determine whether one is in a state of wishfully believing that *p* or in a state of being self-deceived in believing that *p*.[21]

V. SELF-DECEIVING ONESELF INTO BELIEVING CONTRASTED WITH OTHER FORMS OF UNINTENTIONAL SELF-MISLEADING

Self-deceivers are, given my account of self-deceiving, self-misleaders, but they do not intend or even foresee the misleading. Rather, self-deceivers see themselves as being unbiased in acquiring their beliefs – as being, for example, non-partial in seeking, interpreting, and weighing the evidence. Why, however, should unintentionally misleading oneself of the special form described in the four conditions be identified with self-deceiving oneself?

There are, of course, frequent cases of people unintentionally acquiring beliefs that are false that one has no inclination to regard as

[20] Talbott suggests that we distinguish cases of believing that *p* as the non-intentional consequence of the desire that *p*, which he takes to be the usual notion of *wishful thinking*, from believing that *p* owing to the undesirability of not-*p* (for example, owing, as Johnston maintains, to anxiety that not-*p*). The latter kind of thinking he refers to as *aversive thinking*. See "Intentional Self-Deception in a Single Coherent Self," p. 59. Wishful thinking, so understood, would not satisfy the four conditions.

[21] For example, Legrandin wishfully, and self-deceptively, believes that he is not thought a snob. A student wishfully believes that she will pass her exam, but if she will in fact pass it, she is not self-deceived in believing that she will pass. A husband can, self-deceptively, but not wishfully, believe that his wife is unfaithful. Or imagine that a man has a stronger felt desire that his wife be faithful and desires, all things considered, that his wife be faithful, and believes that she is unfaithful, and it turns out that she is unfaithful.

cases of self-deceiving. Emotions, for example, in the absence of any anxious desire, cause people to have false beliefs, and yet we are not inclined in these cases to say that they have self-deceived themselves into having these beliefs. We are perhaps also disinclined in these cases to say that they have unintentionally ***misled*** themselves.

For example, Lucinda, desiring to go to Ludwig's masquerade, and having some reason to expect an invitation to it, is angry with Ludwig when she does not receive one. Because she is angry with him, she believes that he has wronged her, and people who we think have wronged us are typically seen by us in negative terms, as having character flaws. Lucinda thus believes that Ludwig is ungenerous and unkind. I do not believe that we are in this case inclined to think of Lucinda's belief about Ludwig as self-deceptive. On my analysis of self-deceiving oneself, Lucinda would not have self-deceived herself. While her belief that Ludwig is ungenerous and unkind was caused by her anger, it does not function to reduce that anger. Let us suppose that she has no anxious desire that causes her to believe that Ludwig is ungenerous or unkind, and that this belief does not function to reduce any anxiety. She does not, for example, anxiously desire to be justified in her anger, for she believes that she has adequate justification. Nor does the defeat of her expectation generate anxiety about why it was defeated. If the defeat did generate anxiety, say about the possibility of her being unpopular, then we could get self-deception.

One gets self-deceiving oneself and self-deception only if an anxious desire is assumed. Suppose, therefore, that Lucinda anxiously desires not to have any shortcoming. She is anxious that she might, since she was not accepted by Ludwig and believes that his non-acceptance might indicate some shortcoming. When she does not receive an invitation to his masquerade, she takes this as a sign of his non-acceptance, but believes that his lack of generosity and kindness explains his behavior. Having this belief enables her to dismiss the possibility that she has some shortcoming. If she has been biased in coming to her belief about Ludwig, if her only evidence for his alleged defects is his non-acceptance of her, and she has, moreover, dismissed out of hand instances of his generosity and kindness, and if she believes nonetheless that she is justified in her belief, then Lucinda might well have self-deceived herself into believing, and be self-deceived in believing, that Ludwig is ungenerous and unkind. While strong emotions often cause us to form beliefs which are mistaken, in the absence of some anxiety that causes the belief whose purpose is to reduce that anxiety, there is no self-deception.

The absence of an anxious desire also explains why in another sort of case[22] there is no self-deception. In cases of this sort, a person intentionally deceives another, and, by so doing, unintentionally misleads himself. While we want to say the person who takes himself in is deceived, we do not want to say he is a self-deceiver. T. S. Champlin cites the case of a military-camouflage expert who has intentionally disguised a gun to look like a tree in order to deceive the recruits in his charge but who himself gets taken in as well.[23] The expert's action of disguising the gun is not intentional under the description "an attempt to deceive myself" but is intentional under the description "an attempt to deceive the recruits."

While Champlin says the camouflage expert "inadvertently deceives himself," the inadvertent or unintentional deceiving of oneself that goes on in this case is not to be identified with the self-deceiving of oneself I specified in the four conditions. While the unintentional deceiving of oneself here is dependent upon an intentional project to deceive others, the self-deceiving of oneself defined by the four conditions is not thus dependent. Moreover, even in cases where one has an intentional project to deceive others and one gets taken in by it – one unintentionally deceives oneself – one need not fulfill the four conditions requisite for self-deceiving oneself. The camouflage expert does not fulfill these conditions, for he has no anxious desire that causes his belief that a particular gun was a tree, nor is the purpose of this belief to reduce any anxiety.

"To inadvertently deceive oneself," as Champlin uses the phrase, or unintentionally deceiving oneself, is to be the unintended victim of one's intentional attempt to deceive others. There are countless occasions when an other-deceiver unintentionally becomes his own victim. People, in their attempt to deceive others, frequently lie or pretend and end up believing their lie or the pretense. Whether these people self-deceive themselves will depend on whether they fulfill the four conditions.

As we saw earlier, self-deceiving oneself takes place in the course of a person's doing other things. One of the other things a person may be

22 In this sort of case it seems natural to talk of self-misleading, whereas in the first sort of case it did not.

23 See *Reflexive Paradoxes*, p. 12.

doing is intentionally trying to deceive others. But neither does self-deceiving oneself require any such intentional project, nor does it follow that, when there is such an intentional project, and one has become the unintentional victim of it, one has self-deceived oneself. Self-deceiving oneself is, I am claiming, distinct from unintentionally (or inadvertently) deceiving oneself.

In the case of the camouflage expert, no anxious desire was associated with the deception. But even in cases where an anxious desire is present, it does not follow that if one has become the unintentional victim of an intentional deception of others, one has self-deceived oneself. The person who anxiously desires that *q* and who, in his attempt to relieve his anxiety, deceives others into believing that *p*, and himself comes to believe that *p*, is not automatically self-deceiving himself. Let us look at some cases which illustrate this.

Imagine that an aspiring politician believes that a distinguished war record would advance his career. Knowing that he does not have one, but anxious to advance his career, he intentionally exaggerates his wartime accomplishments. Eventually he comes to believe his own lies.

Or imagine that a man anxiously desires not to be thought a coward. While he knows he is a coward, he nevertheless pretends not to be one, aping the outward appearance of courage but remaining nevertheless careful not to get into situations where his courage will be tested. He deceives others into believing he is not a coward, and in the course of time he comes to believe that he is not one. The man, however, remains a coward and would, if his courage were tested, fail the test.

In these two situations people have unintentionally misled themselves. But in neither case does it follow that they are also self-deceivers.

Let us look at the first case. The aspiring politician's anxious desire to advance his career, an advancement he believes is linked to being seen as having a distinguished war record, causes him to lie about that record. His anxiety is relieved if he believes that people believe his lie. If people do, and he correctly believes that they do, he is no longer anxious that his career will not be advanced. Having become accustomed to people's assuming he has a distinguished record, however, he eventually comes to believe that he does. While the man in this situation would be deceived in believing that he had a distinguished record, he would not, I believe, have self-deceived himself into believing this. He would not because he would not satisfy the second of the four conditions. Condition 2 requires that the purpose of his believing that he has a distinguished war record be to reduce his anxiety that his career won't be advanced because he is not seen as having a distinguished war record. But that is not the purpose of his belief. It is his lying that has that purpose. His belief that people have been taken in by his lies about his war record has relieved his anxiety about advancing his career. He has, however, by lying, been responsible for his false belief about his war record, for he has caused that record to be misrepresented, a misrepresentation that he is eventually taken in by.

The coward's anxious desire not to be thought a coward is relieved by his believing, truly, that people do not think him one, for they are taken in by his pretense. Because he has so long aped the role of a brave man, and because he is taken to be one, he believes he is one. He is deceived in so believing, but he too has not self-deceived himself into believing this. He is taken in by appearances, and, of course, he is responsible for setting up these appearances. But, like the politician, he does not satisfy condition 2. It is not the purpose of his believing that he is not a coward to relieve his anxiety that he is thought a coward. That anxiety has been relieved by his believing that people have been taken in by his pretenses.

Neither the politician's nor the coward's anxiety essentially concerned whether they themselves believed what they wanted others to believe. While they were disposed to be partial in acquiring beliefs that reduced their anxiety about what others believed, in the cases discussed there was no need for this partiality to operate and no need to resist its operation. People were taken in by their misrepresentations and, therefore, their anxiety-reducing beliefs about what these people thought were justified. Their beliefs – "I have a distinguished war record," "I am not a coward" – did not serve to reduce the initial anxiety. Reducing that anxiety did not necessarily involve getting oneself to believe that one had a distinguished war record, or that one was not a coward.

Could we change the circumstances in these cases so as to make them not only cases of unintentionally misleading oneself, but also clear cases of self-deceiving?

Suppose that a man anxiously desires not to be a coward. He suspects that he might be one, for he is extremely fearful. He pretends, when fearful, that he is not, and people, believing that he is not fearful, believe that he is not a coward. The man deceives others into believing that he is not a coward, and over time he comes to believe that he is not one. Let us suppose, however, that he is a coward. If he has been biased in acquiring his belief that he is not a coward, if he regards his fear as a surface phenomenon, as something that all non-cowards have, and if he ignores the fact that he avoids all situations of danger, he may well have self-deceived himself into believing, and be self-deceived in believing, that he is not a coward. His belief that he is not a coward has been caused by his anxious desire that he not be a coward, and the purpose of the occurrence of the belief is to reduce his anxiety that he is a coward.

What the discussion of these three situations suggests is that the unintentional misleading of oneself that counts as self-deceiving oneself depends not on whether one is intentionally deceiving others, but on whether the four conditions that I listed previously are satisfied. In the first two situations – the politician who anxiously desires to advance his career by being seen as having a distinguished war record, and the coward who anxiously desires not to be thought a coward – condition 2 was not satisfied; in the third situation – a man anxiously desires not to be a coward – all four conditions were satisfied. Whether in the course of reducing anxiety one deceives others or not is not, therefore, crucial to whether one is self-deceiving oneself.

While many people would concede that one could unintentionally deceive oneself, since all that is meant by this is that one is the unintentional victim of an intentional attempt to deceive others, some people would balk at calling the sort of anxiety reducing I have described in the four conditions self-*deceiving* oneself. In the first instance, deceiving remains intentional; in the second it does not.

Some actions are thought to be intentional under one description in particular. Deceiving someone or lying to someone, unlike poisoning or killing someone, are thought to be actions that must be intentional under the respective descriptions "deceiving someone" and "lying to someone." Deceivers or liars must know what they are up to in order for their actions to constitute deceiving or lying, although their actions need not be intentional under all the descriptions they know apply to it.

Deceiving a specific person, be it another or myself, must, one might be tempted to think, be intentional under the description "deceiving someone." In unintentionally deceiving oneself (the camouflage expert) this condition is satisfied; in self-deceiving oneself it is not. The person who intentionally deceives others but gets taken in himself acts under the description "deceiving someone." Because he is not an intended object of the deception, we are willing to say he inadvertently or unintentionally deceived himself. Deception was intentional; what was unintentional was that a certain person, namely himself, was deceived. If, believing you are my friend's employer, I lie to you about my friend's state of health and it turns out you are his tennis partner, I don't unintentionally lie. We can say I have unintentionally lied to you, but only if we understand this to mean that I have intentionally lied, but that you are not the intended audience for my lie.

If what I am claiming is correct, however, self-deceiving oneself is unlike deceiving others in that it is not intentional under the description "deceiving someone." The description of the process of self-deceiving oneself is not a description that could apply if self-deceiving oneself were the reflexive instance of deceiving someone. But as some philosophers have pointed out, the description of the process of teaching oneself in self-teaching is not the description that would apply if teaching oneself were the reflexive instance of teaching others.[24]

We are now in a position to compare the process of deceiving another into believing something with the process of self-deceiving oneself into believing something.

If I deceive you into believing that *p*, then it seems plausible to assume that

1. You have a false belief that some proposition (*p* or something else) is the case.
2. You have arrived at your belief that *p* in a way that typically[25] makes me culpable.
3. I intentionally introduce into your situation something such that I believe there is a real possibility that that something will cause you

[24] See, for example, Mike Martin, *Self-Deception and Morality*. See also Champlin's *Reflexive Paradoxes*.

[25] There are, as we shall see in Chapter 9, cases of interpersonal deception where the deceiver is not culpable.

to believe that *p*, and I take that something to provide neither adequate evidence for *p* nor direct sensory awareness that *p*.[26]

4. You believe (wrongly) that you are justified[27] in believing that *p*. You believe, for example, that you have adequate evidence for *p* or direct sensory awareness that *p*, when you have neither adequate evidence for *p* nor direct sensory awareness that *p*.[28]

We have seen that there is a process of intentionally deceiving oneself that is parallel to this process, but that it is a process which is not a process of self-deception. Recall the man in Davidson's example who intentionally deceives himself into believing that a meeting is on such-and-such a day.

Here is a reparsing of the four conditions for self-deceiving oneself to bring them into line for comparison with the conditions for deceiving others:

If I self-deceive myself into believing that *p* (if I am self-deceiving), then

1. I have a false belief that some proposition (*p* or something else) is the case.
2. I have arrived at my belief that *p* in a way that makes me an appropriate target of criticism.[29]
3. I have some anxious desire that *q* that causes me to believe that *p*, and the purpose of my believing that *p* is to reduce my anxiety that not-*q*.
4. I fail to make a high enough estimate of how much my anxious desire that *q* contributes to the reason why I believe that *p*. I believe, wrongly, that my belief that *p* is justified. I do not have adequate evidence for *p*, nor do I have direct sensory awareness that *p*.

[26] See Chapter 1 for a discussion of why a stronger epistemic condition is not satisfied.

[27] "Justified" is being used throughout in its less controversial sense, a sense that does not take Goldman-type cases into account. See the discussion in Chapter 1.

[28] As I noted in note 11, a child can satisfy the four conditions for self-deceiving. A child can also satisfy the conditions for deceiving another. If a child understands that seeing a rabbit in the garden is a reason for believing there is a rabbit in the garden, the child can give others reasons for believing something that the child does not take to be a good enough reason for that something. The child who holds an apple behind her back while telling her brother the apples have all been eaten is giving her brother a reason for believing there are no apples that she does not take to be a good enough reason for there being no apples.

[29] As we shall see in Chapter 9, I become an appropriate target of *prima facie* criticism.

While there are parallels between conditions 1, 2, and 4 in both processes (some conditions being more nearly parallel than others), there is not a similar parallel between the two conditions 3. Condition 3 for deceiving another is an epistemic condition; condition 3 for self-deceiving oneself is, in contrast, a radically non-epistemic condition. But both conditions pinpoint the source of the deceiver's shortcoming: in one instance the deceiver is aware that he is deceiving; in the other, he is not. One process involves an intentional act of deception, the other does not. While they are significantly different processes, the claim is that they share enough characteristics to make it understandable that we speak of both as deception processes.

If one is deceived in believing that *p*, then

1. One's belief that *p* is false.
2. Either (a) one has been intentionally deceived into believing that *p* by another or by oneself, or (b) one has self-deceived oneself, where the self-deceiving is purposive but not intentional, or (c) one has been deceived by appearances, where there is neither purposive nor intentional deceiving.[30]

I am not denying that one can be deceived by appearances where the deception has been intentional. When the undercover agent

[30] Loyal Rue in his recent book *By the Grace of Guile* attempts to give a definition of deception that is broad enough to cover interactions in the entire animate world: "[D]eception occurs when the designs embedded in the morphology and/or behavior of one organism can defeat the designs embedded in the perceptual structures and/or strategies of another organism" (p. 104). "A deceiver is an organism (*A*) whose agency contributes by design to the ignorance or delusion of another organism (*B*). Self-deception may be said to occur when *A* and *B* are the same organism" (p. 88). "By design" is not, however, to be given an intentional reading. "[An] African bug . . . is clearly acting by design when it covers itself with dead ants for the deceptive purpose of undetected entry into the ant colony. But there is no question here of intentionality" (p. 90).

Rue emphasizes what is similar to all deception. The deceiver contributes causally to the deceived's being ignorant or mistaken. But his requirement that the deceiver's contribution be by design – purposive but not intentional – is too stringent to cover cases of deception by appearances where the relevant causal contribution is neither purposive nor intentional; and not stringent enough to capture cases of interpersonal deception where the relevant causal contribution is intentional. There may well be at least four distinct deception kinds – self-deception, inter*personal* deception, deception by appearances, and a non-human but interanimate deception, the latter of which is captured by Rue's characterization. And, of course, humans deceive non-human animals and non-human animals deceive humans.

intentionally dresses like a potential drug user, he is intentionally using appearances to deceive the drug dealers. When the homeless man dresses as he does, he is not intentionally using appearances to deceive passing pediatricians. I am using "deceived by appearances" here to refer only to those cases where there is no one who is intentionally using these appearances. Cases where there is someone intentionally using the appearances are to be classified under heading (a).

8

Irrationality

Are self-deceivers irrational? I shall argue that whether they are or not depends upon the kind of rationality being considered. One kind is epistemic or cognitive rationality.

While there is widespread agreement that the epistemic rationality of a belief is compatible with its falsity – the person who adds 67, 81, 37 and gets 175, having forgotten to carry the 1, can be epistemically rational although he believes something false – there is disagreement about what epistemic rationality is. Is epistemically rational belief, for example, belief that is the outcome of a reliable belief-forming process, or is it belief that is well founded on reasons?[1] While I concentrate in this discussion on the latter way of understanding epistemic rationality, and argue that on that way of understanding it the self-deceiver is not epistemically rational in believing that which he deceives himself into believing, nevertheless, given that the self-deceiver is, as I have argued, biased, the self-deceiver would not be epistemically rational in his belief on the reliabilist's conception either. The process of self-deception does not yield beliefs most of which are true.[2]

As I shall understand epistemic rationality, if one's belief state lacks epistemic rationality, and that belief state is not an immediate per-

[1] Some philosophers think it is both. See Robert Nozick, *The Nature of Rationality* (Princeton, N.J.: Princeton University Press, 1993), p. 64: "When is a belief rational? . . . Two themes permeate the philosophical literature. First, that rationality is a matter of reasons . . . Second, that rationality is a matter of reliability . . . Neither theme alone exhausts our notion of rationality. Reasons without reliability seem empty, reliability without reasons seems blind. In tandem these make a powerful unit . . ."

[2] If the reliabilist's desideratum were not true beliefs over the long run but some sort of weighted disjunction of true beliefs and useful beliefs, the self-deception process might be a reliable producer of desirable beliefs. But then the rationality would no longer look epistemic.

ceptual belief, an immediate experiential belief, or a belief in a necessary truth, then one's belief state is epistemically irrational. Every actual belief token (barring the exceptions mentioned) is either epistemically rational or epistemically irrational. In showing, therefore, that self-deceivers are not epistemically rational in believing that *p*, I will be showing that self-deceivers are epistemically irrational in believing that *p*.

The philosophers who adhere to the good-reasons conception of epistemic rationality just mentioned agree that – at least if we set aside immediate perceptual beliefs, immediate experiential beliefs, and beliefs in necessary truths – if a person is epistemically or cognitively rational in his or her belief that *p* (or a person's belief that *p* is epistemically rational), then that person's belief that *p* is well founded on reasons the person has.[3] It is, of course, notoriously difficult to specify a sufficient condition of a person's belief that *p* being well founded on reasons the person has.[4]

For the purposes of this discussion, however, all that we will need are sufficient conditions of a person's belief that *p not being* well founded on reasons the person has. For if, as I claim, a self-deceiver's belief that *p* **always satisfies** one of these sufficient conditions, then the self-deceiver's belief that *p* is never well-founded on reasons the

[3] Davidson is among those who hold that a belief's rationality depends upon its being well founded on reasons the person has. Mental states rationalize a belief if they stand in the appropriate relations to the belief. The appropriate relations require that the mental states non-waywardly cause the belief; that the contents of the mental states provide reasons for thinking that what is believed is true. The mental states provide a cognitive reason for the belief.

Davidson believes that a belief is not rational in the absence of the appropriate relations. In some cases of wishful thinking, for example, a desire causes a belief but gives no reason for thinking that what is believed is true.

[4] For an indication of the complexity of the task, consider, for starters, the following conditions which seem to be among the necessary conditions: (1) the person's belief that *p* is (immediately) caused non-waywardly by beliefs, e.g., *q* and *r*; (2) *q* and *r* together support *p* argumentatively; (3) *q* and *r* are to some extent justified; (4) there do not exist further beliefs q' or r', of the person's, occurrent or dispositional, which give as much or more argumentative support to not-*p* than *q* or *r* give to *p*; (5) there do not exist further propositions q'' or r'' which support not-*p* and which the person doesn't believe but should (if epistemically responsible) believe. I am not claiming that these conditions would do the job. Moreover, they put a lot of weight on the unexplained notion of non-waywardness.

self-deceiver has. And the self-deceiver's belief that *p* is never an immediate perceptual or experiential belief, or a belief in a necessary truth. So, given that, apart from beliefs of those three kinds, a person's belief that *p* being well founded on reasons the person has is necessary for that person's being epistemically rational in believing that *p*, the self-deceiver is never epistemically rational in believing that *p*. Moreover, given my principle that a person's not being epistemically rational in believing that *p* is sufficient for the person's being epistemically irrational in believing that *p*, any self-deceiver is epistemically irrational in believing that *p*.

There is another sort of rationality – prudential or instrumental or practical rationality.[5] This rationality is concerned with securing what one most prefers. While being epistemically irrational does not prevent one from being prudentially rational, self-deceivers are, I claim, not prudentially rational in deceiving themselves. But neither are they prudentially irrational.

My overall conclusion with respect to epistemic rationality is that although self-deceivers are always epistemically irrational, they are not, contrary to what many have claimed, deeply epistemically irrational. If self-deceivers, in the process of deceiving themselves, knowingly violated one of their own standards of epistemic rationality, if they came to believe that which they judged the preponderance of their evidence was against, then they would be deeply epistemically irrational. So too would they be deeply epistemically irrational if in the state of self-deception they knowingly held contradictory beliefs. But I deny that such knowing violation occurs or that the self-deceiver even has contradictory beliefs. While it is true that self-deceivers ought to have known better than to believe that *p* – if they had been unbiased they presumably would have known better – they do not, when self-deceived, "know better."

My overall conclusion with respect to prudential rationality is that while self-deceivers always get something they want as a result of their deception – their anxiety is reduced – and while they sometimes get to do the things they want to do – if they had not deceived themselves they would not have been able to do these things – self-deceivers do not satisfy the conditions for prudential rationality.

[5] I leave open the possibility that there may be further forms of rationality. However, the two I consider are the two around which most discussion revolves.

I. EPISTEMIC IRRATIONALITY

I discuss several conditions, each of which is sufficient for a person's belief that *p* ***not*** being well founded on reasons the person has. My contention is that, given their partiality, self-deceivers always satisfy one or another of these conditions or some similar condition. The examples I give will illustrate how in typical cases the self-deceiver's essential partiality accounts for his or her violation of one or another of these conditions. I contend, moreover, that something of this kind always happens in self-deception.

While a number of philosophers have thought that self-deceivers satisfy another sufficient condition, a condition which, if satisfied, would make the self-deceiver deeply irrational, I argue that not only do self-deceivers never satisfy this other condition, it is difficult to see how self-deceivers could satisfy this condition. While these other philosophers are right about self-deceivers being epistemically irrational, they are wrong about what kind of epistemic irrationality is involved in self-deception and why self-deceivers are epistemically irrational.

When is a person's belief that *p* not well founded on reasons the person has? Obviously, if the person's beliefs do not give argumentative support for his or her belief that *p*, that belief is not well founded on reasons the person has. One sufficient condition for a person's belief that *p* not being well founded on the reasons the person has is thus:

> *If a person's belief that p is caused by beliefs, e.g., q and r, whose content does not give an argument for p, then that person's belief that p is not well founded on reasons the person has.*[6]

As a result of their bias, self-deceivers may have risibly inadequate reasons for their beliefs that *p* – the reasons would not in any normal context be good reasons for thinking that the beliefs were true. That a person says good morning to a colleague is typically not a good reason for anyone to believe that the person is intimate with that colleague. Believing that someone has done something wrong and that he deserves punishment are not good reasons for believing that you are

[6] The causing of the belief that *p* by beliefs *q* and *r* should be thought of as right-way causing.

the appropriate person to carry out that punishment. That a fortune-teller predicts that you are going to have marital difficulties is not a good reason for believing that your spouse is having an affair. But the man who anxiously desires to leave his wife may, owing to being biased, take the fact that his wife says good morning to her colleague as evidence for her intimacy with that colleague, or he may take the fact that a fortune-teller predicts that he is going to have marital difficulties as evidence for her having an affair. And a woman who anxiously desires to kill her husband, who she believes is guilty of wrong-doing, and establish her paramour in his place may, if she is biased, reason in the way just suggested to the conclusion that she is the appropriate person to mete out his punishment. The beliefs mentioned in these cases do not give the believers argumentative support for their beliefs that *p*.

The risibility of the reasons is, of course, to be seen from a perspective which the self-deceiver does not, while he or she is self-deceived, occupy. We assume, however, that the person is in some sense capable of appreciating this risibility – he or she normally would appreciate it in contexts in which the relevant anxious desire is absent. Interests other than anxious desires can, of course, also prevent a person from appreciating something he or she would otherwise appreciate.

> One girl tells another how she has changed her mind in love; and the friend sympathizes with the friend, and perhaps applauds. Had the story been told in print, the friend who has listened with equanimity would have read of such vacillation with indignation. She who vacillated herself would have hated her own performance when brought before her judgment as a matter in which she had no personal interest.[7]

[7] Anthony Trollope, *The Last Chronicle of Barset* (Penguin Classics, 1986), p. 592. Bringing to their attention the fact that they treat relevantly similar cases differently (*quid rides? Mutato nomine, de te fabula narrator* [Why do you laugh? Change the name and the story is told of you.]) often enough does not convince self-deceivers, for they insist that the cases are significantly dissimilar. "I know that my son (or husband or . . .) could not have done —— " is a familiar kind of response. In a recent execution-style murder case, the suspect's father said of his son, "I swear on my father's grave he's a perfect kid – going to college . . . He only does good things." The difference in beliefs is explained by the presence of a special knowledge ("I know the person in a way that others cannot") and not by the presence of anxious desires.

In other cases, while the reasons a person has do support argumentatively his or her belief that *p*, those reasons themselves are not justified. Another sufficient condition for a person's belief that *p* not being well founded on reasons the person has is thus:

If the beliefs q and r which cause the belief that p do give an argument for p, but q or r are not justified, then the person's belief that p is not well founded on reasons the person has.[8]

A man believes that his wife and another man are passionately embracing, because he believes that he sees them doing this. He believes that such an embrace is indicative of sexual intimacy, and thus believes that his wife and this man are sexually intimate. If his supporting beliefs were to some extent justified, his belief about their sexual intimacy could be well founded. However, imagine that the husband, anxiously desiring to leave his wife, misperceives – the woman embracing the man is not his wife. Because he is biased in favor of beliefs that reduce his anxiety, he does not consider the possibility (a very real possibility in the circumstances, let us suppose) that he may be misperceiving. In such circumstances the man's belief that his wife and the other man were sexually intimate would not be well founded on the reasons he has.

In the case just considered, one of the supporting beliefs was not merely not justified, that belief was also false. Suppose, however, that the supporting belief, though not justified, is nonetheless true. Suppose that a man who anxiously desires to leave his wife believes that his wife spent the weekend with another man, and that this belief is true. Given what he believes in general about women who do this, he believes that she is having an affair with that man. Suppose, however, that the man is not justified in believing that she spent the weekend with that man. His friend, who he knows is unreliable about such matters, tells him that she spent the weekend with that man. While the man described would have argumentative support for his belief – his premises are true, the form is truth preserving – there is epistemic irrationality here, nonetheless. The man is not justified in believing one of his premises. That it is true is a matter of epistemic

[8] See Richard Foley, *The Theory of Epistemic Rationality* (Cambridge, Mass.: Harvard University Press, 1987). Foley speaks of a richer and less rich sense of epistemic rationality. I am in this discussion speaking of the richer sort of epistemic rationality.

luck, not of epistemic rationality. In this case, as in the former, the man's belief that *p* is not well founded on the reasons he has. It is the supporting belief's own lack of justification that is crucial here, not whether the supporting belief is true or false.

Sometimes, the reasons the self-deceiver relies on might be good reasons for the self-deceptive belief if they were the only reasons that were relevant. But they are not the only reasons relevant. A third condition, sufficient for a person's belief that *p* not being well founded on the reasons the person has, is therefore:

> *If a person's belief that p is caused by beliefs q and r; beliefs q and r are to some extent justified; but beliefs q′ and r′ (which are also to at least that same extent justified) give more support to not-p than q and r give to p, then the person's belief that p is not well founded on the reasons he or she has.*

A father's belief that his daughter is unloving because her words to him are untender might be well founded on the reasons he has, if, for example, there were no history of good relations between them. However, the father's belief would not be well founded if, for example, there had always been affectionate relations between them. Suppose the father, anxiously desiring to retain power, sees the untender words as a threat to that power. Believing that she is unloving could reduce his anxiety by enabling him to exercise power. His anxious desire could cause him to be partial, to respond to a certain subset of his beliefs and to fail to respond to the rest.

The case just discussed relies on the self-deceiver's having other reasons which in fact give more argumentative support for not-*p* than the reasons he relies on give for *p*, although he does not recognize that these other reasons do this.[9] But there are cases of self-deception where, although there are other reasons which in fact give more argumentative support for not-*p*, the self-deceiver is not aware of them, and, more importantly, he is at fault for not being aware of them. Another condition sufficient for a person's belief that *p* not being well founded on the reasons he or she has is thus:

[9] It can happen that a person has – not a dispositional, but – an occurrent belief *q′* which gives not-*p* more support than his occurrent belief *q* gives to *p* and yet the person does not recognize that it does. A man acknowledges that his mother loves him but nonetheless believes, self-deceptively, that she wants him to fail.

If a person's belief that p is caused by beliefs q and r; beliefs q and r are to some extent justified; there exist further propositions q′ and r′ (belief in which would be to at least the same extent justified) which give more support to not-p than q and r give to p, and which the person should believe but does not believe because he or she is biased, then the person's belief that p is not well founded on the reasons he or she has.

Suppose that a person, anxious that his finances may be insufficient to allow him to continue living as he has been living, neglects to inquire about them. By focusing on ill-founded rumors about a general economic recovery, he comes to believe, self-deceptively, that his finances are sufficient. However, had the man not been biased, he would have been aware of the reasons for believing that his finances were insufficient.

Given the sufficient conditions I have discussed, a self-deceiver's belief that *p* is not well founded on the reasons he has because (1) some of the reason-giving beliefs, which cause the person's belief that *p*, are not justified (the man's belief that his wife is embracing another man is not justified); or (2) the reason-giving beliefs which cause the belief that *p* are justified or, at least, not unjustified, but do not provide adequate argumentative support for the belief in any normal context (one colleague saying good morning to another is not adequate argumentative support for believing them to be sexually intimate); or (3) the beliefs which cause the belief that *p* are justified or, at least, not unjustified, and would provide adequate evidence in some normal contexts, but would not provide evidence in others, and the context under consideration is one of the others. (Speaking untender words would in some contexts provide evidence for a belief in the speaker's being unloving, but in others it would not.)

I argued in an earlier chapter that although self-deceivers are often enough not epistemically responsible – they do not do all they should to ensure that their beliefs are true – they are always biased in acquiring their belief that *p*. As a consequence of their partiality, their beliefs that *p* are not well founded on the reasons they have. And their beliefs are not well founded for reasons such as the reasons I have been discussing. While the reasons I have been discussing are not exhaustive, they are the reasons in typical cases why a self-deceiver's belief is not well founded.

Self-deceivers are epistemically irrational because they satisfy one or another of the conditions I have given or some similar condition. Let us now look at another condition which some suppose self-deceivers satisfy. This condition, if satisfied, would also make self-deceivers epistemically irrational; indeed, would make them deeply irrational. My contention is that the self-deceiver *qua* self-deceiver never satisfies this condition.

II. DEEP EPISTEMIC IRRATIONALITY

If a person believes that p when that person judges (or recognizes) that he or she has better reasons for believing not-p, then that person's belief that p is not well founded on the reasons he or she has.

Davidson, we saw, believes that self-deceivers satisfy this condition; that there is an incoherence or inconsistency in the thought of the self-deceiver. Satisfaction of this condition is sufficient for deep epistemic irrationality. On the characterization of self-deception I have been arguing for, insofar as one is self-deceived in believing that *p*, one does not judge or recognize that one has better reasons for believing not-*p* than for believing *p*. Self-deceivers are, therefore, not deeply epistemically irrational in this way. Moreover, as I pointed out in in my earlier discussion of Davidson, it is difficult to see how self-deceivers *could* be deeply irrational in this way.

Everyone, of course, acknowledges that cognitive failures occur, that people, for example, believe inconsistent things, or fail to reason in the ways required by their own standards of rationality. A woman believes that she might find her son at a friend's house, completely forgetting that he told her the day before that he would be staying late at school. Forgetfulness, fatigue, carelessness, depression, a penchant for selective focusing and evidence gathering, a partiality for vivid and salient data, for confirmation rather than disconfirmation of hypotheses are cited among the reasons why such cognitive failures are common even in non-anxiety situations.[10] But in all these sorts of cognitive failure people do not recognize that their evidence supports the denial of what they come to believe.[11] They do not knowingly violate their own standards of rationality. Those described by the

[10] See Mele, *Irrationality*, chapter 10.

[11] Getting occasional or fleeting glimpses of the truth is not sufficient for recognizing that the evidence supports the denial of what one comes to believe, as I use that expression.

condition under discussion must recognize that the totality of their evidence points to not-*p*, yet at the same time go on to believe that *p*.

Davidson, as we saw, postulates an irrational mental step – the self-deceiver segregates the requirement that he give credence to that which the totality of his evidence supports, thereby making it possible for him to believe that *p* on the basis of only some of his evidence. Once the relevant norm of rationality and whatever doxastic states with respect to not-*p* it brings with it are segregated, it becomes possible for the self-deceiver to believe that his remaining evidence (the evidence favorable to *p* or unfavorable to not-*p*) supports his self-deceptive belief that *p*.[12]

Davidson's partitioning was introduced to explain how there can be an incoherence or inconsistency in the self-deceiver's own pattern of thought, how the self-deceiver can knowingly violate his own standard of rationality and, in particular, how he can knowingly violate the Requirement of Total Evidence. But if partitioning occurred, it is not, as I pointed out earlier, clear that the self-deceiver knowingly violates this standard of rationality or that there is any incoherence in his own pattern of thought. For, in order to come to believe that *p*, the self-deceiver must first "exile"[13] the troublesome standard as well as whatever doxastic state he is in with respect to not-*p*. Otherwise, the deception cannot take place. But if he does the exiling, then it seems the violation of his own standard of rationality is not a knowing one.

Davidson not only believes that the process of deceiving oneself is irrational, but also that the resultant state of self-deception is irrational. It is irrational either because the self-deceiver has contradictory beliefs – he believes that *p* and believes that not-*p* – or because

[12] In interpersonal deception the deceived need not be irrational to believe that *p* on the basis of the evidence available to him, although he would not be rational to believe this if he had access to the evidence possessed by the deceiver. In intrapersonal deception segregation would allow the self-deceiver to believe, using partial evidence, what it would not be rational for him to believe given all his evidence. Self-deceivers' minds are partitioned in such a way, according to Davidson, that in each part mental states are related in appropriate rational ways to the mental states they cause, although a mental state from one part can cause a mental state in another part without being rationally connected to it. (See John Heil, "Going to Pieces," in *Psychopathology: A Book of Readings*, ed. G. Graham and L. Stephens [Cambridge, Mass.: MIT Press, 1994].) Davidson believes that he can thus explain how self-deceivers can be deeply irrational.

[13] For a discussion of "exiling" see Chapter 2.

the self-deceiver believes that *p* and believes that the totality of his evidence favors not-*p*. This state would not be deeply irrational for the same sort of reason the process was not deeply irrational. The partitioning ensures that the self-deceiver is not aware that he has all of these beliefs.[14]

If my account of self-deception is correct, the self-deceiver *qua* self-deceiver does not have contradictory beliefs, nor does he believe that

[14] In a recent paper, "Self-Deception and Internal Irrationality," Scott-Kakures argues that the state of self-deception is nonetheless deeply irrational. I find difficulties, however, both with the kind of belief-state transition he relies on – it is an anomalous belief-state transition in which "the subject comes, just like that, to believe that not-*p* for reasons" (p. 47) – and with the fact that he requires the self-deceiver to recognize that his belief-state transition is odd.

I see no reason to believe, as Scott-Kakures requires, that a self-deceiver ever believes that she has come to believe that not-*p* (while I use *p* to refer to the self-deceptive belief, Scott-Kakures uses not-*p*) in an epistemically suspicious manner, that "she possesses a second order belief that she ought not have come to believe what she currently has [by her lights] sufficient reason for believing" (p. 53). I find it implausible to think, for example, that the self-deceived alcoholic recognizes that his evidence once led him to believe that he was an alcoholic, and although he now believes he has sufficient reason for believing that he is not an alcoholic, he realizes that the transition to this belief state is odd, that he has come to believe that he is not an alcoholic in a way which makes for a violation of his principles of reason. The alcoholics I have encountered in real life or in fiction, who sincerely believe they are not alcoholics, deny, or would deny, that their coming to believe that they were not alcoholics was odd in the way Scott-Kakures suggests. They firmly believe that the reasons that they give others and themselves for why they are not alcoholics are the reasons which caused them in the standard way to believe they are not alcoholics; they are reasons which justify their believing this. They are of course mistaken, for the reasons they give for their beliefs do not justify them, nor are they aware that other factors play crucial causal roles in their coming to believe what they do.

I believe, moreover, that a self-deceiver need not recognize that he is an alcoholic before coming to believe self-deceptively that he is not one. He may very well be made anxious that he might be an alcoholic. I do not want to deny that the self-deceived alcoholic may feel discomfort, that the state of self-deception may be unstable, but I would locate the source of any discomfort or instability in new confrontations with reality, not in the sort of internal irrational state Scott-Kakures postulates. A source of discomfort may come when yet another friend takes the alcoholic aside to talk about his drinking problem.

If I am correct, the puzzling thought Scott-Kakures needs for his account is not there. So even if there were an anomalous belief transition, the self-deceiver would not know of it.

p while also believing that the totality of his evidence favors not-*p*.[15] I shall discuss the second alternative first.

While in many of the central cases of self-deception discussed in the literature it is plausible to view the self-deceiver as having some uncertainty about whether *p* is the case – the self-deceiver recognizes that not-*p* is possible – it does not follow that the self-deceiver also recognizes that the totality of his evidence favors not-*p*. In many cases of self-deception an anxious desire that *q* is an anxious desire that *p*. Consider Legrandin, who was anxious that people would think him a snob, and his self-deceptive belief that he was not thought a snob. While Legrandin recognized that it was possible that he would be thought a snob, he did not also recognize that the totality of his evidence favored the proposition that he was thought a snob.

In other cases of self-deception the relevant anxiety that not-*q* is not to be equated with an anxiety that not-*p*. In these cases the self-deceiver may not have had any reasons for thinking that not-*p*. Clarissa, when she misread the description of the side effects of her asthma medicine, did not judge that the totality of her evidence favored the asthma medicine's not being the cause of her joint pains, nor did she believe that this was the case, before coming to believe that the asthma medicine was the cause of her joint pains. Recognizing that the totality of one's evidence favors not-*p* is not, as I argued earlier, necessary for self-deception, and therefore those who like Davidson claim that it is required are mistaken.

It seems clear that there are cases of self-deception in which recognizing that the totality of one's evidence favors not-*p* is not required. However, this leaves open the possibility that such recognition may occur in some cases of self-deception. I contend that even if such recognition occurs at some point concurrent with the self-deceiving process, its occurrence would be extraneous to the elements of the case which comprise the self-deception occurring in the case. That is, even if a self-deceiver momentarily recognizes that the totality of his evidence favors not-*p*, this recognition is most parsimoniously viewed as an epiphenomenon; it is not part of what self-deception essentially involves. Indeed, I argue, self-deception essentially excludes such a recognition. I claim that all the essential phenomena of every (realistic)

[15] Mele also argues that the self-deceiver does not believe that his prior beliefs rule out his self-deceptive belief.

case of self-deception not only ***can*** be accounted for without appeal to the disputed recognition, they ***must*** be accounted for without appeal to this recognition, for the disputed recognition is inconsistent with an element of all self-deception. Let us see why this is so.

There are cases in which self-deceivers, prior to their believing that *p*, have recognized that the totality of their evidence favored not-*p* and have believed that not-*p*. One way to look at these cases, and the way I recommend, is to assume that the judgment about evidence which led to the belief that not-*p* ***is revised*** in the course of the self-deceiving process. For example, a father, who truly believed that his daughter was loving until she spoke untender words, would not still judge, after she had spoken these words, that the totality of his evidence favored the view that she was loving, nor would he any longer believe that she was loving. What he previously had taken to be adequate evidence for her being loving would be ignored or reinterpreted in light of what he took to be new and salient evidence. I suggest that all self-deceivers always find, as did the father, that their "new evidence" offsets the old.

The suggestion is that the alcoholic, the overweight, the bald, who are anxious that their evidence suggests that they are these things, do not, when they self-deceptively believe that they are not alcoholic, overweight, or bald, judge that the totality of their evidence suggests otherwise. They believe that the totality of their evidence suggests they are not alcoholic, not overweight, not bald, and they believe this because they have given, for example, undue weight to some of the evidence, and not enough to other evidence.

If we look at cases of self-deception in this way, we are, I claim, able to explain all that essentially happens in self-deception without appealing to the disputed recognition. If at some point concurrent with the self-deceiving process, the self-deceiver does momentarily recognize that his total evidence favors that not-*p*, then this momentary recognition does not interact in any important way with the elements of the self-deceiving process.

The epistemic irrationality of self-deception, I am claiming, does not involve the self-deceiver's being in a state in which he believes that *p* and also believes that the totality of his evidence favors not-*p*. If a person should be in such a state, it is not in virtue of being a self-deceiver; something else is going on that is independent of self-deception. Let us see why this is so.

Imagine, for example, that a person believes that *p* and also believes that his evidence for not-*p* is stronger than his evidence for *p*. If we asked such a person, "Why do you believe that *p*?" he would be unable to answer that question. An alcoholic who believes that he is not an alcoholic and also believes that his evidence that he is an alcoholic is stronger than his evidence that he is not an alcoholic would be unable to say why he believes he is not an alcoholic. Such an alcoholic would not be a self-deceiver, for a self-deceiver can always answer the question "Why do you believe that *p*?" Indeed, anyone who could not answer this question would be in worse shape with regard to epistemic irrationality than merely being self-deceived.

Or imagine that a person believes that *p* when he believes that although his evidence for not-*p* is somewhat stronger than his evidence for *p*, that evidence is significantly incomplete. This person has the option of suspending judgment with regard to *p*, but he would have no grounds to give for not exercising that option, yet would not exercise it. The self-deceiver, however, will always give grounds for not suspending judgment. The person in this case, like the person in the preceding case, would be in worse shape with regard to epistemic irrationality than merely being self-deceived. Self-deception, as these cases are meant to show, essentially excludes a recognition that one's evidence favors not-*p*.

If on the other hand, we imagine that a person believes that future evidence will support *p*, a father, for example, has feelings, intuitions, etc. that his son did not commit the murder *despite* the police's evidence that he did – then that person could be brought to agree that these feelings etc. are evidence for his son's innocence. Such a person would not believe that his evidence for not-*p* is stronger than his evidence for *p*; he could, therefore, self-deceive himself into believing in his son's innocence.

If self-deceivers *qua* self-deceivers do not, when they believe that *p*, judge that the totality of their evidence favors not-*p*, they also do not believe that *p* when they believe that not-*p*. The bald, alcoholic, or overweight who believe that they are not bald or alcoholic or overweight do not also believe that they are bald, alcoholic, or overweight. Self-deceivers, *qua* self-deceivers, do not have contradictory beliefs.

Some who would agree with my claim that self-deceivers do not recognize or judge that their evidence favors not-*p* when they come to believe that *p* would, nevertheless, disagree with my contention that self-deceivers *qua* self-deceivers do not have contradictory beliefs.[16] They are persuaded by cases like the following.

Imagine that a woman says sincerely that her lover is intelligent, and that we have no reason to doubt the sincerity of her assertion. However, the woman treats her lover in ways which seem inconsistent with a belief in his intelligence.[17] For example, she condescends to him in discussion, seldom takes his views seriously, and hesitates to recommend him for a job. Given that we attribute beliefs to people on the basis of what they do as well as what they say, on the basis of what the woman does the best explanation of her behavior might seem to be that she believes that her lover is not intelligent. The suggestion is that if beliefs are attributed on the basis of both what people sincerely claim to believe (their avowals) and how they behave, then it seems plausible to conclude that the woman has contradictory beliefs. She believes that her lover is intelligent and she also believes that he is not intelligent.

My contention is that these cases do not compel one to attribute contradictory beliefs to the self-deceiver. Equally plausible explanations exist for every case of the relevant sort cited in the literature.

Let us look at the case just mentioned. I maintain that it is at least as plausible to think that if the woman is a self-deceiver, then either (a) the best explanation of her behavior is not that she believes that her lover is unintelligent or (b) if the best explanation of her behavior is that she believes her lover is unintelligent, then despite her sincerity she is mistaken about what she believes.

Is it always plausible to think that the best explanation of such a woman's behavior is that she believes that her lover is unintelligent? Suppose the woman agrees that she sometimes condescends to her

[16] Although, as note 17 points out, they need not take the having of these contradictory beliefs to indicate that self-deceivers are deeply epistemically irrational. They do, however, believe that having contradictory beliefs is essential to self-deception.

[17] See Georges Rey, "Toward a Computational Account of *Akrasia* and Self-Deception," in *Perspectives on Self-Deception*, ed. Brian McLaughlin and Amelie Oksenberg Rorty (Berkeley: University of California Press, 1988), pp. 264–96. He introduces this example to illustrate that self-deceivers can have contradictory beliefs without being deeply irrational. There are central beliefs and avowed beliefs. Although Rey's way of explaining self-deception is an alternative to any of those I have discussed, I believe (but shall not argue here) that if you analyze beliefs in the way that he suggests, while you do get contradictory beliefs you do not have self-deception. If you analyze beliefs in the ways I suggest, you do have self-deception but you do not have contradictory beliefs.

lover – he does, she acknowledges, say foolish things. She also acknowledges that she did not recommend him for a job because she thought he would not do well in it. But she explains her behavior and beliefs in terms of her lover's lack of will, not in terms of his lack of intelligence. He is lazy and therefore ignorant and inefficient.

If she is self-deceived in believing that he is intelligent, then this belief, on my account of self-deception, would have been caused by, e.g., an anxious desire to continue her relationship with him. Being uncertain whether he is unintelligent – he says foolish things – and believing that if he were unintelligent, she would have to end the relationship, something she does not want to do, she could, by being partial, have come to believe self-deceptively that he is intelligent. The woman would not both believe that he is intelligent and believe that he is not intelligent. She began uncertain whether he was intelligent, and came to believe that he is intelligent; there is no belief that he is not intelligent at any stage.

Another option that is compatible with the assumption that she does not simultaneously believe that he is intelligent and believe that he is not intelligent is to regard her as mistaken about what she really believes. Assume that the best explanation of her behavior is that she thinks he is unintelligent. She thought she believed he was intelligent, but when her behavior is brought to her attention, she acknowledges that this shows that she had not really believed that he was intelligent. She had self-deceived herself into believing that she believed one thing when she really believed another. Here an anxious desire not to end the relationship – if she believed that he is not intelligent, she would have to end the relationship – causes her to believe, mistakenly, that she believes that he is intelligent. Her avowal of a belief that he is intelligent was all along a mistake; so our attribution to her of the belief on, simply, the basis of the avowal was all along a mistake. The belief was never there.

The fact that the woman would in other circumstances believe that a person who did what her lover did was not intelligent, or the fact that she did believe that a woman who did what she did would not believe that her lover was intelligent, would not prove that the woman in the case described knows or believes at any stage that her lover is not intelligent, or prove that she knows or believes that she believes her lover is not intelligent. While she is biased in the case of her lover, she would not be so in the other case. She views the "evidence" differently in the two cases. What is obvious to a person in one situation, where he or she has no anxious desire, need not be obvious to the same person in a situation where he or she does have an anxious desire.

It is true that people whose self-deception is revealed to them and who are able to acknowledge it, not infrequently ***say*** that they **knew** all along that not-*p*. This, too, does not prove that they held contradictory beliefs. They need not have known all along that not-*p*. It is often easier to say that one knew something, but because of its disturbing nature concealed it, than to admit that one really did not know it, even though it was obvious to everyone else.

While multiple personalities, or people who have had traumatic or very disturbing experiences which they repressed, may believe that *p* and believe that not-*p*, ordinary self-deceivers do not similarly simultaneously believe that *p* and believe that not-*p*.[18] Alternative and equally plausible explanations which do not postulate such simultaneous believing can be given for all cases of self-deception. This is not, of course, to deny that self-deceivers are epistemically irrational. It is, however, to rule out one characterization of their irrationality.

III. PRUDENTIAL RATIONALITY AND IRRATIONALITY

Prudential or instrumental or practical rationality, in contrast to epistemic or cognitive rationality, is concerned with securing what one prefers. Since knowing what is the case, especially in complicated environments, is often conducive to securing what one prefers, it might seem prudentially rational for one to try to be always epistemically rational. The starving man, who anxiously desires to eat, had sometimes better not believe as a result of this anxious desire that those mushrooms he has found are not poisonous, that is, if he prefers to be around to have further desires. But prudential rationality is compatible with epistemic irrationality, for being epistemically rational is not always advantageous to creatures preferring that their desires be satisfied; their having true beliefs does not always secure them what they prefer.[19] It can, therefore, sometimes be prudentially rational to allow

[18] Self-deceivers may, like the rest of us, unknowingly believe inconsistent things, but with respect to their self-deceptive belief that *p*, they do not simultaneously believe that not-*p*, or, even if they do, the not-*p* belief is entirely extraneous to the self-deception dynamics.

[19] I am not of course claiming that the connection between epistemic rationality and securing what one prefers is an arbitrary one.

oneself *not* to be (or even to cause oneself not to be) epistemically rational rather than to be epistemically rational.[20] Immobilizing anxieties about the non-satisfaction of desires can, for example, sometimes be allayed by self-deceptive beliefs.[21] I suggest that an unreliable belief procedure with regard to the goal of truth can, in some circumstances, have survival value.

While, for some *p*, it might not be epistemically rational for people ***to believe that p***, it might be prudentially rational for them ***to prefer that they believe p*** and also prudentially rational for them ***to try to make something happen that brings about their believing p***. Let us look, therefore, at some cases which illustrate epistemic irrationality's compatibility with prudential rationality.[22]

It may, for example, be epistemically irrational for a man to believe that his wife is sexually intimate with another man, when, for example, he has no reason for believing that she is, and reasons for believing that she is not. What may be prudentially rational for him, however, ***is preferring that he believe*** she is sexually intimate with

[20] See Derek Parfit, *Reasons and Persons* (Oxford: Oxford University Press paperback, reprinted 1986), pp. 12–13, for a vivid case of its being prudentially rational to cause oneself not to be epistemically rational.

[21] Johnston talks of the advantages of treating such anxieties with doses of hopeful belief.

[22] There are cases where it is not possible to determine what it is epistemically rational to believe although it is possible to determine what it would be prudentially rational to believe. Pascal believed there were cases where, although one could not determine which of two conflicting beliefs it was epistemically rational to hold (one might say it was epistemically rational to suspend judgment), it was possible to determine which of the beliefs had the better consequences and thus which of the beliefs people should prefer that they hold and which they should try to bring it about that they hold. He assumes that the evidence available to us is not sufficient to justify either the belief that God is or the belief that God is not. But if we think of the benefits of believing that God is, we will see that the effects of believing that He is are better than the effects of believing that He is not. If we believe the former, and God is, we gain all, and if God is not, we lose nothing, so, he urged, "wager, then, without hesitation that He is."

There are other cases where one prefers having a certain belief because one knows that having such a belief will make it more likely that what is believed is the case. The contestant in the beauty pageant knows that if she believes she will win, she will have a better chance of winning. It is prudentially rational for her to prefer that she believe that she will win and also prudentially rational for her to try to bring it about that she believes this. Here, however, having the belief that she will win provides her with some evidence for the truth of the belief. In more typical cases, the having of a belief does not provide one with evidence for its truth.

another man, or preferring that he comes to believe this. What may also be prudentially rational for him ***is trying to make something happen that brings about his believing this***. Assume that believing his wife is sexually intimate with another man would allow him to leave his wife, something he anxiously desires to do. Since prudential rationality permits one to prefer that one believe something if believing that something gets one what one prefers, and he prefers to leave his wife, in such a situation it is not prudentially irrational for him to prefer that he believe she is unfaithful to that he believe that she is faithful. The former, but not the latter, belief would enable him to leave her. While it may thus be prudentially rational to prefer that one have a certain belief, it does not follow that it is epistemically rational to believe it.

Prudential rationality requires of us that we try to do what we believe will secure what we most prefer.[23] Reason requires the man, who most prefers to leave his wife, to try to do what he believes will best secure that end. If he believes that he would leave his wife if he believed that she were unfaithful, then he has a reason to look for evidence for her infidelity, if that is the best way to get himself to have that belief.

Or imagine that a man wants to live in a certain community. He knows that unless he believes that the head of the community is divine, he will not be able to do so. It is prudentially rational for him to prefer that he believe in the divinity of this individual and for him to try to bring it about that he believes this. It would be prudentially rational for him to try to bring it about that he has a belief which is not epistemically rational.[24]

[23] See "Common mentalistic explanation seems to depend upon the plausibility of some version of a law of practical reason: e.g., people (try to) do what they believe will best secure what they most prefer." Rey, "Toward a Computational Account of *Akrasia* and Self-Deception," p. 264. There are of course critics of this alleged law of practical reason.

[24] Another example where prudential rationality does not demand epistemic rationality is provided by Alfred Mele, *Irrationality*, p. 111. "[A] person who has epistemic values – for example, a pro-attitude toward his having only epistemically warranted beliefs – may take these values to be overridden by others in certain cases. Consider, for example, the undergraduate who sincerely states in the final exam for his philosophy of religion course that although he is now convinced that the bulk of the evidence supports the claim that the Christian God does not exist, he still finds himself believing that there is such a God, and, what is more, sincerely maintains that, all things considered, it is quite *rational* for him to hold this belief, given that the strong evidence against Christian theism is not

Having cognitive reasons for beliefs, as Davidson pointed out, is distinct from having evaluative reasons for wanting to be, and for taking steps to get oneself to be, a believer in a proposition. An evaluative reason of the sort in question, unlike a cognitive reason, does not provide evidence in light of which it is reasonable to think that the belief is true. Rather it provides "a motive for acting in such a way as to promote having a belief."[25]

Although being prudentially rational is compatible with not being epistemically rational, are self-deceivers prudentially rational? By having self-deceptive beliefs, self-deceivers sometimes secure what they most prefer. However, I shall argue, even when this occurs, self-deceivers are not being prudentially rational.

Prudential or means–end rationality requires believingly going after the best outcome, given your preferences. If you want an apple, and believe that apples can be gotten at the local greengrocer with less difficulty and cost than they can be gotten elsewhere, and getting an apple with the least cost and difficulty is what you most prefer, then when, given these desires and belief,[26] you go to the greengrocer to get the apple, you have believingly gone after the best outcome, given your preferences. But, if my description of what goes on in self-deception is correct, the self-deceiver does not do this. Self-deceivers do not *believingly* get themselves to believe something such that if they believe it, it will secure them something they prefer. Self-deceivers, assuming my characterization of them is correct, do not do any of the many things they do under the kind of description needed in order for them to be prudentially rational. They do not try to get themselves to believe something in the belief that believing it will relieve their anxiety, will allow them to believe that something they feared would happen will not happen.

entirely conclusive and that he would be unbearably unhappy as an atheist or an agnostic. Such a person believes against his *epistemic* judgment but in accordance with his better *all-things-considered judgment*."

Mele suggests the person "may, from an epistemic point of view, believe irresponsibly." I would agree that the student, as described, is not epistemically rational in believing that God exists, although he might be prudentially rational in preferring that he believe God exists. This case is similar to Pascal's, but whereas Pascal left open which cognitive belief it was epistemically rational to hold, Mele (but not the student) does not.

25 Davidson, "Deception and Division," p. 86.

26 Assume that your desires and belief cause in the right way your action.

People who knowingly set out, given their preferences, to try to get themselves to believe something because believing it would enable them to secure what they prefer, could be prudentially rational. But people like this – say, a person who puts down in his calendar the wrong date of an appointment, knowing that by the time he reads the calendar he will have forgotten what he did and therefore will believe that the appointment is on the day written – would not be self-deceivers. Self-deceivers, to be sure, get something they prefer, and – in the sense of the expression to which my account calls attention – they deceive themselves because they get something they prefer; they believe what they do *because* believing this relieves their anxiety. But they do not believingly try to get themselves to believe this. Rather, by failing to take precautions against their disposition towards bias in the circumstances they are in, they come to believe this. Their bias for beliefs that reduce their anxiety is what keeps them, as it were, on course. Since knowing what one is doing is necessary for prudential rationality, self-deceivers are not prudentially rational. But while they are not prudentially rational, they are not thereby prudentially irrational either. Knowing what one is doing is necessary for ascriptions of both prudential irrationality and rationality.

While we have seen cases where not being epistemically rational is compatible with being prudentially rational, it seems that self-deceivers are not prudentially rational when they come to believe that p. My overall conclusion with respect to prudential rationality is that self-deceivers are neither prudentially rational nor prudentially irrational in coming to believe that p.

While prudential rationality is compatible with epistemic irrationality, prudential rationality would, nonetheless, seem to require that people try to be epistemically rational a good deal of the time.[27] This is due to the fact that lack of epistemic rationality can make it impossible for a person to secure what he or she most prefers. Self-deceivers always have an evaluative reason for wanting to be a p-believer, believing that p always gets them something they want, namely a reduction in anxiety; but they may have other wants whose satisfaction is

[27] Epistemic rationality ensures that your beliefs are well founded on the reasons you have. While it doesn't ensure truth, the person who is epistemically rational is more likely to have true beliefs than is the epistemically irrational person. And having true beliefs is in general a more reliable way to get what you want than having false beliefs.

incompatible with being a p-believer. The self-deceiver gets something he prefers by being partial, but he may also get other things he does not prefer. For example, a father may prefer that his son have the most effective education available, but, by believing self-deceptively that his child is not learning-disabled, he may make it impossible for his son to get such an education.

Self-deceivers are not, I contend, irrational in the way that Davidson believes makes conceptual trouble. They are not deeply irrational. Self-deceivers are epistemically irrational if we understand that to mean that their beliefs that p are not well founded on the reasons they have. Their response to the evidence has been skewed by their anxiety, an anxiety which causes them to be partial, to believe certain things which are not in the situation good reason for believing that p is the case. Self-deceivers are also not prudentially rational even if the self-deception allows them to secure what they most prefer. Nor are they prudentially irrational if the self-deception prevents them from securing what they most prefer.

There are other ways in which self-deceivers can be irrational, although they would not be irrational *qua* self-deceivers. For example, the self-deceiver could be irrational for being anxious that not-q. An anxiety itself may be irrational if, for example, it is based on an unjustified false belief.[28] Self-deceivers can be epistemically irrational not only about their self-deceptive beliefs but about the beliefs that generate their anxiety.

For example, consider a prospective bride who, because of her uncertainty about whether it will rain, is anxious that her outdoor wedding will be ruined. Her anxiety causes her to be biased in coming to her belief that it will not rain. In her horoscope there is talk of good weather, and she takes this to be evidence for its not raining. Suppose, however, that her uncertainty about the weather, a source of the anxiety, is based on a patently false belief that the weather station's barometer is malfunctioning. Her anxiety is irrational. While she is not self-deceived in believing that it will not rain – let us suppose that it will not – she could, nonetheless, have self-deceived herself into believing that it would not. An irrational anxiety causes her to have an unjustified – although, in this case, true – belief.

[28] See Ronald de Sousa, *The Rationality of Emotion* (Cambridge, Mass.: MIT Press, 1987), who claims that anxieties can be irrational in another way.

A student who had difficulty with the review questions for an examination may be anxious that she will lose her fellowship. She is uncertain whether she will do badly on the examination, and believes that if she does badly she will lose her fellowship. Her anxious desire causes her to be biased in coming to believe that she will do well, when in fact she will not. Suppose her belief that she will lose her fellowship if she does badly is patently false. The examination in question is a minor one, and she has done well on the major ones. Her anxiety is irrational, not because she was not justified in being uncertain about whether she would do badly – she was right to be uncertain – but because she was unjustified in believing that if she did badly she would lose her fellowship. This belief is both false and unjustified. While an irrational anxiety is the cause of a self-deceptive belief, an unjustified false belief is the source of the irrational anxiety. What causes the unjustified false belief responsible for her irrational anxiety is left open. It may be caused by an anxious desire (and be self-deceptive), or it may be caused by something else.

Not all self-deceivers are irrational in the way just discussed, for not all their anxieties are based on unjustified false beliefs. The father's anxiety about losing power, a man's anxiety about not leaving his wife, may well be rational anxieties, although the beliefs the men form in response to them may not be rational.

Self-deceivers are epistemically irrational because their beliefs are not well founded on the reasons they have and that ill-foundedness is sufficient for epistemic irrationality. They are not prudentially rational, because they do not satisfy the preconditions for ascriptions of prudential rationality. While self-deceivers sometimes secure what they most prefer, their securing it was not a matter of their believingly pursuing their objective in the most efficient and effective way. When self-deceivers do not secure what they most prefer, their not securing it is not a matter of their believingly pursuing their objective in some way that is inefficient or ineffective. Whether self-deceivers are irrational in other ways – for example. whether they have irrational anxieties – depends upon the particular circumstances of the case.

9

What, if anything, is objectionable about self- and other-deception?

"Most of us agree that there is something objectionable about self-deception,"[1] but we do not agree about what is objectionable. This lack of agreement stems in part from a lack of agreement about what self-deception is. Self-deceivers have been charged, for example, with falseness of heart, insincerity, and hypocrisy,[2] yet these require an intentionality that some of us argue is lacking in self-deception.

I take the most telling of the charges against self-deception to be that of epistemic cowardice. One who self-deceives oneself is, as Johnston points out, accused "of mental cowardice, of flight from anxiety (or angst), a failure to contain one's anxiety, a lack of courage in matters epistemic."[3] The self-deceiver is "held responsible for an episode that evidences a defect of character, in this case a lack of the negative power that is reason, i.e., the capacity to inhibit changes in beliefs when those changes are not grounded in reasons."[4]

While the charge of epistemic cowardice is always an appropriate one to level against self-deceivers, and epistemic cowardice is a non-admirable character trait, having this trait is not, I contend, sufficient for *prima facie* moral badness. I claim, moreover, that self-deception is not always *prima facie* morally bad, nor is other-deception always *prima facie* morally wrong. Neither deception is in all cases morally objectionable. I shall first look briefly at other-deception.

Interpersonal deceiving is intentional activity; it is appropriate to ask whether it is *prima facie* morally wrong. If it were always *prima facie*

[1] Marcia Baron, "What is Wrong with Self-Deception?" in *Perspectives on Self-Deception*, ed. Brian McLaughlin and Amelie Oksenberg Rorty (Berkeley: University of California Press, 1988), p. 431.

[2] See, for example, Bishop Joseph Butler, "Upon Self-Deceit," Sermon X in *Fifteen Sermons* (London: SPCK, 1970), pp. 90–8; Mike Martin, *Self-Deception and Morality*.

[3] "Self-Deception and the Nature of the Mind," p. 85.

[4] Ibid., pp. 85–6.

morally wrong, it would be wrong either intrinsically or because of its consequences.

While I believe that ***not all*** interpersonal deception is intrinsically *prima facie* morally wrong, one kind of interpersonal deception is. It is taken for granted that in some situations people not only expect, but ***are entitled to expect***, honesty from one another. Intimate personal relations are, paradigmatically, relations in which an entitlement to honesty is presumed, but such entitlement is also present in many ordinary social interactions,[5] interactions, for example, between customers and merchants, between employers and employees. Where people are entitled to trust one another, they have a right not to have their trust violated.[6] Deceivers in such situations violate the deceived's right not to have his or her trust violated.[7] Since violating a right is intrinsically *prima facie* morally wrong, deceiving another in this situation is intrinsically *prima facie* morally wrong.

Situations in which honesty is expected are not, however, always situations in which people are entitled to expect honesty. For example, an obstinate stranger who sets himself down on your doorstep may trust you to take care of him, but given that you neither asked for, nor want, his trust, you would not have violated any right of

5 It is well known that if people did not standardly trust one another, social interactions would be very inefficient. See Rue, *By the Grace of Guile*.

6 It is, of course, not inappropriate to be suspicious in some situations where one has a right not to have one's trust violated. *Caveat emptor* is good advice in ordinary purchasing transactions, for even where people are entitled to trust, those whom they trust are not always trustworthy.

However, in intimate personal relationships where much effort has gone into establishing that one is trustworthy, suspicion is thought to be not only unnecessary, but inappropriate. But, if there is any truth in Oscar Wilde's quip "the one charm of marriage is that it makes a life of deception absolutely necessary for both parties," a healthy dose of suspicion might not be inappropriate even in intimate relations. It is obviously appropriate in those relations of feigned sincerity and intimacy that successful salesmen and saleswomen, be they on the lot or on the screen, establish with their audience.

7 Claudia Mills in her discussion of covert persuasion – and deception is one form of such persuasion – makes betrayal of trust the distinctive wrong. "Influence: Coercion, Manipulation, and Persuasion," unpublished Ph.D. thesis, Princeton University, 1991, chapter 4 ("Manipulation"). T. S. Champlin distinguishes deceptive behavior from deceitful behavior in the following way: deceit is deception where the victim is entitled not to expect it. "Deceit, Deception and the Self-Deceiver," *Philosophical Investigations*, vol. 17, no. 1 (January 1994), pp. 53–8.

his not to have his trust violated if you deceived him into going elsewhere.[8]

In other situations people neither expect, nor are they entitled to expect, honesty from one another. For example, in highly competitive situations where the aim is to defeat opponents, honesty is not expected with regard to certain matters. The goalie does not expect the opposition soccer player to reveal to him where he will aim his kick; the German commanders in World War II did not expect their Allied counterparts to be honest with them about where they intended to stage an invasion. A corporation does not expect its competitor to reveal its marketing strategies. In situations of this sort interpersonal deceivers do not violate the deceived's right not to have his or her trust violated. Violation of people's right not to have their trust violated is not, therefore, sufficient for making ***all*** other-deception intrinsically *prima facie* morally wrong.

If violating a right is, as I believe, the most plausible candidate for making other-deception *intrinsically prima facie* morally wrong,[9] then not all such deception is **intrinsically** *prima facie* morally wrong. Is all

[8] It is not always clear when someone has a right not to have his or her trust violated. Ordinarily a commander is entitled to expect that the soldiers under his command will be honest in their dealings with him. Consider, however, a soldier who lies to his commander about a couple's religion in order to prevent them from being sent to Dachau. The commander is prevented from getting what he wants – he wants to deport all people of a certain religion to concentration camps – but it is agreed that he should be so prevented. If we believe that a right is violated here, then this case would show that sometimes a violation of another's right not to have his or her trust violated may be the only feasible way to prevent harm or to produce good.

[9] Kant in his *Doctrine of Virtue* (trans. Mary J. Gregor [New York: Harper and Row, 1964]) suggests another reason why other-deception is intrinsically morally wrong. In his discussion of lying, he claims that "the harm that can come to others from it is not the characteristic property of this vice (for if it were, the vice would consist only in violating one's duty to others)." Neither does it consist in "the harm that the liar brings on himself; for then a lie, as a mere error in prudence, would be contrary to the pragmatic maxim, not to the moral maxim, and it could not be considered a violation of duty at all. – By a lie a man throws away and, as it were, annihilates his dignity as a man. A man who himself does not believe what he tells another . . . has even less worth than if he were a mere thing." He "makes himself a mere deceptive appearance of man, not man himself" (p. 93).

If by deceiving one threw away one's dignity, then this would be a reason for thinking other-deception was intrinsically *prima facie* morally wrong. I am skeptical that the Allied commanders who lied in order to get the German commanders to believe that the Allies intended to stage an invasion at Calais threw away or annihilated their dignity by so lying.

other-deception nonetheless morally wrong because of its consequences? "[O]n reflection it becomes obvious that the cultural bias against acts of deceiving is derived from the more fundamental belief that one is harmed by being deceived."[10]

On certain understandings of harm, harm is not always caused to the deceived.[11] If, for example, we understand harm as either causing people to have less happiness than they would otherwise have, or causing people to have less desire fulfillment through their life than they would otherwise have, then there are many examples that suggest that deception does not always cause the deceived harm. A woman deceives an elderly relative in order to get him to make a needed medical appointment. A friend lies to another in order to keep the surprise party intended for her a secret.[12]

If there exist kinds of things that are good or bad for one regardless of what one wants, and if one harms someone by causing him or her to have a thing of this kind, then the deceiver may always cause the deceived harm. For example, if being deceived was intrinsically bad,[13] then the deceiver would always cause the deceived harm. If being deceived were necessarily associated with something that was intrinsically bad, then the deceiver would also always cause the deceived

[10] Rue, *By the Grace of Guile*, p. 6.

[11] Derek Parfit distinguishes between three theories about self-interest – the Hedonistic Theory, the Desire-Fulfillment Theory, and the Objective List Theory. These theories are the source of the various conceptions of harm I allude to. See *Reasons and Persons*, p. 4.

[12] But as Sisela Bok points out in *Lying: Moral Choice in Public and Private Life* (Brighton: Harvester Press, 1978), paternalistic lies are often a dicey business. See p. 212: "One reason for the appeal of paternalistic lies is that they, unlike so much deception, are felt to be without bias and told in a disinterested way to be helpful to fellow human beings in need. On closer examination, however, this objectivity and disinterest are often found to be spurious. The benevolent motives claimed by liars are then seen to be mixed with many others much less altruistic – the fear of confrontation which would accompany a more outspoken acknowledgment of the liar's feelings and intentions; the desire to avoid setting in motion great pressures to change, as where addiction or infidelity are no longer concealed; the urge to maintain the power that comes with duping others (never greater than when those lied to are defenseless or in need of care). These are motives of self-protection and of manipulation, of wanting to retain control over a situation and to remain a free agent. So long as the liar does not see them clearly, his judgment that his lies are altruistic and thus excused is itself biased and unreliable."

[13] Parfit includes being deceived on the list of things that might be bad for a person. *Reasons and Persons*, p. 4.

harm. For example, if having false beliefs were intrinsically bad,[14] then since being deceived is necessarily associated with having false beliefs, one would always be harmed by being deceived.[15]

However, even if interpersonal deception always (in every case) caused the deceived harm, it would not follow that the deception was always morally wrong. In general, if one harms a person by causing him to have something intrinsically bad for him – e.g., pain – it does not follow that one has done something morally wrong. A nurse who gives a patient his requested flu shot may cause that patient pain, but she ordinarily does not do anything morally wrong. In situations where the deceived is caused to have something intrinsically bad, it does not follow that the deception is morally wrong. The Allied commanders caused the German commanders and their troops harm when they deceived them, but it is generally assumed that this causing of harm does not make their deception morally wrong.[16] In this example – and examples like this are commonplace – it is taken for

[14] A case can be made that having false beliefs is generally instrumentally bad. If one's beliefs are not idle, then when one acts on false beliefs one's behavior is guided not by what is the case, but by what one mistakenly believes is the case. But being guided by what is not the case is not a generally reliable way to get what one wants. One is substantially less likely to get what one wants and hence less likely to have maximum happiness and desire satisfaction. While a self-deceiver's false belief always gets him something he wants – his anxiety is reduced and often enough a desire associated with the anxiety is satisfied – when he acts on his self-deceptive belief he frequently enough gets things he does not want. The person who is deceived by another is not assured of getting anything he wants as a result of the deception.

Having false beliefs is not instrumentally bad because it *always* causes the person who has them less happiness or less desire fulfillment. Rather having false beliefs is instrumentally bad because it *tends* to cause the person who has them either less happiness or desire fulfillment or to have something bad – his agency limited or undermined – or to do something bad – e.g., cause unintentional harm.

[15] Other items that might be intrinsically bad – e.g., unhappiness, or limitation of agency – and which have been linked with being deceived would not ensure that the deceived was always harmed. Being deceived does not always result in unhappiness or limitation of agency. Recall the recalcitrant relative who, when deceived, makes a needed medical appointment. He may as a result become healthier and hence better able to do the things he wants to do. He may be happier as well.

[16] Some might want to respond to the claim that causing the deceived harm is not sufficient for the moral wrongness of deception in the following way. They might grant that the examples that have been given show that causing harm on a particular occasion is not sufficient for the moral wrongness of deception, but claim that the tendency of an arbi-

granted that it is not *prima facie* morally wrong for the deceiver to deceive the deceived. All interpersonal deception is not, therefore, *prima facie* morally wrong because of its consequences.[17]

Some of what has been said about other-deception also applies to self-deception. For example, if a person is harmed (i.e., is caused to have a bad thing) and if having false beliefs is an intrinsically bad thing, then self-deceivers, who necessarily have false beliefs, are harmed. But causing this sort of harm is not sufficient for moral badness. If we understand harm as causing people to have less happiness or less desire-fulfillment, then there are examples that suggest that self-deception, like other-deception, does not always cause the deceived harm. An academic self-deceives himself into believing that his tenure chances are good, thereby enabling himself to write.

Some of what has been said about other-deception, however, does not apply to self-deception. In other-deception, a deceiver may violate the deceived's right not to have his trust violated, but no such violation occurs in self-deception. While we talk of trusting ourselves – I do or do not trust myself to make an important decision or to do something difficult – when I deceive myself I do not betray a trust to myself, any more than when I do not give myself enough to eat I betray a trust to myself. In contrast, not giving my child enough to eat is to betray a trust to him.[18]

If self-deception were always *prima facie* morally bad, it would be bad either intrinsically or because of its consequences. While epistemic cowardice makes self-deception intrinsically *prima facie* objectionable, I contend that it does not make all self-deception intrinsically *prima facie* morally bad.

If one is a self-deceiver one fails, as Johnston points out, "to contain

trary instance of deception to cause harm, or the harmfulness of deception considered as a practice, is sufficient for moral wrongness. However, I myself do not see how if causing harm is not sufficient for moral wrongness, the tendency to cause harm would be sufficient, although perhaps there is some story to tell here.

[17] Nor, even when a deception is intrinsically *prima facie* morally wrong, does it follow that the deception is *all things considered* morally wrong. That a deception has good consequences for the deceived – the deceived elderly relative, by making a medical appointment, gets better health, something he very much wants, or the deceived friend is happily surprised – may override the intrinsic *prima facie* moral wrongness of violating the relative's or friend's right not to have his or her trust violated.

[18] Assuming, of course, that I am in a position to give him enough to eat.

one's anxiety and face the anxiety-provoking."[19] We regard people who can face the anxiety-provoking as epistemically courageous; those who cannot (at least to some extent) face the anxiety-provoking as epistemically cowardly. Self-deceivers' belief-acquisition processes exhibit partiality and bias partly because it takes courage in the circumstances they are in to prevent this biasing or partiality and they lack this courage.[20]

Cowardice, like envy or spite, is a vice, and hence the self-deceiver, whose response is epistemically cowardly, is never, for this reason, altogether exempt from *prima facie* criticism with regard to his or her own deception.

Cowardice, to be sure, can take various forms, and not all forms of cowardice are equally objectionable. For example, those unwilling to prepare or eat unfamiliar food, wear unfamiliar clothes, or venture into unfamiliar places may be culinary or fashion or travel cowards. These cowards are unadventurous and give priority to safety over novelty. Giving priority to safety over novelty is not, however, regarded as a serious character defect, but giving priority to safety over truth, as the epistemic coward does, is regarded as a potentially more serious character shortcoming.

Commonsense thought takes it for granted that there is something noble and courageous about facing up to a painful truth, and something not to be admired and cowardly about avoiding it.

> [A]n incurable cancer victim may, in a sense we can all understand, benefit from his ability to misread or deceive himself about the evidence that he has terminal cancer . . . But we commonly regard such a person as less to be admired than someone who faces similar facts squarely, who has the courage to look death in the face, who is less dishonest with himself, even when or if we are willing to concede that the latter may suffer and be worse off for the knowledge he refuses to evade.[21]

[19] "Self-Deception and the Nature of the Mind," p. 85.

[20] In situations of anxious desire, self-deceiving is typically the default response. It is easier if one's anxious desire skews one's belief-forming process than if one takes steps to prevent this, especially if taking such steps may bring one face to face with an unwelcome truth.

[21] Michael Slote, *From Morality to Virtue* (New York: Oxford University Press, 1992), p. 130. See also Patricia Greenspan, "Guilt and Virtue," *Journal of Philosophy*, vol. 91, no. 2 (February 1994), p. 61: "[E]ven in a case where real redemption is impossible, we still

Facing up to a painful truth is, admittedly, always an admirable response, considered in isolation. But in light of the crippling effect facing up to this sort of truth can sometimes have, is it always epistemic cowardice to avoid such facing up? Is the ideal of always facing up to the truth, however painful that truth may be, a vanity of a certain individualistic *aesthetic*; an aesthetic which, moreover, dubiously assumes that people have enough strength to resist their inclination to avoid such truth?

Certainly there are many cases where despite the great cost and difficulty of facing up to the truth, one is epistemically cowardly for failing to do so. Consider a father who self-deceives himself into believing that his son is not learning-impaired. Moreover, however painful it is for people to face up to the fact that their assessments of their own abilities may be overblown, that it is their lack of ability, rather than the niggardliness of their assessors or the difficulty or irrelevance of tests, that is at fault; that their children have committed heinous crimes; that they are addicted to alcohol or drugs; that their marriage or career is failing; or that they themselves, or those about whom they care, are lazy, dishonest, cruel, selfish, vengeful, or less important, less knowledgeable, less interesting, etc. than they think they are, such people too are epistemically cowardly if by deceiving themselves they avoid facing up to these truths.

While being epistemically cowardly is compatible in many situations with its being very difficult or costly for the individual involved to be epistemically brave, are there ***any*** circumstances sufficiently difficult or costly that the avoidance of a painful truth is not a sign of epistemic cowardice? Suppose that a recently widowed parent of a terminally ill child would, if she faced the truth about her child's illness, be crippled by this knowledge; she would not be able to fulfill her obligations to the dying child and to her other children. She deceives herself into believing that the child has a good chance of recovering, and she is thus able to take proper care of her children. The woman in this case does not deceive herself in order to allow herself to cope; her being able to cope is a consequence of her having deceived herself. Her self-deceptive belief that her child's chances of recovery are good

seem to place a value just on facing up to the past. We admire someone who insists on doing so at some cost to his own peace of mind – and perhaps even to his effectiveness as a moral agent in certain cases. The notion of a noble character seems to include a kind of heightened sensitivity to one's own moral wrongs."

functions to reduce her anxiety, which reduction enables her to cope. The deception occurs because she is anxious that her child is dying and she does not resist her partiality for beliefs that reduce her anxiety. That her child has a good chance of recovery is obviously an anxiety-reducing belief.

If, as I believe, epistemic cowardice is displayed in giving priority to safety over truth,[22] then the widowed mother is epistemically cowardly. Although she does not intentionally choose safety over truth, in not resisting her partiality to anxiety-reducing beliefs she gives safety such priority. The widowed mother, the cancer victim, display, as do all self-deceivers, epistemic cowardice. It does not, however, follow that all self-deceivers are, thereby, *prima facie* morally bad.

While I believe there is always something (epistemic cowardice) that is intrinsically *prima facie* objectionable (non-admirable) about self-deception, this does not entail that there is always something that is intrinsically *prima facie* morally bad about self-deception. The widowed mother is not in virtue of being epistemically cowardly morally bad. Is there, however, anything with which self-deception can be identified that would make all self-deception, including the widowed mother's self-deception, intrinsically *prima facie* morally bad? I contend there is not. I shall show that the three most plausible candidates with which self-deception can be identified – self-partiality, dishonesty, and bad faith – do not establish that all self-deception is intrinsically *prima facie* morally bad.

On one understanding of self-partiality, not all self-deception involves self-partiality, and hence being self-partial cannot show that self-deception is always intrinsically *prima facie* morally bad. We take people to be self-partial if, as I said earlier,[23] they tend in their responses to favor themselves more than they favor others and their favoring is unwarranted.[24]

[22] The epistemically courageous person, on the other hand, gives the right relative weight to truth as opposed to safety.

[23] See Chapter 5.

[24] It is not sufficient for self-partiality in this sense to regard our own interests as more important to ourselves than are the interests of others, for we may well be warranted in regarding our interests in this way. However, if we believe, and act on our belief, that our own interests are more important than are other people's interests and our belief about this is unwarranted, then we would be self-partial. Suppose tennis rackets are being distributed to the tennis team and Nigel chooses the best racket. He does this because he

For example, people are self-partial if they think better of themselves than they do of others; if it takes more evidence for them to believe propositions unfavorable to themselves than it does to believe propositions unfavorable to others, or more evidence to believe propositions favorable to others than it does to believe propositions favorable to themselves. Self-deceivers are not, however, necessarily self-partial in this sense of self-partiality. While people frequently deceive themselves into believing things that allow them to think better of themselves than of others, people sometimes deceive themselves into believing, for example, that they are less talented, more selfish, and so on than others. It sometimes takes less evidence, not more, for a self-deceiver to believe something unfavorable about himself than to believe something unfavorable about others. Therefore, self-deceivers are not always self-partial if self-partiality requires that they unwarrantedly think better of themselves than they do of others.[25]

Bishop Butler, who believed that self-partiality made self-deception possible, describes as self-partial those who have a "wrong way of thinking and judging" about matters "relating to themselves."[26] Self-deceivers would always be self-partial only if we understand "in matters relating to themselves" as "in matters in which they have an

knows, as do his teammates, that he is the best tennis player on the team and deserves the best racket. He is not being self-partial in these circumstances. He would, however, be self-partial if despite the fact that he is the worst player on the team, he demands the best racket for himself.

[25] Moreover, as Patrick Gardiner pointed out, "it is far from clear that the primary or most frequent objects of self-deception are such things as a man's own character traits or his motives and intentions. Misapprehensions concerning how things stand in the world confronting him are equally plausible candidates, and very common. Thus a general's misappreciation of the military state of affairs in which he is placed may be described in these terms; and a politician, engaged upon a project on which he has staked the reputation of himself or his country, may be spoken of as sinking deeper and deeper into self-deception regarding the objective chances of a successful outcome." "Error, Faith and Self-Deception," *Proceedings of the Aristotelian Society*, vol. 70 (1969–70), p. 223.

[26] "Upon Self-Deceit," Sermon X, p. 92. This self-partiality gives rise to self-ignorance. People are ignorant of their own character. There is a suggestion in Butler that not simply does self-partiality give rise to self-ignorance, but that without such self-partiality, self-ignorance could be easily overcome. "[I]f it were not for that partial and fond regard to ourselves, it would certainly be no great difficulty to know our own character" (p. 91).

anxious desire."[27] If people who judge and think wrongly about matters in which they have an anxious desire, but do not judge and think this way about matters in which they have no anxious desire, are self-partial, then self-deceivers are self-partial. Self-deceivers think and judge wrongly about matters about which they are anxious. But thinking and judging wrongly in situations of anxiety is not thereby morally bad.

Dishonesty is typically an intentional activity – the intentional activities of lying and cheating are sufficient for dishonesty – but neither lying nor cheating can be the source of the self-deceiver's dishonesty. Can we, however, make sense of a non-intentional dishonesty? I suggest that we may be able to, but any such dishonesty will ultimately rest upon epistemic cowardice, and epistemic cowardice is not, I claimed, sufficient for moral badness. That is, we may be able to think of a self-deceiver as dishonest insofar as he does not face up to unwelcome truths and his being epistemically cowardly is a part of his not facing up. There is no conscious decision on the self-deceiver's part not to face up to such truths, but a non-intentional, although motivated, failure to face up to unwelcome truths may plausibly be thought of as a kind of dishonesty. While this sort of dishonesty is not to be admired, it is not sufficient for moral badness.

Bad faith does not show that self-deception is intrinsically *prima facie* morally bad, even if we could agree that the self-deceiver is a bad-faith-believer. Bad faith is a notion Sartre uses in connection with self-deception, but it is by no means clear what exactly he means by it. Suppose, as has been suggested,[28] that Sartrian bad faith essentially involves a recognition on the part of a believer that beliefs, adopted as integrating responses to the world, are always inadequate to their task. What separates believers of bad faith from believers of good faith, who also recognize that beliefs are inadequate in this way, is their response to this inadequacy. The believer of bad faith is content with the imperfection, maintaining his beliefs by consciously directing his attention towards those aspects of the world his beliefs integrate and away from those aspects which challenge his beliefs. In contrast, the believer of

[27] There is of course good reason not to understand self-partial as being limited to matters in which one has an anxious desire.

[28] I am making use of Allan Wood's interpretation of Sartre: see his "Self-Deception and Bad Faith," in *Perspectives on Self-Deception*, ed. Brian McLaughlin and Amelie Oksenberg Rorty (Berkeley: University of California Press, 1988), pp. 207–27.

good faith is discontent with the imperfection, always subjecting his beliefs to further critical scrutiny, always allowing for the possibility that his beliefs might need to be altered in light of new evidence.

I leave aside the question of whether beliefs are inadequate to their task as integrating responses to the world. Insofar as we think of the believer of bad faith as one who does not call his beliefs into question – a calling into question which would require him to be epistemically responsible – and the believer of good faith as one who does call his beliefs into question – he is epistemically responsible – the self-deceiver who is epistemically irresponsible is a believer of bad faith. But, as we saw in Chapter 5, not all self-deceivers are epistemically irresponsible.[29] A self-deceiver may try to prevent bias, and so may not be charged with epistemic irresponsibility, even though he does not succeed in preventing it. Moreover, being epistemically irresponsible is not sufficient for moral badness.

While it is a defect to be epistemically irresponsible, it is not always morally bad. A person can, by a careless addition, come to believe that his last month's expenses were higher than they were, but the person need not be morally bad. Self-deceivers' epistemic cowardice frequently enough results in their being epistemically irresponsible, but even such motivated epistemic irresponsibility is not sufficient for moral badness.

If there is no factor which makes self-deception intrinsically *prima facie* morally bad, is all self-deception bad because of its consequences? As the cases I have discussed show, some self-deceiving may have good consequences. Recall the widowed mother. By self-deceiving herself she is able to take proper care of her children. It is, of course, morally wrong for a parent not to take such care, and while it would be noble and admirable if she could face the truth and also take care, we understand that many people in her situation might not have enough strength to do this. That she lacks such strength in such circumstances does not make her morally bad.[30] In this situation we would probably

[29] Recall the Nixon example.

[30] If, as some claim, combat readiness is adversely affected when soldiers make realistic assessments of enemy forces, and positively affected if they deceive themselves about the enemy's strength, then although it would be more admirable if soldiers could make realistic assessments and still be combat-ready, given that this is something most soldiers cannot do, their self-deception does not render them morally bad. See Manuel Davenport, "False Reports: Misperceptions, Self-Deceptions or Lies?," *Southwest Philosophy Review*, vol. 6, no. 1 (January 1990), pp. 113–21.

withhold all criticism, given the good that is obtained in exchange for her epistemic cowardice. While epistemic cowardice is *prima facie* non-admirable, it may not be, all things considered, non-admirable.

A self-deception does not have to have good consequences to escape moral censure. When a self-deception is trivial or limited, we also withhold such censure. Consider the person who self-deceives himself into believing that his tie is bright, not garish, that the apple he has just eaten was not riddled with worms, that the dessert he consumed was not high in calories.

Cases of trivial or limited self-deception also show why a number of other charges leveled against the self-deceiver do not make *all* self-deception *prima facie* morally bad. In trivial and limited cases of self-deception, the self-deceiver need not manifest *moral weakness*, nor need there be a *gradual corroding of his own belief-forming processes*, nor need it be the case that either his *moral integrity is threatened* or his *agency or ability to function morally is undermined*, nor need he *have shirked responsibility*.[31] I am not, of course, denying that self-deception often enough does involve these things and that when it does, its involving them contributes to the moral badness of particular self-deceptions.

For example, contrast the mother who cannot face the truth about her offspring's horrendous illness with a father who cannot face the truth about his offspring's horrendous behavior. While we saw that the mother's self-deception enables her to do what she is obligated to do, it is not difficult to imagine that the father's self-deception could prevent him from doing what he is obligated to do or enable him to do something he ought not to do. The bad consequences of a particular self-deception can make *that* self-deception *prima facie* morally bad, but *all* self-deception is not *prima facie* morally bad because of its consequences.

The literature on self-deception is not without those who defend self-deception, who point to its good consequences. On the positive side, self-deception is said to reduce the burden of painful thoughts or to reduce anxiety; to prevent harm; to produce good by allowing one to cope with a bad situation or by offering an imaginative solution to a perplexing problem; to facilitate romantic love and certain kinds of loyalty and dedication;[32] to be instrumental in achieving intrapsychic

[31] Marcia Baron also points out in "What Is Wrong with Self-Deception?" that some cases of self-deception are not morally objectionable.

[32] See Martin, *Self-Deception and Morality*, p. 118. Martin is considering Amelie Rorty's view.

harmony; to negotiate a confluence of interests within a social system.[33] It has been thought by some to be virtually indispensable: without it certain kinds of self-knowledge would not be attainable, or without it ordinary humans would be unhappy, despairing, self-contemptuous. Playwrights and novelists remind us of the dire consequences that can attend the unmasking of self-deceivers.

I have already acknowledged that self-deceiving oneself may sometimes have good consequences and that having good consequences may cause us to withhold both moral and non-moral criticism. Focusing, however, on the good consequences can make one lose track of the fact that the consequences of self-deception are frequently enough not on balance good.

If self-deceptive beliefs function to reduce anxiety, that one's anxiety is relieved is generally regarded as a good consequence. But the self-deception, which relieves the anxiety, may, nonetheless, have overall bad consequences. Even in the seemingly trivial cases of self-deception – one deceives oneself into believing that one's tie is not garish, one's garden not overgrown – it might be better, all things considered, to face up to the fact that one has bad taste or that one is slovenly. It ordinarily would have better consequences if, instead of deceiving oneself into believing that one's lying to one's spouse is done in order to protect the spouse, or that one's child is not a bully although he brutalizes the neighborhood children, one faced up to the fact that one is a controlling, and not a beneficent, person, or that one is a bad parent.

Moreover, it is not clear to me that many of the alleged good consequences of self-deception are in fact good consequences. While I believe that self-deception is a prevalent and widespread phenomenon,[34] it is not clear to me, for example, that it is psychologically nec-

[33] See Rue, *By the Grace of Guile,* especially chapter 4, "Deception and Social Coherence."

[34] There is a large psychological literature documenting cases of self-deception. See, for example, George A. Quattrone and Amos Tversky, "Self-Deception and the Voter's Illusion," in *The Multiple Self,* ed. Jon Elster (Cambridge: Cambridge University Press paperback, reprinted 1988), pp. 35–58: C. R. Synder, "Collaborative Companions: The Relationship of Self-Deception and Excuse Making," in *Self-Deception and Self-Understanding: New Essays in Philosophy and Psychology*, ed. Mike Martin (Lawrence: University Press of Kansas, 1985), pp. 35–51. Martha Knight's article "Cognitive and Motivational Bases of Self-Deception: Commentary on Mele's *Irrationality*" makes reference to some of this literature. See also the bibliography in Alfred Mele, "Recent Work on Self-Deception," pp. 15–17.

essary for people who want self-knowledge to self-deceive themselves. I am dubious whether, as Marcia Baron suggests, "self-deception is, for most of us, virtually indispensable. And this is the case not merely because there are episodes in most lives in which we cannot bear to face the truth; it has more to do with the opacity of self-knowledge."[35] The suggestion is that it is not "reasonable to expect ourselves to always avoid the obfuscation of self-knowledge" that deceiving oneself involves. We cannot be expected to "get it right the first time"; rather, it seems, we sometimes need to "stumble along confusedly settling on *some* plan of action and *some* picture of what is going on." For "it is not that easy to figure out what we are about; discovering it may at times have to arise *through* self-deception." The "have to" in the last sentence suggests a psychological necessity, although perhaps the suggestion is canceled by the "may."

Certainly no one thinks that achieving self-knowledge in situations of anxiety is an easy matter, and no doubt people sometimes achieve a belated self-knowledge by (or despite) wallowing in their self-created muddles. But people achieve self-knowledge in this way because they are epistemically cowardly in the face of their anxiety. And it is not clear to me that there is something about people, or about their situations, that requires them to be epistemically cowardly, that requires that people come to the requisite self-knowledge via self-deception.

Moreover, learning via self-deception is by and large a bad way to learn – the harm the self-deceiver does while deceived is very likely to offset any eventual gain in self-knowledge.

It is also more likely that people who deceive themselves will persist in self-deception rather than obtain self-knowledge through it. As Baron notes, "self-deception often requires, for its efficacy, further self-deception. The need to see things in a certain way, despite the evidence,"[36] leads to interpretations of what one sees which support

Sufficient evidence of self-deception can also be found in everyday life. It is not difficult to find examples of self-deceiving in other people, to find, for example, that others regularly self-deceive themselves about the importance of themselves in relation to others, about their degree of selfishness, about their sexual attractiveness, about their strength, independence, ability to cope, about their children, about how cultured or intelligent they are, about their honesty, about their losses, about their friends' and lovers' characters and characteristics.

[35] "What Is Wrong with Self-Deception?" p. 441. The other quotations in the paragraph appear on the same page. [36] Ibid., p. 437.

the original self-deceptive belief. She also is aware that "too much self-deception, or more typically, self-deception that one struggles desperately to maintain, corrodes one's belief-forming processes."[37] Furthermore, learning via self-deception is not the only way to learn when one is trying "to understand a complicated series of events, or a stage in one's life, or a relationship between oneself and another."[38]

Why is self-deception, for most of us, so prevalent a phenomenon if it is neither a matter of psychic necessity nor the result of the opacity of knowledge? Why do we so frequently lack the epistemic courage required to obtain self-knowledge?[39] I think the answer is simple and stark: truth is abundant and often ugly.[40]

While Baron defends self-deception for its potential role in self-knowledge, Loyal Rue defends both self- and other-deception as adaptive strategies. Deception, in moderation, can, he suggests, help us to achieve "personal wholeness"[41] ("a sense of individual well-being, integrity, equilibrium, homeostasis, mental health, self-fulfillment")[42] and "social coherence" ("an acceptable level of collective order and stability, a sense of security, solidarity, predictability and communication of purpose")[43].

[37] Ibid., p. 443. [38] Ibid., p. 442.

[39] We are more like Golenishchev in Tolstoy's description in *Anna Karenin* than we are like Vronsky. "The same thing happened to him that happened to Golenishchev, who felt he had nothing to say and went on deceiving himself with the idea that his theories had not yet matured, that he was working them out and collecting material. But while Golenishchev grew bitter and irritable, Vronsky was incapable of self-deception and self-torment and even more incapable of exasperation. With characteristic decision, without explanation or apology, he left off painting" (p. 505). Vronsky, of course, might not have been anxious about lacking talent for painting.

[40] Harry Frankfurt in his American Philosophical Association, Eastern Division Philosophical Address, 1991 (*Proceedings and Addresses*, vol. 66, no. 3 [1992], pp 5–16), suggested that "the faintest human passion – both the least salient and the least robust – is our love of the truth about ourselves." Since many truths about ourselves are ugly and anxiety-making, we commonly deceive ourselves about ourselves, acquiring beliefs that allow us to retain a positive self-image, that explain how we could do something that seems to fall below our or others' standards. For many people self-knowledge is not, despite what Aristotle thought, a most pleasing thing.

We also commonly deceive ourselves about the world, acquiring beliefs that allow us to think the world is such that our desires can be satisfied, that downgrade inaccessible options. [41] *By the Grace of Guile*, p. 183.

[42] Ibid., p. 127. [43] Ibid.

No doubt self-deception allows most of us to maintain a consistent (if overly flattering) picture of ourselves. It may even be true that self-deception, given its prevalence, has some evolutionary payoff. But operating with a false view of ourselves is not, of course, an appropriate way to operate if the general admirability of behavior is at stake. Having such a view tends to prevent us from appreciating what the relevant reasons are for doing or not doing something.

In some situations, self-deceiving oneself can, I have said, prevent one from performing the action that should be done, or it can ensure that one performs the action that should not be performed. The man who self-deceives himself into believing that his daughter is unloving is unable to appreciate the central reason – that she is loving – for not disinheriting her.

In other situations, self-deceivers may perform the action that should be performed, but they perform it for the wrong reason. Consider a man who does not recommend a rival for a job, not, however, because he knows that the rival lacks the requisite intelligence to do the job, but because he has self-deceived himself into believing that his rival is dishonest.

Operating with a false view of oneself is also not an advisable way to operate if one wants to secure what one most prefers. While it is true that self-deceivers not infrequently get what they want as a result of the deception – had they accurate descriptions of their actions, they might be loath to perform the actions under those descriptions – Rue himself points out that while "short term, occasional and moderate uses of deceptive and self-deceptive strategies are generally conducive to personal wholeness . . . chronic uses are generally counterproductive."[44]

Furthermore, the social coherence that is gained by self-deception may be a very vulnerable one. Rue tells us that

> [p]arents usually hold unrealistically positive views of their children's appearance, abilities and character . . . children will have grossly biased estimates of their parents. Positive illusions of this sort serve to maintain high levels of affection and respect, which enhance the frequency of cooperative interactions within the family.[45]

[44] Ibid., p. 183. [45] Ibid., p. 228.

But that parents exhibit partiality or bias in forming their beliefs about their children (or vice versa) is not sufficient for them to have self-deceived themselves into believing these things. Their overestimations may simply be the result of their partiality for beliefs that favor those about whom they care. And if their overestimation is a result of anxious desire – one suspects one's child or one's parent is, for example, mean-spirited – then the family coherence that is achieved in the short run may be undermined in the long run.

I have been assuming throughout this discussion that self-deceivers are not to be admired for self-deceiving themselves, given that epistemic cowardice is not to be admired. But the activities, including the failures to act, that exhibit epistemic cowardice are, I have also said, not intentional under the relevant descriptions. Self-deceivers do not intentionally deceive themselves; they are not intentionally epistemically cowardly. We, however, regularly criticize people not merely for the actions they do intentionally but for their unintentional omissions. Self-deceivers can be criticized for failing to take steps to prevent themselves from being biased;[46] they can be criticized for lacking courage in situations where having courage is neither superhumanly difficult nor costly.

We have also seen that self-deception can have instrumental disvalue. While we do not admire self-deceivers for being epistemically cowardly, we blame self-deceivers for certain unintentional omissions and commissions that result from their cowardice. A mother who self-deceives herself into believing her husband is not sexually abusing her daughter is blamed for failing to stop this abuse even if she has self-deceived herself into believing there is no abuse. A father who insists on sending his son to a regular school because he has self-deceived himself into believing that the son is not learning-impaired does damage, however unintentionally, to his son, damage for which he is to be blamed.

Philip Larkin is said to have chosen his title *The Less Deceived*, for its "sad-eyed realism." If what has been said in this book about self-deception is correct – if epistemic bravery in the face of anxiety is required to avoid it – then being among the less deceived may very well be the best that most of us are able to achieve.

46 For supporting argumentation, see Alfred Mele, *Autonomous Agents* (New York: Oxford University Press, 1995), chapter 5.

References

Adams, Don, "Love and Impartiality," *American Philosophical Quarterly*, vol. 30, no. 3 (July 1993), pp. 223–234.

Audi, Robert, "Acting for Reasons," *Philosophical Review*, vol. 95, no. 4 (October 1986), pp. 511–546.

Barnes, Annette, "On Deceiving Others," *American Philosophical Quarterly*, vol. 29, no. 2 (April 1992), pp. 153–161.

"When Do We Deceive Others?" *Analysis*, vol. 50, no. 3 (June 1990), pp. 197–202.

Baron, Marcia, "What Is Wrong with Self-Deception?" in *Perspectives on Self-Deception*, ed. Brian McLaughlin and Amelie Oksenberg Rorty (Berkeley: University of California Press, 1988), pp. 431–449.

Bok, Sisela, *Lying: Moral Choice in Public and Private Life* (Brighton: Harvester Press, 1978).

Butler, Bishop Joseph, "Upon Self-Deceit," Sermon X in *Fifteen Sermons* (London: SPCK, 1970), pp. 90–98.

Champlin, T. S., "Deceit, Deception and the Self-Deceiver," *Philosophical Investigations*, vol. 17, no. 1 (January 1994), pp. 53–58.

Reflexive Paradoxes (London: Routledge, 1988).

Clifford, W. K., "The Ethics of Belief," reprinted in *Philosophy: Contemporary Perspectives on Perennial Issues*, ed. E. D. Klemke, A. David Kline, and Robert Hollinger, 4th ed. (New York: St. Martin's Press, 1994), pp. 66–71.

Cohen, G. A., *History, Labour and Freedom* (Oxford: Clarendon Press, 1988).

Karl Marx's Theory of History (Oxford: Clarendon Press, 1978), chapters 9 and 10.

Cook, Thomas, "Deciding to Believe without Self-Deception," *Journal of Philosophy*, vol. 84 (August 1987), pp. 441–446.

Davenport, Manuel, "False Reports: Misperceptions, Self-Deceptions or Lies?" *Southwest Philosophy Review*, vol. 6, no. 1 (January 1990), pp. 113–121.

Davidson, Donald, "Deception and Division," in *The Multiple Self*, ed. Jon Elster (Cambridge: Cambridge University Press paperback, reprinted 1988), pp. 79–92.

"Paradoxes of Irrationality," in *Philosophical Essays on Freud*, ed. R. Wollheim and J. Hopkins (Cambridge: Cambridge University Press, 1982), pp. 289–305.

de Sousa, Ronald, *The Rationality of Emotion* (Cambridge, Mass.: MIT Press, 1987).

Elster, Jon, "Deception and Self-Deception in Stendhal," in *The Multiple Self*, ed. Elster (Cambridge: Cambridge University Press paperback, reprinted 1988), pp. 93–113.

Fingarette, Herbert, *Self-Deception* (London: Routledge and Kegan Paul, 1969).

Foley, Richard, *The Theory of Epistemic Rationality* (Cambridge, Mass.: Harvard University Press, 1987).

Frankfurt, Harry, "The Faintest Passion," *Proceedings and Addresses of the American Philosophical Association*, vol. 66, no. 3 (1992), pp. 5–16.

Freud, Sigmund, "Repression" (1915), *The Ego and the Id* (1923), and "Splitting of the Ego in the Process of Defense" (1938), in *The Standard Edition of the Complete Psychological Works*, ed. James Strachey, Anna Freud, Alix Strachey, and Alan Tyson (London: Hogarth Press and the Institute of Psychoanalysis, 1954–74).

Gardiner, Patrick, "Error, Faith and Self-Deception," *Proceedings of the Aristotelian Society*, vol. 70 (1969–70), pp. 221–243.

Goldman, Alvin, "Discrimination and Perceptual Knowledge," *Journal of Philosophy*, vol. 73, no. 20 (1976), pp. 771–791.

Gombay, Andre, review of Mike W. Martin's *Self-Deception and Morality*, *Philosophical Review*, vol. 98, no. 3 (July 1988), pp. 442–444.

Gordon, Robert, *The Structure of Emotions* (Cambridge: Cambridge University Press, 1987).

Greenspan, Patricia, "Guilt and Virtue," *Journal of Philosophy*, vol. 91, no. 2 (February 1994), pp. 57–70.

Haigh, Christopher, *Elizabeth I* (London: Longman, 1988).

Hampshire, Stuart, "Justice Is Strife," *Proceedings and Addresses of the American Philosophical Association*, vol. 65, no. 3 (1991), pp. 19–27.

Heil, John, "Going to Pieces," in *Philosophical Psychopathology: A Book of Readings*, ed. G. Graham and L. Stephens (Cambridge, Mass.: MIT Press, 1994), pp. 113–133.

Johnston, Mark, "Self-Deception and the Nature of the Mind," in

Perspectives on Self-Deception, ed. Brian McLaughlin and Amelie Oksenberg Rorty (Berkeley: University of California Press, 1988), pp. 63–91.

Kant, Immanuel, *The Doctrine of Virtue*, translated by Mary J. Gregor (New York: Harper and Row, 1964).

Knight, Martha, "Cognitive and Motivational Bases of Self-Deception: Commentary on Mele's *Irrationality*," *Philosophical Psychology*, vol. 1, no. 2 (1988), pp. 179–188.

Kornblith, Hilary, "Justified Belief and Epistemically Responsible Action," *Philosophical Review*, vol. 92, no. 1 (January 1983), pp. 33–48.

Martin, Mike W., *Self-Deception and Morality* (Lawrence: University Press of Kansas, 1986).

McLaughlin, Brian, "Exploring the Possibility of Self-Deception in Belief," in *Perspectives on Self-Deception*, ed. McLaughlin and Amelie Oksenberg Rorty (Berkeley: University of California Press, 1988), pp. 29–62.

"Mele's *Irrationality*: A Commentary," *Philosophical Psychology*, vol. 1, no. 2 (1988), pp. 189–200.

Mele, Alfred, *Autonomous Agents* (New York: Oxford University Press, 1995), chapter 5.

Irrationality: An Essay on Akrasia, Self-Deception and Self-Control (New York: Oxford University Press, 1987).

"Recent Work on Self-Deception," *American Philosophical Quarterly*, vol. 24, no. 1 (January 1987), pp. 1–17.

Mills, Claudia, "Influence: Coercion, Manipulation and Persuasion," unpublished Ph.D. thesis, Princeton University, 1991, chapter 4 ("Manipulation").

Nozick, Robert, *The Nature of Rationality* (Princeton, N.J.: Princeton University Press, 1993).

Parfit, Derek, *Reasons and Persons* (Oxford: Oxford University Press paperback, reprinted 1986).

Pears, David, *Motivated Irrationality* (Oxford: Clarendon Press paperback, 1986).

"Self-Deceptive Belief-Formation," *Synthese,* vol. 89 (1991), pp. 393–405.

Proust, Marcel, *Swann's Way*, translated by C. K. Moncrief (New York: Vintage, 1970).

Quattrone, George A., and Amos Tversky, "Self-Deception and the Voter's Illusion," in *The Multiple Self*, ed. Jon Elster (Cambridge: Cambridge University Press paperback, reprinted 1988), pp. 35–58.

Rey, Georges, "Toward a Computational Account of *Akrasia* and Self-

Deception," in *Perspectives on Self-Deception*, ed. Brian McLaughlin and Amelie Oksenberg Rorty (Berkeley: University of California Press, 1988), pp. 264–296.

Rue, Loyal, *By the Grace of Guile: The Role of Deception in Natural History and Human Affairs* (Oxford: Oxford University Press, 1994).

Sanford, David, "Self-Deception as Rationalization," in *Perspectives on Self-Deception*, ed. Brian McLaughlin and Amelie Oksenberg Rorty (Berkeley: University of California Press, 1988), pp. 157–169.

Scott-Kakures, Dion, "Self-Deception and Internal Irrationality," *Philosophy and Phenomenological Research*, vol. 56, no. 1 (March 1966), pp. 31–56.

Searle, John, *Intentionality* (Cambridge: Cambridge University Press, 1983).

Shakespeare, William, *The Winter's Tale*, in *The Complete Works of Shakespeare* (Oxford: Clarendon Press, 1986), pp. 1241–1274.

Siegler, Frederick, "An Analysis of Self-Deception," *Nous*, vol. 2 (1968), pp. 147–164.

Simon, David, *Homicide: A Year on the Killing Streets* (Boston: Houghton Mifflin, 1991).

Slote, Michael, *From Morality to Virtue* (New York: Oxford University Press, 1992).

Synder, C. R., "Collaborative Companions: The Relationship of Self-Deception and Excuse Making," in *Self-Deception and Self-Understanding: New Essays in Philosophy and Psychology*, ed. Mike Martin (Lawrence: University Press of Kansas, 1985), pp. 35–51.

Szabados, Bela, "Self-Deception," *Canadian Journal of Philosophy*, vol. 4, no. 1 (1974), pp. 51–68.

Talbott, William, "Intentional Self-Deception in a Single Coherent Self," *Philosophy and Phenomenological Research*, vol. 55, no. 1 (March 1995), pp. 27–74.

Thernstrom, Melanie, "Diary of a Murder," *New Yorker*, June 3, 1996, pp. 62–71.

Tolstoy, Leo, *Anna Karenin* (Penguin Classics, 1986).

Trollope, Anthony, *The Last Chronicle of Barset* (Penguin Classics, 1986).

van Fraassen, Bas, "The Peculiar Effects of Love and Desire," in *Perspectives on Self-Deception*, ed. Brian McLaughlin and Amelie Oksenberg Rorty (Berkeley: University of California Press, 1988), pp. 123–156.

Wood, Allan, "Self-Deception and Bad Faith," in *Perspectives on Self-Deception*, ed. Brian McLaughlin and Amelie Oksenberg Rorty (Berkeley: University of California Press, 1988), pp. 207–227.

Index

anxiety, characterized, 39–41, 67
anxiety, reduction of
  characterized, 36, 47–8, 67
  typical modes of, 67–74

bad faith, 168–9
belief, wishful, 1–3, 23, 31–4, 51–4, 124–5
biasing
  intentional, 78–9, 88–95, 123
  non-intentional, 3, 78–82, 88, 95–7, 119–22

consciousness, false
  failure of estimation, 99–101, 107–8
  lack of a high enough estimation, 99–100, 102–3, 105, 107–8
  overestimation, 99, 101–8
  underestimation, 99–108

deceived in believing as distinct from into believing, 9
deception by appearances, 4, 13, 19, 110, 129, 133–4
deception in nature, 19, 94n40, 133n30
deception of oneself
  intentional, 24, 110–15, 124, 132
  non-intentional, 3, 111, 127–31
deception of others
  intentional, 1, 4, 5n1, 6–18, 110, 127–8, 130–3
  and lying, 13, 23, 127–31, 168
  non-intentional, 5n1
  and *prima facie* moral wrong, 158–63
  standard account, 1, 4–8, 18
deception, self-
  and compulsive belief, 46n29
  and division, 1, 3, 20, 22, 25, 30, 123, 144–5
  and epistemic cowardice, 158, 163–6, 168, 170, 172–3, 175
  and epistemic irresponsibility, 77, 83–8, 118, 142, 169
  functioning to reduce anxiety, 36, 38, 42–4, 57–64, 67–8, 74–6, 79, 104, 106, 117, 132, 171
  and good consequences, 161, 169–74
  intentional, 1, 4, 22–4, 29, 32–3
  and irrationality, 3, 135–8, 141–3, 147, 156–7
  and lying to oneself, 23–4, 33
  non-intentional, 1–2, 31,–3, 36, 59, 111, 116–17, 119, 123–5, 130–1, 133, 175
  and objectionability, 158, 164, 166, 170, 175
  and *prima facie* moral badness, 163, 166, 168–71, 175
  process of, characterized, 117–19, 132
  seemingly unmotivated, 46–7n29
  seemingly unwelcome, 23, 34, 41–6, 48, 51
  state of, characterized, 118–19, 133
  welcome, 54–7
  and wishful belief, 1–3, 23, 31–4, 42, 51–4, 124–5
description, desirability-characterizing as distinct from identifying, 49
desire
  ambivalence, 48–53
  anxious, 31, 33, 37–9, 40n19
  for its own sake, 39, 40n19
  satisfaction, 58, 62–4, 66–8

intentions
  inferentially recognizable, 93
  non-inferentially recognizable, 89–95

intentions (*cont.*)
non-inferentially unrecognizable, 89–90, 92, 94–6
unrecognized, 89–96
irrationality
cognitive or epistemic, 136–43, 151–7
deep, 25, 29–30, 137–8, 143–51, 156
instrumental or practical or prudential, 137, 151, 153, 155–6

justification, strong, 12–13

paradox
doxastic, 2–3, 5–6, 13–14, 16–21
strategic, 6–7, 13–14, 15n17, 16–21

rationality
cognitive or epistemic, 135–7, 141, 151, 153, 155
instrumental or practical or prudential, 137, 151–7
reasons
anticipatory, 101, 109
ostensible, 101–2, 104, 109
relations, causal and functional, 60–1

tropisms, 31–2

walling off, 22, 25–30
and forgetting, 27–8, 30